Brief Contents

 LearningCurve activity is available for this topic. Visit **bedfordstmartins.com/reinteractive.**

Real
Essays
INTERACTIVE

Real
Essays
INTERACTIVE

A Brief Guide to
Writing Essays

Susan Anker

Bedford/St. Martin's
Boston ◆ New York

For Bedford/St. Martin's

Publisher for College Success and Developmental Studies: Edwin Hill
Executive Editor for Developmental Studies: Alexis Walker
Developmental Editor: Jill Gallagher
Senior Production Editor: Bridget Leahy
Senior Production Supervisor: Dennis Conroy
Marketing Manager: Christina Shea
Copy Editor: Steve Patterson
Indexer: Melanie Belkin
Senior Art Director: Anna Palchik
Text Design: Claire Seng-Niemoller
Cover Design: Billy Boardman
Composition: Graphic World Inc.
Printing and Binding: RR Donnelley and Sons

President, Bedford / St. Martin's: Denise B. Wydra
Editorial Director for English and Music: Karen S. Henry
Director of Development: Erica T. Appel
Director of Marketing: Karen R. Soeltz
Production Director: Susan W. Brown
Director of Rights and Permissions: Hilary Newman

Manufactured in the United States of America.

8   7   6   5   4   3
f   e   d   c   b   a

For information, write: Bedford/St. Martin's, 75 Arlington Street, Boston, MA 02116
   (617-399-4000)

ISBN 978-1-4576-5409-1

Acknowledgments

Contents

Part Two
Writing Different Kinds of Essays

Part Four
Grammar, Punctuation, and Mechanics

LearningCurve activity is available for this topic. Visit **bedfordstmartins.com/reinteractive**.

Preface

Real Essays Interactive has a two-fold goal: to show students that writing is essential to success in the real world and to help them develop the skills they need to achieve that success in their own college, work, and everyday lives. In support of this message, the book provides practical advice on writing different kinds of essays, step-by-step grammar instruction, and an abundance of readable student and professional reading selections, all in a brief, affordable format.

Real Essays Interactive (like *Real Skills Interactive* and *Real Writing Interactive*) reframes writing for students who view it as irrelevant and impossible—instead it presents writing and the work of the writing class as eminently learnable and potentially life-altering, and therefore worthy of students' best efforts. *Real Essays Interactive* is written in a new interactive format that brings grammar practice to life via LearningCurve, a game-like, adaptive quizzing system that helps students learn as they go.

Core Features

- **Brief, Affordable Format.** The text offers what's essential for the essay level course—process-oriented writing instruction and focused grammar lessons—in a concise and affordable format.

- ✓ **Interactive Grammar Practice via LearningCurve.** LearningCurve's innovative adaptive online quizzing lets students learn at their own pace, and a game-like interface encourages them to keep at it. Quizzes are keyed to grammar instruction in the book, so what is taught in class gets reinforced at home. Instructors can also check in on each student's activity in a grade book.

  A student access code is printed in every new student copy of *Real Essays Interactive*. Students who do not buy a new print book or e-book can purchase access by going to **bedfordstmartins.com/reinteractive**. Instructors can also get access at this site.

  NOTE: LearningCurve is also available in WritingClass or SkillsClass, so if you're using either Class, encourage your students to use it there.

- **Real-World Examples.** Samples of real students' writing demonstrate the concepts covered and give students confidence that good writing skills are achievable. These models address such real-world issues and concerns as parenting, peer pressure, and the importance of getting involved on campus and in the community.

- **Four Basics Boxes.** Presenting essay writing in manageable increments, these boxes break down the essentials of topics such as revision, good paragraphs, and narration.

Most college courses require writing. So do most jobs, which may surprise you. Good communication skills, including good writing, will help you achieve success in life.

Four elements are key to good writing. Keep them in mind throughout the writing process.

IDEA JOURNAL Think of something you do well and how you got to be good at it.

Four Basics of Good Writing

1. It considers the needs and knowledge of the audience.
2. It fulfills the writer's purpose.
3. It includes a clear, definite point.
4. It provides support that explains or proves the main point.

This chapter discusses audience and purpose first because they are essential to effective writing. Purpose determines what a writer's main point is, and audience determines how the writer makes that point.

The chapter shows you how to structure your writing to meet the four basics of good writing, outlines the steps of the writing process, and asks you to apply the critical thinking skills you have learned. It also explains the criteria your instructor may use to grade your writing.

For more on making a point, see Chapter 6. For more on supporting a point, see Chapter 7.

- **Focus on the Four Most Serious Errors.** *Real Essays Interactive* concentrates first on the four types of grammatical errors that matter most: fragments, run-ons, errors in subject-verb agreement, and errors of verb tense and form, and helps students avoid making them. Once students master these four topics and start building their editing skills, they are better prepared to tackle the grammar errors treated in later chapters.

You Get More with *Real Essays Interactive*

Real Essays Interactive does not stop with a book. Online, you will find more resources to help students get even more out of the book and your course. You will also find free, convenient instructor resources, such as a downloadable instructor's manual.

For more information, visit **bedfordstmartins.com/reinteractive /catalog**.

STUDENT RESOURCES

Premium Resources

- **Writing Class** provides students with a dynamic, interactive online course space preloaded with exercises, diagnostics, video tutorials, and more. WritingClass helps students stay focused and lets instructors see how they are progressing. It is available at a significant discount when packaged with the print text. To learn more about WritingClass, visit **yourwritingclass.com**.

■ **SkillsClass** offers all that WritingClass offers, plus guidance and practice in reading and study skills. This interactive online course space comes preloaded with exercises, diagnostics, video tutorials, and more. It is available at a significant discount when packaged with the print text. To learn more about SkillsClass, visit **yourskillsclass.com**.

■ *Re:Writing Plus,* **now with VideoCentral,** gathers all of our pre-mium digital content for the writing class into one online collection. This impressive resource includes innovative and interactive help with writing a paragraph; tutorials and practices that show how writing works in students' real-world experience; VideoCentral, with over 140 brief videos for the writing classroom; the first ever peer-review gam, *Peer Factor*; plus hundreds of models of writing and hundreds of readings. *Re:Writing Plus* can be purchased separately or packaged with *Real Essays Interactive* at a significant discount.

Free* with the Print Text

■ The *Bedford/St. Martin's ESL Workbook* includes a broad range of exercises covering grammatical issues for multilingual students of varying language skills and backgrounds. Answers are at the back. ISBN: 978-0-312-54034-0

■ The *Make-a-Paragraph Kit* is a fun, interactive CD-ROM that teaches students about paragraph development. It also contains ex-ercises to help students build their own paragraphs, audio-visual tutorials on four of the most common errors for basic writers, and the content from *Exercise Central to Go: Writing and Grammar Practices for Basic Writers*. ISBN: 978-0-312-45332-9

■ The *Bedford/St. Martin's Planner* includes everything that stu-dents need to plan and use their time effectively, with advice on preparing schedules and to-do lists plus blank schedules and calen-dars (monthly and weekly). The planner fits easily into a backpack or purse, so students can take it anywhere. ISBN: 978-0-312-57447-5

    NOTE: **There is a limit of one free supplement per order.** Additional supplements can be packaged at a significant discount.

E-Book Options

■ *Real Essays Interactive* e-book. Available as a value-priced e-book, either as a CourseSmart e-book or in formats for use with computers, tablets, and e-readers—visit **bedfordstmartins.com/reinteractive /catalog** for more information.

INSTRUCTOR RESOURCES

- *Practical Suggestions for Teaching Real Essays Interactive* provides helpful information and advice on teaching developmental writing. It includes sample syllabi, tips on building students' critical thinking skills, resources for teaching nonnative English speakers and speakers of nonstandard English dialects, ideas for assessing students' writing and progress, and up-to-date suggestions for using technology in the writing classroom and lab. To download, see **bedfordstmartins.com/reinteractive/catalog**.

- *Additional Resources for Teaching Real Essays Interactive* is a collection of resources that supplements the instructional materials in the text. It contains a variety of extra exercises and tests, transparency masters, planning forms, and other reproducibles for classroom use. To download, see **bedfordstmartins.com/reinteractive/catalog**.

- *Answer Key for Real Essays Interactive* contains answers to the practice exercises in the printed book. To download, see **bedfordstmartins.com/reinteractive/catalog**.

Acknowledgments

As with the rest of the Anker series, *Real Essays Interactive* grew out of a collaboration with teachers and students across the country and with the talented staff of Bedford / St. Martin's. I am grateful for everyone's thoughtful contributions.

REVIEWERS

I would like to thank the following instructors for their many good ideas and suggestions for this edition. Their insights were invaluable.

Nikki Aitken, Illinois Central College
Valerie Badgett, Lon Morris College
Michael Briggs, East Tennessee State University
Andrew Cavanaugh, University of Maryland University College
Jeff Kosse, Iowa Western Community College
Mimi Leonard, Wytheville Community College
Shannon McCann, Suffolk Community College
Loren Mitchell, Hawaii Community College
Jim McKeown, McLennan Community College
Virginia Nugent, Miami Dade College
Lisa Oldaker Palmer, Quinsigamond Community College
Anne Marie Prendergast, Bergen Community College
Gina Schochenmaier, Iowa Western Community College

Karen Taylor, Belmont College
Elizabeth Wurz, College of Coastal Georgia
Svetlana Zhuravlova, Lakeland Community College

STUDENTS

Many current and former students have helped shape *Real Essays Interactive*, and I am grateful for all of their contributions.

Among the students who provided paragraphs and essays for the book are Joseph Ameur, John Around Him, Florence Bagley, Deshon Briggs, Jordan Brown, Rui Dai, Islam Elshami, Roberta Fair, Daniel Flanagan, Shannon Grady, Michael Jernigan, Dylan Marcos, Luz Medina, Heaven Morrison, Donnie Ney, Jennifer Orlando, Tam Nguyen, Anna Puiia, Liliana Ramirez, Beth Trimmer, Katie Whitehead, Kevin Willey, Meagan Willey, and Carson Williams. Thanks to these students and the many others who submitted their work.

I would also like to thank the nine former students who provided inspirational words of advice and examples of workplace writing which are central to the book. They are Monique Rizer, Juan Gonzalez, Alex Espinoza, Patty Maloney, Rebeka Mazzone, Gary Knoblock, Garth Vaz, Jolanda Jones, and Shawn Brown.

A Note to Students from Susan Anker

For the last twenty years or so, I have traveled the country talking to students about their goals and, more important, about the challenges they face on the way to achieving those goals. Students always tell me that they want good jobs and that they need a college degree to get those jobs. I designed *Real Essays Interactive* with those goals in mind—strengthening the writing, reading, and editing skills needed for success in college, at work, and in everyday life.

Here is something else: Good jobs require not only a college degree but also a college education—knowing not only how to read and write but how to think critically and learn effectively. So that is what I stress here, too. It is worth facing the challenges. All my best wishes to you, in this course and in all your future endeavors.

Critical Thinking, Reading, and Writing

Making Connections

In order to become a better writer, you need to use critical thinking and reading skills. This chapter explains critical thinking and reading strategies and explores the important connections among critical thinking, reading, and writing.

Critical Thinking

Critical thinking is a process of actively questioning what you see, hear, and read to come to thoughtful conclusions about the information presented. Critical thinking also involves making connections between existing impressions and new ones, and among various beliefs, claims, and bits of information.

   We all think critically in our lives when we assess situations. For example, consider the following situation.

PRACTICE 1   Analyzing a Situation

You walk into a party and see two men yelling and swearing at each other with a group of others crowded around them. The men are in each other's faces, and they are angry.

1. What is going on?

2. What elements of the situation do you notice to assess how bad the situation is?

3. What do you think will happen?

✓ LearningCurve For extra practice in the skills covered in this chapter, visit
bedfordstmartins.com/reinteractive.

1

Four Basic Critical Thinking Questions

1 Be alert to assumptions made by you and others.

2 Question those assumptions.

3 Consider and connect various points of view—even those different from your own.

4 Keep an open mind and avoid hasty conclusions.

Assumptions—ideas or opinions that we do not question and that we automatically accept as true—can get in the way of clear, critical thinking. In college, work, and everyday life, we often make judgments based on assumptions that we are not even aware of. By identifying these assumptions and questioning them, we stand a better chance of seeing things as they are and responding to them more effectively.

When questioning assumptions, try to get a bit of distance from them. Imagine what people with entirely different points of view might say. You might even try disagreeing with your own assumptions. Take a look at the following examples.

Questioning Assumptions

SITUATION	ASSUMPTION	QUESTIONS
COLLEGE: I saw from the syllabus that I need to write five essays for this course.	That sounds like too much work.	What obstacles might be getting in my way? What might be some ways around those obstacles? What have others done in this situation?
WORK: Two of my coworkers just got raises.	My own raise is just around the corner.	Did my coworkers accomplish anything that I did not? When was their last raise, and when was mine?
EVERYDAY LIFE: My neighbor has been cool to me lately.	I must have done something wrong.	Is it possible that this has nothing to do with me? Maybe he is going through something difficult in his life?

You need to be aware not only of your own hidden assumptions but also of any assumptions hidden in what you read, see, and hear. However confidently a claim is made, never assume that it cannot be questioned.

In addition to assumptions, be aware of **biases**, one-sided and sometimes prejudiced views that may blind you to the truth of any situation. Here is just one example:

All politicians are dishonest.

This is an extreme statement that could be contradicted with specific examples of politicians who have no history of fraud or unethical behavior.

Be on the lookout for bias in your own views and in whatever you read, see, and hear. When a statement seems one-sided or extreme, ask yourself what facts or points of view might have been omitted.

Critical Reading

When you practice **critical reading**, you apply your critical thinking skills to your reading. To do this, you need to read actively, paying close attention to the text and asking yourself questions about the author's purpose, his or her main point, the support he or she gives, and how good that support is. It is important to think critically as you read, looking out for assumptions and biases (both the writer's and your own). You should also consider whether you agree or disagree with the points being made.

Here are the four steps of the critical reading process:

2PR The Critical Reading Process

- **Preview** the reading.

- **Read** the piece, double underlining the <u>thesis statement</u>, underlining the <u>major support</u>. Consider the quality of the support.

- **Pause** to think during the reading. Take notes and ask questions about what you are reading. Imagine that you are talking to the author.

- **Review** the reading, your marginal notes, and your questions.

2PR   Preview the Reading

Before reading any piece of writing, skim the whole thing, using the following steps.

- **Read the title, headnote, and introductory paragraphs** to determine the topic and main point of the reading.

CRITICAL
READING
- Preview
- Read
- Pause
- Review

- **Read headings, key words, and definitions** to help follow the author's main ideas and important concepts.

- **Look for summaries, checklists, and chapter reviews** to make sure you understand the main points.

- **Read the conclusion** to confirm the reading's main idea.

- **Ask a guiding question**—a question you think the reading might answer—to help keep you focused as you read.

CRITICAL
READING
■ Preview
■ Read
■ Pause
■ Review

2PR   Read the Piece: Find the Main Point and the Support

After previewing, begin reading carefully for meaning, trying especially to identify the writer's main point and the support for that point.

MAIN POINT, PURPOSE, AND AUDIENCE

For more on
main points,
see pages
31-38.

The **main point** of a reading is the central idea the author wants to communicate. The main point is related to the writer's **purpose**, which can be to explain, to demonstrate, to persuade, to entertain, and to inform his or her intended **audience,** which can range from specific (say a particular person) to general (any reader of a periodical). Writers often introduce their main point early, so read the first few paragraphs with special care. If the writer has stated the main point in a single sentence, double-underline it.

SUPPORT

Support is the evidence that shows, explains, or proves the main point. The author might use statistics, facts, definitions, and scientific results for support. Or he or she might use memories, stories, comparisons, quotations from experts, and personal observations.

For more on
support, see
pages 39-43.

Not all support is good support. When you are reading, ask yourself: What information is the author including to help me understand or agree with the main point? Is the support (evidence) valid and convincing? If not, why not?

In the paragraph below, the main point has been double-underlined and the support has been underlined.

Neighbors who are too friendly can be seen just about anywhere. I mean that both ways. They exist in every neighborhood I have ever lived in and seem to appear everywhere I go. For some strange reason these people become extremely attached to my family and stop in as

<u>many as eight to ten times a day.</u> No matter how tired I appear to be, nothing short of opening the door and suggesting they leave will make them go home at night. (I once told an unusually friendly neighbor that his house was on fire, in an attempt to make him leave, and he still took ten minutes to say goodbye.) <u>What is truly interesting about these people is their strong desire to cook for us even though they have developed no culinary skill whatsoever.</u> (This has always proved particularly disconcerting since they stay to watch us eat every bite as they continually ask if the food "tastes good.")

— From Jonathan R. Gould Jr., "The People Next Door"

· ·

PRACTICE 2 Finding the Main Point and Support

Read each of the following paragraphs. Double underline the main point and underline the support.

1. When we see people chewing gum, we might think it gives an impression of immaturity or unprofessionalism. We all remember teachers in elementary school forbidding gum-chewing, though we never knew why. But new research indicates that chewing gum can actually improve certain kinds of thinking and memory. Subjects in a study conducted by Andrew Scholey in England showed that people who chewed gum during challenging mental tasks performed significantly better than subjects who did not chew gum doing the same tasks. Scholey speculated that the chewing increased heart rate, and therefore increased oxygen flowing to the brain while lowering stress and anxiety. Still, it is not a good idea to chew gum during a job interview as the negative impression of chewing is widespread.

2. In communities around the United States, people are "time banking," giving their individual skills in return for another's, and building a sense of community in the process. For example, one person might not have a driver's license or a car but needs transportation to a regular appointment. That same person is a good baker, and so offers to make cakes, pies, or cookies in return for transportation to her appointment. Individuals offer up their skills and get what they need in return, when they need it. Time banking in some large cities is funded by AmeriCorps because the groups are large and need a central administration. People involved in time banking are highly satisfied with the practice because it is local, it saves money, and

it connects people who might not otherwise meet, strengthening community ties. It also reminds individuals that they have something to contribute as they offer up their skills to their neighbors.

2PR   Pause to Think

READING ACTIVELY

Taking notes and asking questions as you read will help you understand the author's points and develop a thoughtful response. As you read:

CRITICAL READING
■ **Preview**
■ **Read**
■ **Pause**
■ Review

- Double-underline the <u>main idea</u> or write it in the margin.
- Note the <u>major support points</u> by underlining them.
- Note ideas that you agree with by placing a check mark next to them (✓).
- Note ideas that you do not agree with or that surprise you with an ! or X.
- Note ideas you do not understand with a question mark (?).
- Note any examples of an author's or expert's assumptions or biases.
- Jot any additional notes or questions in the margin.
- Consider how parts of the reading relate to the main point.

WATCHING FOR LOGICAL FALLACIES

As you read, look for examples of faulty reasoning. Certain kinds of errors in reasoning are so common that they have their own name: **logical fallacies**. Here are some of the most common examples of faulty reasoning:

Either/Or Extremes.   Assuming that there are only two extreme choices with nothing in between.

> **EXAMPLE:**   My country, love it or leave it.
>
> [**Faulty reasoning:** Should people really either applaud everything a government does or move to a different country?]

Bad Analogy.   Comparing items or circumstances that are not enough alike to make a meaningful comparison.

> **EXAMPLE:**   A human fetus should have the same rights as a human adult.
>
> [**Faulty reasoning:** While some specific rights may be shared by a fetus and an adult, saying they should have all the same rights does not make sense because they are different in many ways. Should a fetus be able to vote, for example?]

Circular Reasoning.   Supporting a position by restating part of it.

EXAMPLE: I deserve a raise because I need to make more money.

[**Faulty reasoning:** While this may be true, it will not persuade your boss. You need to offer reasons why you are worth more than you are being paid.]

"Everyone Knows."   Appealing to people's general desire to be like the majority by supporting a statement with a claim that all or most other people believe something. A common occurrence of this is when a child says to a parent, "Everybody else's parents are letting them do *X*." This kind of faulty reasoning is also called "the bandwagon effect."

EXAMPLE: Everyone knows that Apple makes the best computers.

[**Faulty reasoning:** While a certain brand of computer may be popular, it is not likely that all people would agree on a single brand being the best.]

Mistaken Causes or Effects.   Assuming that one thing caused another simply because it occurred beforehand.

EXAMPLE: The opening of the new liquor superwarehouse caused old Mr. Jones to close up his shop.

[**Faulty reasoning:** Mr. Jones might have closed for a variety of reasons. Your assumption is not evidence of his real reason for closing.]

Overgeneralization.   Making a broad statement that is not supported by enough evidence.

EXAMPLE: Having grown up with three brothers, I know firsthand that boys are more violent than girls.

[**Faulty reasoning:** A sample of one family is not enough to assume that all boys act in a particular way.]

Oversimplification.   Making something seem simple when it is not simple.

EXAMPLE: If more parking spaces were available on campus, most students would come to class.

[**Faulty reasoning:** Students miss class for many reasons, so saying parking is the problem is too simple.]

2PR   Review and Respond

After reading, take a few minutes to look back and review. Go over your guiding question, your marginal notes, and your questions—and connect with what you have read. Consider, "What interested me? What did I learn? How does it fit with what I know from other sources?" When you

For more on writing critically about readings, see pages 3-15.

have reviewed your reading in this way and fixed it well in your mind and memory, it is much easier to respond in class discussion and writing. To write about a reading, you need to generate and organize your ideas, draft and revise your response, and above all, use your critical thinking skills.

CRITICAL
READING
▪ Preview
▪ Read
▪ Pause
▪ Review

A Critical Reader at Work

Read the following piece. The notes in the margin show how one student applied the process of critical reading to an assigned reading.

Deborah Tannen

It Begins at the Beginning

Deborah Tannen is a professor of linguistics at Georgetown University in Washington, D.C. Linguistics — the study of human language — reveals much about people and their culture. Part of Tannen's research in linguistics has focused on differences in how women and men use language and how those differences affect communication. The following excerpt, adapted from her book *You Just Don't Understand* (1990), describes how girls' and boys' language and communication patterns differ from an early age.

GUIDING QUESTION
How do boys and girls differ in their play and the language they use in their play?

Main point

Even if they grow up in the same neighborhood, on the same block, or in the same house, girls and boys grow up in different worlds of words. Others talk to them differently and expect and accept different ways of talking from them. Most important, children

She will have to prove this point.

learn how to talk, how to have conversations, not only from their parents, but from their peers. . . . Although they often play together,

Signals important purpose

boys and girls spend most of their time playing in same-sex groups.

What about computers?

And, although some of the activities they play at are similar, their favorite games are different, and their ways of using language in their games are separated by a world of difference.

Examples (boys' play)

Boys tend to play outside, in large groups that are hierarchically structured. Their groups have a leader who tells others what to do and how to do it, and resists doing what other boys propose. It is by giving orders and making them stick that high status is

! But don't boys & girls play together— at least sometimes?

negotiated. Another way boys achieve status is to take center stage by telling jokes, and by sidetracking or challenging the stories and jokes of others. Boys' games have winners and losers and elaborate systems of rules, and the players frequently boast their skill and argue about who is best at what.

3   Girls, on the other hand, play in small groups or in pairs; the center of a girl's social life is a best friend. . . . In their most frequent games, such as jump rope and hopscotch, everyone gets a turn. Many of their activities (such as playing house) do not have winners or losers. Though some girls are certainly more skilled than others, girls are expected not to boast about it, or show that they think they are better than the others. Girls don't give orders; they express their preferences as suggestions, and suggestions are likely to be accepted. Anything else is put down as bossy. They don't grab center stage—they don't want it—so they don't challenge each other directly. And much of the time, they simply sit together and talk. Girls are not accustomed to jockeying for status in an obvious way; they are more concerned that they be liked.

More examples (girls' play)

Does Tannen think these differences affect how adult men and women work together?

Writing Critically about Readings

WRITING
CRITICALLY
■ Summarize
■ Analyze
■ Synthesize
■ Evaluate

There are different types of writing in college. In Chapters 2 through 4, we examine the writing process in general and learn how to draft and revise paragraphs and essays. In Chapters 5 through 13, we explore the different techniques for developing an essay, such as narration and illustration, and in Chapter 14, we cover the research essay.

In this section, we discuss the key college skill of writing critically about what you read. In any college course, your instructor may ask you to summarize, analyze, synthesize, or evaluate one or more readings to demonstrate your deep understanding of the material. When you do so, you answer the following questions.

Writing Critically

■ **Summarize**
- What is important about the text?
- What is the purpose, the big picture?
- Who is the intended audience?
- What are the main points and key support?

■ **Analyze**
- What elements have been used to convey the main point?
- Do any elements raise questions? Do any key points seem missing or undeveloped?

■ **Synthesize**

- What do other sources say about the topic of the text?
- How does your own (or others') experience affect how you see the topic?
- What new point(s) might you make by bringing together all the different sources and experiences?

■ **Evaluate**

- Based on your application of summary, analysis, and synthesis, what do you think about the material you have read?
- Is the work successful? Does it achieve its purpose?
- Does the author show any biases? Are there any hidden assumptions? If so, do they make the piece more or less effective?

The pages that follow will explain when and how to use summary, analysis, synthesis, and evaluation. The passage below, "Daily Hassles," from *Discovering Psychology*, fifth edition, by Don H. Hockenbury and Sandra E. Hockenbury, is used as the basis for each type of writing that follows.

Daily Hassles
That's Not What I Ordered!

What made you feel "stressed out" in the last week? Chances are it was not a major life event. Instead, it was probably some unexpected but minor annoyance, such as splotching ketchup on your new white T-shirt, misplacing your keys, or discovering that you've been standing in the wrong line.

Stress researcher **Richard Lazarus** and his colleagues suspected that such ordinary irritations in daily life might be an important source of stress. To explore this idea, they developed a scale measuring **daily hassles**—everyday occurrences that annoy and upset people (DeLongis & others, 1982; Kanner & others, 1981). The *Daily Hassles Scale* measures the occurrence of everyday annoyances, such as losing something, getting stuck in traffic, and even being inconvenienced by lousy weather.

Are there gender differences in the frequency of daily hassles? One study measured the daily hassles experienced by married couples (Almeida & Kessler, 1998). The women experienced both more daily hassles and higher levels of psychological stress than their husbands did. For men, the most common sources of daily stress were financial and job-related problems. For women, family demands and interpersonal conflict were the most frequent causes of stress. However, when women *do* experience a stressful day in the workplace, the stress is more likely to spill over into their interactions with their husbands and other family members (Schulz & others, 2004). Men, on the other hand, are more likely to simply withdraw.

How important are daily hassles in producing stress? The frequency of daily hassles is linked to both psychological distress and physical symptoms, such as headaches and backaches (Bottos & Dewey, 2004; DeLongis & others, 1988). In fact, the number of daily hassles people experience is a better predictor of physical illness and symptoms than is the number of major life events experienced (Burks & Martin, 1985).

Why do daily hassles take such a toll? One explanation is that such minor stressors are *cumulative* (Repetti, 1993). Each hassle may be relatively unimportant in itself, but after a day filled with minor hassles, the effects add up. People feel drained, grumpy, and stressed out. Daily hassles also contribute to the stress produced by major life events. Any major life change, whether positive or negative, can create a ripple effect, generating a host of new daily hassles (Maybery & others, 2007; Pillow & others, 1996)

Summary

WRITING CRITICALLY
■ Summarize
■ Analyze
■ Synthesize
■ Evaluate

A **summary** is a condensed, or shortened, version of something—often, a longer piece of writing, a movie or television show, a situation, or an event. In writing a summary, you give the main points and key support in your own words.

Here is a summary of the textbook excerpt "Daily Hassles." The main point is double-underlined, and the support points are underlined.

Hockenbury and Hockenbury tell us that daily hassles often cause more stress than major problems do. According to studies, men and women report different kinds of daily stress and react to stress differently, though both experience psychological and physical symptoms. Some research shows that daily hassles produce stress because their effects are cumulative—that is, they add up over time to create major stress.

A summary is a useful way to record information from a reading in a course notebook. You can put the main points of an article into your own words for later review. You may also be asked to provide summaries in homework assignments or on tests in order to show that you read and understood a reading. In addition, summary is an important tool for keeping track of information for a research project.

Analysis

WRITING CRITICALLY
■ Summarize
■ Analyze
■ Synthesize
■ Evaluate

An **analysis** breaks down the points or parts of something and considers how they work together to make an impression or convey a main point. When writing an analysis, you might also consider points or parts that seem to be missing or that raise questions in your mind. Your analysis of a reading provides the main points as well as your own reaction to the piece.

Here is an analysis of "Daily Hassles." The main point is double-underlined, and the support points are underlined.

We have all read about stress, but Hockenbury and Hockenbury have something new and interesting to say about it: It is not the big life crises but the million petty hassles we face every day that get to us. They mention a number of different studies on hassles and their effects on us. Two of these studies explore gender differences, and they conclude that men and women report different kinds of daily hassles and respond to them differently.

These studies seem to involve only married men and women, however, which raises areas for further exploration. Do *all* men and women really experience and respond to hassles differently? For example, would unmarried male and female students be affected in the same ways that married men and women are? In a future paper, I would like to examine the kinds of daily hassles my college friends — both male and female — react to and what symptoms those hassles produce. The subject of hassles and how we react to them seems particularly relevant to students, whose lives are full of stress.

In any college course, your instructor may ask you to write an analysis to show your critical thinking skills and your ability to respond to a reading.

WRITING CRITICALLY

■ Summarize
■ Analyze
■ Synthesize
■ Evaluate

Synthesis

A **synthesis** pulls together information from additional sources or experiences to make a new point. Here is a synthesis of "Daily Hassles." Because the writer wanted to address some of the questions she raised in her analysis, she incorporated additional details from published sources and from people she interviewed. The various sources the writer pulls together are underlined. Her synthesis of this information helped her arrive at a fresh conclusion.

In *Discovering Psychology*, Hockenbury and Hockenbury present evidence that males and females react to different sources of stress and respond differently to them. The studies they use as evidence discuss only married couples, however, and they provide few details about the actual kinds and symptoms of stress. Several other studies, as well as original research done among unmarried college students, provide some additional insights into these questions.

The Mayo Clinic's Web site, produced by the staff at the Mayo Clinic, suggests that there are two main types of stress: acute stress, which is a response to specific and isolated situations (such as a car accident, a performance, or an exam) and chronic stress, which is longer term and cumulative. Acute, short-term stress can be good for people, prompting them to act. Chronic stress, however, tends to have negative effects, both physical and psychological. Daily hassles can produce either or both types of stress. Physical symptoms include headaches, back pain, stomach upset, and sleep problems. Psychological symptoms include anxiety, anger, depression, and burnout. The site offers numerous articles on stress and stress management, including a stress assessment test.

The Web site *Diabetes at Work* gives a list of the "Top 10 Daily Hassles," among them the illness of a family member, home repairs, loss of work, and crime. It includes the same symptoms of stress that the Mayo Clinic site does, such as shortness of breath, forgetfulness, reduced concentration, trouble making decisions, and irritability. Neither the *Diabetes at Work* Web site nor the Mayo Clinic site distinguishes between male and female stress sources or symptoms.

To these sources, I added interviews with eight friends—four men and four women—who all reported these top five daily hassles: worries about money, transportation problems, waiting in lines, unfair bosses, and automated phone systems that take forever and never get you an answer.

The only significant difference in the kind of hassles reported by the men and women I talked to was that several women (but not men) mentioned worries about physical safety (for example, while traveling home from school at night). When I asked my friends to report how they dealt with their stress, they seemed to confirm the Hockenburys' claim that women's stress spills over into the family and men tend to withdraw. Two men reported no psychological symptoms of stress, whereas the remaining six people (four women and two men) emphasized both psychological and physical symptoms.

These sources suggest that there might be some gender differences in the hassles that people experience and the symptoms that result from these hassles, but they might not be as major as the Hockenburys' passage led me to expect. Most of the stresses mentioned seem to be caused by having to do too much in too little time. Perhaps this is a comment on the quality of modern life, which affects both men and women equally.

Works Cited

Hockenbury, Don H., and Sandra E. Hockenbury. *Discovering Psychology.* 5th ed. New York: Worth, 2010. 543. Print.

Mayo Clinic Staff. "Stress Symptoms: Effects on Your Body, Feelings, and Behavior." *Mayo Clinic.* The Mayo Clinic, 20 Feb. 2009. Web. 13 Oct. 2010.

"Top 10 Daily Hassles." *Diabetes at Work.* United States Dept. of Health and Human Services, 27 May 2007. Web. 10 Oct. 2010.

Synthesizing is important for longer writing assignments and research papers, in which you need to make connections among different works. Many courses that involve writing, such as history and psychology, require papers that synthesize information from more than one source.

**WRITING
CRITICALLY**
■ Summarize
■ Analyze
■ Synthesize
■ Evaluate

Evaluation

An **evaluation** is your *thoughtful* judgment about something based on what you have discovered through your summary, analysis, and synthesis. To evaluate something effectively, apply the questions from the Writing Critically box on pages 9–10.

Here is an evaluation of "Daily Hassles."

Hockenbury and Hockenbury present important information and raise some interesting questions about how daily hassles affect our lives. In a few paragraphs, they present a great deal of information on the subject of daily hassles — what they are, who developed the scale of daily hassles, how men and women differ in their reactions to daily hassles, and how the stress of daily hassles negatively affects people. They provide numerous credible references to support their points. Other sources — such as the Mayo Clinic's Web site, the Web site *Diabetes at Work*, and a gender-based poll I conducted — provide more details about some aspects of daily hassles and raise questions about the extent to which women and men are differently affected by them. However, the Hockenburys present a good overview of the subject in a short piece of writing. I think the authors do a great job of pulling together good information for students.

When you do college-level work, you must be able to evaluate the readings and other sources you encounter. Instructors may ask you to write evaluations in order to demonstrate your ability to question and judge sources.

PRACTICE 3 Making Connections

As you work through this exercise, refer to the Writing Critically box on pages 9–10.

WRITING CRITICALLY
- Summarize
- Analyze
- Synthesize
- Evaluate

1. **Summary:** Summarize Deborah Tannen's essay on pages 8-9.

2. **Analysis:** Write a paragraph analyzing the points Tannen presents.

3. **Synthesis:** Read additional opinion pieces or blog postings on the social differences between boys and girls. In one paragraph, state your position on the subject according to your reading of these materials. Also, explain the range of opinions on the subject.

4. **Evaluation:** Write a paragraph that evaluates Tannen's essay.

Any time you write in response to assignments, you may want to review the "Writing about Readings" checklist that follows.

CHECKLIST

Writing about Readings

FOCUS

☐ Carefully read the writing assignment.

ASK

☐ Does the assignment include any words that indicate the type of writing required (*summarize, analyze, describe, give examples of, compare,* and so on)?

☐ Is the writing supposed to be in response to the reading alone, or are you expected to bring in other sources and points of view?

☐ Are you supposed to quote from the reading to support your point?

☐ Does the assignment ask you to evaluate the reading?

WRITE

☐ Apply your critical reading skills to the reading, and write a response to the reading that fulfills the requirements of the writing assignment.

2

Getting Ready to Write

Form, Process, and Purpose

Four elements are key to good writing. Keep them in mind throughout the writing process.

Four Basics of Good Writing

1 It considers the needs and knowledge of the audience.

2 It fulfills the writer's purpose.

3 It includes a clear, definite point.

4 It provides support that explains or proves the main point.

For more
on making
a point, and
supporting
a point, see
Chapter 3.

This chapter shows you how to structure your writing to meet the four basics of good writing, outlines the steps of the writing process, and asks you to apply the critical thinking skills you have learned. It also explains how to get started by choosing something to write about.

NOTE: AVOIDING PLAGIARISM

In all the writing you do, it is important to avoid plagiarism — using other people's words as your own or handing in information you gather from another source as your own. Your instructors are aware of plagiarism and know how to look for it. Writers who plagiarize, either on purpose or by accident, risk failing a course or losing their jobs and damaging their reputations.

To avoid plagiarism, take careful notes on every source (books, interviews, television shows, Web sites, and so on) you might use in your writing.

✓ **LearningCurve** For extra practice in the skills covered in this chapter, visit
bedfordstmartins.com/reinteractive.

When recording information from sources, take notes in your own words, unless you plan to use direct quotations. In that case, make sure to record the quotation word for word. Also, include quotation marks around it, both in your notes and in your paper. When you use material from other sources—whether you directly quote or put information in your own words (paraphrase)—you must name and give citation information about these sources.

TIP For more on avoiding plagiarism, and citing and documenting outside sources, see Chapter 14. Visit the Bedford/St. Martin's Workshop on Plagiarism at http://bcs .bedfordstmartins .com/plagiarism for online resources on avoiding plagiarism.

Paragraph and Essay Forms

Throughout college and beyond, you will write paragraphs and essays. Each of these has a basic structure.

Paragraph Structure

A **paragraph** is a group of sentences that work together to make a point. A good paragraph has three necessary parts—the topic sentence, the body, and the concluding sentence. Each part serves a specific purpose.

PARAGRAPH PART	PURPOSE OF THE PARAGRAPH PART
1. The **topic sentence**	states the **main point**. The topic sentence is often either the first or last sentence of a paragraph.
2. The **body**	supports (shows, explains, or proves) the main point. It usually contains three to six **support sentences**, which present facts and details that develop the main point.
3. The **concluding sentence**	reminds readers of the main point and often makes an observation.

Essay Structure

Essays vary in length. A short essay may consist of four or five paragraphs, totaling three hundred to six hundred words. A long essay is six paragraphs or more, depending on what the essay needs to accomplish—persuading someone to do something, using research to make a point, explaining a complex concept, or explaining an idea or experience.

PARAGRAPHS VS. ESSAYS FORMS

Paragraph Form

Topic sentence

Main Point: In this case, the topic sentence of the paragraph is the same as the thesis statement of the essay: that doing good can be easy.

Some ways to do good for our world do not require much time, effort, or money. My favorite way is to use click-and-give Web sites, where just going to the site triggers donations to it from another source (not you). Every night before I go to bed, I go to one or more of these sites. The **first site that I click on every night is the** *Animal Rescue Site* **(www.theanimalrescuesite.com). Each click gives food to rescued animals.** Another of my favorite Web sites is *Free Rice* **(www.freerice.com) where I play vocabulary or grammar games. With each correct answer, grains of rice are donated to hungry people.** One site with lots of choices of click-and-give options is the *NonProfits* **(www.thenonprofits .com). It lists hundreds of causes and sites, grouped under "Hunger and Poverty," "Health, Education, Misc.," and "Environment and Animals."** Because I work, have a family, and take two classes, I do not have much extra time or money. Going to these Web sites allows me to feel as if I am contributing and making a small difference, and that feels good.

Support 1

Support 2

Support 3

Support concluding sentence

Support for the main point

Details explaining the support: Usually, 1 to 3 sentences for each support point in paragraphs, and three to eight sentences for each point in essays.

Conclusion

Essay Form

Some ways to do good for our world do not require much time, effort, or money. My favorite way is to use click-and-give Web sites, where just going to the site triggers donations to it from another source (not you). Anyone can help out in any cause they are interested in by just one quick click. Every night before I go to bed, I go to one or more of the sites. I have particular favorites, but there are hundreds to choose from.

Thesis statement

The first site that I click on every day is the *Animal Rescue Site* (**www.theanimalrescuesite .com**). Each click gives food to rescued animals. The Web site provides information about the sponsors of the site and where the donations go. It also has information about the site's projects and the animals who are rescued, a photo contest, and fun online games that you can play to trigger more donations. My favorite is Bubble Burst. People can become involved in "challenges." Most nights I have time only to click to give, which is why I go to this site every single night.

Topic sentence 1

2

Another of my favorite Web sites is *Free Rice* (**www.freerice .com**) where I play vocabulary or grammar games. With each correct answer, grains of rice are donated to hungry people. The games are offered at increasingly difficult levels, and for each correct answer, you are told how many grains of rice you have given. A wooden bowl fills up with the grains as you play. When I go to this Web site, I feel as if I am doing good, having fun, and learning useful words.

Topic sentence 2

3

One site with lots of click-and-give options is the *NonProfits* (**www.thenonprofits.com**). It lists hundreds of causes and sites, grouped under "Hunger and Poverty," "Health, Education, Misc.," and "Environment and Animals." Under "Hunger and Poverty," I go to the site named "One Click One Meal." This site says that one person dies every three seconds of starvation. A quick click will fund "One More Meal," with a donation to the World Food Programme. You can click on "WorldFoodProgramme" and read about the program, about nutrition, and about other related information. Twenty other sites help stop hunger and poverty, and many others are available in categories such as health, education, environment, and animals. Exploring the many choices, I find that each one I click on gives me so much information as well as the opportunity to help others.

Topic sentence 3

Because I work, have a family, and take two classes, I do not have much extra time or money. Still, I know there are many problems in the world, and I would like to help in some way. Going to these Web sites allows me to feel as if I am contributing and making a small difference, and that feels good. So try it: Click and give.

Concluding paragraph

An essay has three necessary parts—an introduction, a body, and a conclusion.

ESSAY PART	PURPOSE OF THE ESSAY PART
1. The **introduction**	states the **main point**, or **thesis**, generally in a single strong statement. The introduction may be a single paragraph or multiple paragraphs.
2. The **body**	supports (shows, explains, or proves) the main point. The body of an essay generally has at least three **support paragraphs**. Each support paragraph begins with a **topic sentence** that supports the thesis statement and continues with facts and details that develop the main point.
3. The **conclusion**	reminds readers of the main point. It may summarize and reinforce the support in the body paragraphs, or it may make an observation based on that support. Whether it is a single paragraph or more, the conclusion should relate back to the main point of the essay.

The parts of an essay correspond to the parts of a paragraph. The **thesis** of an essay is like the **topic sentence** of a paragraph. The **support paragraphs** in the body of an essay are like the **support sentences** of a paragraph. And the **conclusion** of an essay is like the **concluding sentence** of a paragraph. The diagram on pages 18–19 shows how paragraphs and essays are related.

The Writing Process

The **writing process** consists of four basic stages—generating ideas, planning and drafting, revising, and editing. The flowchart on the next page shows the four basic stages of the writing process and the steps within each stage.

THE WRITING PROCESS

Generate Ideas

CONSIDER: What is my purpose in writing? Given this purpose, what interests me? What connections can I make among ideas? Who will read what I am writing? What do they need to know?

- Determine your audience and purpose (pages 22–23).
- Find and explore your topic (pages 23–29).
- Make your point (pages 31–34).
- Support your point (pages 39–43).

Plan and Draft

CONSIDER: How can I organize and present my ideas effectively for my readers?

- Arrange your ideas, and make an outline (pages 44–47).
- Write a draft, including an introduction that will interest your readers, a strong conclusion, and a title (pages 49–56).

Revise

CONSIDER: How can I make my draft clearer or more convincing to my readers?

- Look for ideas that do not fit (pages 58–60).
- Look for ideas that could use more detailed support (pages 60–62).
- Connect ideas with transitional words and sentences (pages 62–65).

Edit

CONSIDER: What errors could confuse my readers and weaken my point?

- Find and correct the most serious errors in grammar (Chapter 16).
- Look for other errors in grammar and style (Chapter 17).
- Check your punctuation and capitalization (Chapter 18).

Audience and Purpose

Your **audience** is the person or people who will read what you write. Whenever you write, always have at least one real person in mind as a reader. Think about what that person already knows and what he or she will need to know to understand your main idea. In most cases, assume that readers will know only what you write about your topic and main point.

The **purpose** of a piece of writing is the reason for writing it. In college, your purpose for writing often will be to show something; to summarize, analyze, synthesize, or evaluate something; or to make a convincing argument. In college writing, you want to demonstrate that you understand the content of the course.

Understanding your purpose for writing is key to writing successfully. In college, to understand your purpose, be sure to read assignments and exam questions critically, highlighting words that tell you what your instructor wants to see in your writing.

The tone and content of your writing will vary depending on your audiences and purposes. The chart that follows explains some different audiences and purposes.

Audience and Purpose

TYPE OF WRITING	AUDIENCE AND PURPOSE	TIPS
COLLEGE: A research essay about the environmental effects of "fracking": fracturing rock layers to extract oil or natural gas	AUDIENCE: The professor of your environmental science class PURPOSE: • To complete an assignment according to your professor's instructions and any research methods discussed in class • To show what you have learned about the topic	When writing to fulfill a course assignment, never make assumptions like, "My instructor already knows this fact, so what's the point of mentioning it?" By providing plenty of relevant examples and details, you demonstrate your knowledge of a subject and make your writing more effective.
WORK: An e-mail to coworkers about your company's new insurance provider	AUDIENCE: Fellow workers PURPOSE: To make sure that coworkers understand all the important details about the new provider	Define or explain any terminology or concepts that will not be familiar to your audience.

TYPE OF WRITING	AUDIENCE AND PURPOSE	TIPS
EVERYDAY LIFE: An electronic comment about an online newspaper editorial that you disagree with	AUDIENCE: • The editorial writer • Other readers of the editorial PURPOSE: To make the editorial writer and other readers aware of your views	Keep all correspondence with others as polite as possible, even if you disagree with their views.

Finding, Narrowing, and Exploring Your Topic

A **topic** is what, who, or where you are writing about. Any topic that you choose to write about should pass the following test.

QUESTIONS FOR FINDING A GOOD TOPIC

- Does this topic interest me?
- Can I find out more about it?
- Can I get involved with this topic? Is it relevant to my life in some way?
- Does it fit the assignment, focusing on a subject neither too broad nor too narrow to treat in the assigned length?

Choose one of the following broad topics or one of your own, and focus on one specific aspect of it that you think would make a good topic for a short essay.

My goals	Something I am proud of
Pet peeves	Something I enjoy doing
Personal responsibility	Reality TV
Relationships	Popular music

Use the general topic you have chosen to complete the practice activities on pages 25 and 29.

Narrowing a Topic

To **narrow** a topic is to focus on the smaller parts of a general topic until you find a more limited topic or an angle that is interesting and specific. In real life, you narrow topics all the time: You talk with friends about a particular song rather than music, about a particular person rather than the human race, or about a class you are taking rather than every class the college offers.

In college writing, you often need to do the same thing. A professor may give you a broad topic like "religion and culture," "cheating in our society," or "goals in life." These topics are too general to write about in a short essay, so you need to know how to narrow them.

ASK YOURSELF QUESTIONS

For the broad essay topic "religion and culture," one student asked the questions below to make it manageable.

GENERAL TOPIC **Religion and Culture**

QUESTIONS   What religion—mine?

Whose culture—mine? This country's? Another country's? Now or in the past?

What kind of culture—like art? Politics?

Serious religion? Or things like Christmas music? Maybe both?

MAP YOUR IDEAS

Use circles and lines to help visually break a general topic into more specific ones. Start in the center of a blank piece of paper, and write your topic. Circle your topic, and ask yourself some questions about it, such as "What do I know about it?" or "What's important about it?" Write your ideas around the topic, drawing lines from your topic to the ideas and then circling them. Keep adding ideas, connecting them with the lines and circles. This technique is called **mapping** or **clustering**. After mapping, look at each cluster of ideas, and consider using one of the narrower topics.

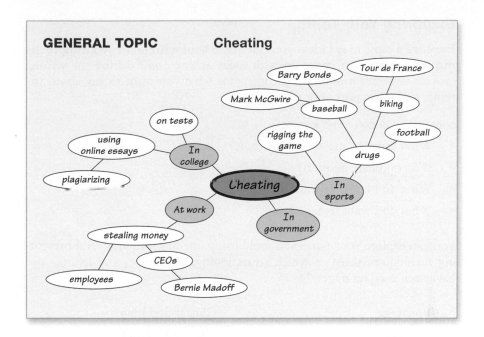

GENERAL TOPIC   Cheating

LIST NARROWER TOPICS

GENERAL TOPIC	NARROWER IDEAS
Personal goals	Stop smoking
	Get a better job
	Get a college degree
	Learn to use my time better

PRACTICE 1   Narrowing a Topic

Use one of the three methods on pages 24–25 to narrow your topic. Then, write your narrowed topic below.

NARROWED TOPIC: _____

Exploring Your Topic

Explore a topic to get ideas you can use in your writing. **Prewriting techniques** are ways to come up with ideas at any point during the writing process—to find a topic, to get ideas for what you want to say about the topic, and to support your ideas.

QUESTIONS FOR EXPLORING A TOPIC

■   What interests me about this topic?

■   Why do I care about it?

■   What do I know or want to know?

■   What do I want to say?

You can explore your narrowed topic using one or more of several prewriting techniques, three of which (questioning, clustering, and listing) you have seen used on pages 24–25.

■   Freewrite   ■   Cluster and map

■   List and brainstorm   ■   Use the Internet

■   Ask a reporter's questions   ■   Keep a journal

■   Discuss

While exploring ideas, just think; do not judge. You can decide later whether your ideas are good or not. At this point, your goal is to get as many ideas as possible. Write down all the possibilities.

The following sections detail techniques for exploring ideas and show how one student used each one of them to get ideas about the topic "Getting a college degree."

FREEWRITE

Freewriting is like having a conversation with yourself on paper. To freewrite, just start writing everything you can think of about your topic. Write nonstop for at least five minutes. Do not go back and cross anything out or worry about using correct grammar or spelling; just write.

> *I don't know, I don't think about goals more than just handling every day—I don't have time. The kids, my job, laundry, food, school, it's a lot. So I just get by day by day but I know that won't get me or my kids anywhere. I really do wish I could get a better job that was more interesting and I wish I could make more money and get my kids better stuff and live in a better place and not be worried all the time about money and our apartment and all that. I really do need to get that degree cause I know we'd have a better chance then. I know I need to finish college.*

LIST AND BRAINSTORM

List all the ideas about your topic that come to your mind. Write as fast as you can for five minutes without stopping.

> So hard to find time to study
> Good in the long run
> Lots of advantages
> Better job
> Better place to live
> More money
> More opportunities
> A big achievement—no one in my family's ever gotten a degree
> But they don't give me support either

ASK A REPORTER'S QUESTIONS

Ask yourself questions to start getting ideas. The following reporter's questions—Who? What? Where? When? Why? and How?—give you different angles on a narrowed topic, but you can also use other kinds of questions that come to you as you explore your narrowed topic.

> Who? Me, a single mother and student
>
> What? Getting a college degree
>
> Where? Stetson Community College
>
> When? Taking classes off and on now, want a degree in next couple of years
>
> Why? Because I want more out of life for my kids and me
>
> How? Working like a dog to finish school

DISCUSS

When you discuss ideas with someone else, you get more ideas and also feedback on them from the other person.

Team up with another person. If you both have writing assignments, first discuss one person's topic and then the other's. Ask questions about anything that seems unclear, and let the writer know what sounds interesting. Give thoughtful answers, and keep an open mind. It is a good idea to take notes when your partner comments on your ideas.

CLUSTER AND MAP

You saw an example of clustering, also called mapping, on page 25. Here is another one.

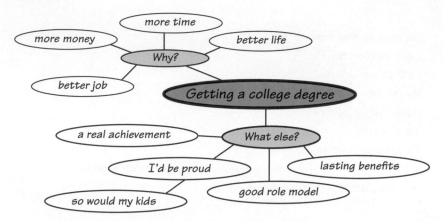

USE THE INTERNET

Do an online search using key words related to your topic, being as specific as possible. The search will probably yield a lot of results that can give you more ideas about your topic.

KEEP A JOURNAL

Another good way to explore ideas and topics for writing is to keep a journal. Set aside a few minutes a day to write in your journal. Your journal will be a great source of ideas when you need to find something to write about.

You can use a journal in many ways:

- To record and explore your personal thoughts and feelings
- To comment on things that happen either in the neighborhood, at work, at your college, in the news, and so on
- To examine situations you do not understand (as you write, you may figure them out)

I've been taking courses at the college for a couple of years but not really knowing whether I'd ever finish or not. It's so hard, and I'm so tired all the time that I sometimes think it would be easier (and cheaper!) to stop or to go one semester and not another, but then it's so easy to get out of the habit. I need to decide whether getting a degree is worth all of the effort it will take, and I'm starting to think it is. I don't want to live like this forever. I want a better life.

PRACTICE 2　Prewriting

Choose *two* prewriting techniques, and use them to explore your narrowed topic. Keep your readers in mind as you explore your topic. Find ideas that will be effective for both your purpose and your readers' understanding.

Writing Assignment

Review your narrowed topic (Practice 1) and some ideas about it (Practice 2). Use the checklist that follows to evaluate your topic and to understand the process of narrowing and exploring a general topic. If necessary, spend some more time clarifying your topic or generating ideas before moving on to Chapter 3.

CHECKLIST

Evaluating Your Topic

FOCUS

☐ Read the assignment carefully and consider your audience and purpose.

ASK

☐ Review the "Questions for Finding a Good Topic" on page 23.

☐ Is the topic too big for a short essay, if that is the assignment?

☐ If it is too big, what are some more limited parts of the topic?

☐ Once I have a narrowed topic, ask the "Questions for Exploring a Topic" on page 26.

☐ Do I or my audience have any assumptions or biases relating to my topic that I should be aware of? If so, what are they?

☐ What can I say about my topic? What ideas do I have about my topic?

☐ Use a prewriting technique to explore ideas about your narrowed topic.

Organizing Your Main Point and Support

Arranging Your Ideas

Thesis Statements

The **thesis statement** of an essay states the main point you want to get across about your topic. It is your position on whatever you are writing about.

| Narrowed topic | + | Main point/position | = | Thesis statement |

Eating disorders are caused by both cultural and psychological factors.

A strong thesis statement has several basic features.

BASICS OF A GOOD THESIS STATEMENT

- It focuses on a single main point or position about the topic.
- It fits the size of the assignment.
- It is specific.
- It is something that you can show, explain, or prove.
- It is a forceful statement written in confident, firm language.

> **WEAK THESIS STATEMENT** I think college is good, and there are lots of them.

The weak statement does not follow the basics of a good thesis statement: It focuses on two points, not one; it is very broad; the word *good* is not specific; and the words *I think* are not forceful or confident.

> **GOOD THESIS STATEMENT** A college degree brings many potential benefits such as better jobs, more career choices, and higher salaries.

✓ LearningCurve **For extra practice in the skills covered in this chapter, visit** bedfordstmartins.com/reinteractive.

This statement has all the basics of a good thesis statement.

A good thesis statement is essential to most good essays. Early in your writing process, you may develop a *draft thesis* (or *working thesis*), a first-try version of the sentence that will state your main point. You can revise it into a final thesis statement later in the writing process.

Focusing on a Single Main Point

Your thesis should focus on one main point. If you try to address more than one main point in an essay, you will not be able to give adequate support for all the points. Also, you risk splitting your focus.

THESIS STATEMENT WITH TWO MAIN POINTS

In the next decade, <u>many high schools will have a drastic shortage of teachers,</u> and <u>high school teachers should have to take competency tests.</u>

The two points are underlined. The writer would need to explain why there will be a shortage of teachers and also why teachers should take competency tests. These are both meaty points, and any writer would have trouble supporting them equally in a single essay.

REVISED

In the next decade, many schools will have a drastic shortage of high school teachers.

or

High school teachers should have to take competency tests.

Although a good thesis statement focuses on a single main point, it may include more than one idea if these ideas directly relate to the main point.

A good thesis may or may not include other information that the essay will include. If you know the points or examples that you will make to support your thesis, you can include them. In the example below, the thesis statement includes some points (shown in *italics*) that support the writer's main point.

The job market for students is tight, but there are things you can do to help get a job in your field, such as *asking for an informational interview, finding a mentor, or getting an internship.*

Fitting the Size of the Assignment

A thesis that is too broad is impossible to support fully in a short essay: There is just too much to cover well. A thesis that is too narrow does not give you enough to write a whole essay on.

TOO BROAD	The Industrial Revolution was important in this country.
	[The Industrial Revolution is too broad to cover in an essay.]
REVISED	During the Industrial Revolution, women workers in the textile industry played an important role in Lowell, Massachusetts.

A thesis that is too narrow leaves the writer with little to show, explain, or prove. It can also make the reader think, "So what?"

TOO NARROW	I tweeted this morning.
REVISED	Tweeting connects me to other people and their ideas.

Being Specific

A good thesis statement gives readers specific information so that they know exactly what the writer's main point is.

GENERAL	Writing is important for my job.
	[Why is writing important for your job, and what kind of job do you have?]
SPECIFIC	Although my primary job, as a nurse, is to care for others, I have found that my ability to write clearly is essential.
	[This thesis tells us that the job is nursing and suggests that the essay will discuss the types of writing a nurse does.]

One good way to be specific is to let your readers know what you will be discussing in your essay. In this way, your thesis prepares your reader for what is to come.

MORE SPECIFIC   As a nurse, my ability to write clearly is essential in documents such as patient reports, status notes to nurses on other shifts, and e-mails to other hospital staff.

[This thesis tells the reader specific kinds of writing the essay will discuss.]

Writing a Thesis That You Can Show, Explain, or Prove

If a thesis is so obvious that it does not need support or if it states a known fact, you will not be able to say much about it.

OBVIOUS   Most teenagers drive.

REVISED   The high accident rates among new teen drivers could be reduced with better and more extended driver training.

FACT   A growing number of American children are over-weight.

REVISED   We must, as a nation, act to reduce obesity in our children.

Being Forceful and Confident

A strong thesis statement should be forceful and definite. Avoid writing a thesis statement that begins, "In this essay I will show . . . ." Do not say you will make a point. Just make it.

WEAK   In this essay, I will prove that high school dropouts have a difficult time in life.

FORCEFUL   High school dropouts can expect to face surprising hardships in life.

Also, some words and phrases—such as "maybe" and "I think"—can indicate you lack confidence in your main point. Avoid them.

WEAK   I think you have to be careful when buying a used car.

FORCEFUL   Before you buy a used car, inform yourself about the basics so that you do not spend more than you need to.

The practices that follow will help you write a good thesis statement. The first practice helps you develop a thesis statement from a narrowed topic. The rest focus on the basics of a good thesis statement (p. 31).

PRACTICE 1 Developing a Thesis Statement from a Narrowed Topic

For each general topic, write a thesis statement from the narrowed topic.

EXAMPLE

GENERAL TOPIC: Foreign languages

NARROWED TOPIC: Learning a foreign language

THESIS: *Learning a foreign language has many benefits.*

GENERAL TOPIC	NARROWED TOPIC
A memory	My first date
Music	My favorite kind of music
Friendship	My best friend
Owning a car	Costs of owning a car
Reality TV	A show that you watch
Politics	Dishonest campaign advertisements

PRACTICE 2 Writing Thesis Statements That Focus on a Single Main Point

Rewrite the following thesis statements so that they focus on just one of the points made. You can add information to make the statements more specific.

> **EXAMPLE:** Juggling college and other responsibilities can be challenging, and rising college costs are putting higher education out of reach for many.

Juggling college and other responsibilities can be challenging.

1.   Planning for college financial aid should begin long before a student's first year of college, and prospective students should also consider how attending college will affect their family life.

2.   My first job taught me the importance of cooperation, and I also learned how to manage my time effectively.

3.   For several reasons, I will never own my own business, but I do have what it takes to be a top athlete.

PRACTICE 3 Writing Thesis Statements That Fit the Size of the Assignment

Read the following thesis statements, and decide whether they are too broad, too narrow, or the right size for a short essay. Rewrite statements that are too broad or too narrow to better fit the size of the assignment. For statements that are the right size, write "OK."

> **EXAMPLE:** My dog will be ten years old next month.
>
> **BROADER:** Dogs make excellent pets because they are social, loyal, and affectionate.

1. Hinduism is a fascinating religion.

2. I love food.

3. Being a vegetarian offers a wide range of healthy food choices.

4. There are many vegetarians in this country.

5. Another gourmet coffee shop opened last week, the third one on a single block.

PRACTICE 4 Writing Thesis Statements That Are Specific

Rewrite each of the following thesis statements by adding at least two specific details.

> **EXAMPLE:** Electronic devices in high schools can be a huge problem.
>
> *Cell phones that ring during a high school class disrupt students' concentration and learning.*

1. I have many useful skills.

2. Studying with a partner can be helpful.

3. I have always had trouble writing.

4. Children have more allergies now than in the past.

5. After I received my first paycheck, I had many feelings.

PRACTICE 5 **Writing Thesis Statements That You Can Show, Explain, or Prove**

Each of the following items is either obvious or a fact and therefore difficult to write about. Rewrite each sentence so that it would give you something to write in an essay.

> **EXAMPLE:** I have lived in this neighborhood for fourteen years. [Fact]
>
> *In the fourteen years I have lived in this town, I have learned a lot about small towns.*

1. Many teenagers experiment with drugs.

2. Every year my college fees go up.

3. I make $8.00 an hour.

4. I have just finished my first college course.

5. Public transportation makes it easier to get to work.

PRACTICE 6 **Writing Forceful Thesis Statements**

Rewrite the weak thesis statements that follow to make them more forceful.

> **EXAMPLE:** In my opinion, students who are involved with the community learn many important lessons.
>
> *Students who are involved with the community learn many important lessons.*

1. I will explain some examples of history repeating itself.

2. This college could have better parking facilities.

3. Given that I have improved my job performance and shown a lot of initiative, I am pretty sure I will get a raise this year.

4. It would be a good idea to warn young people about the possible dangers of prescription drug abuse.

5. In this paper, I will describe three reasons why going to college has been a challenge for me.

. . . .

PRACTICE 7   Revising Thesis Statements

Revise each of the possible thesis statements that you wrote in Practice 1, improving them according to the basics of a good thesis statement (p. 31).

> **POSSIBLE THESIS:**   When the sun is shining, people's moods improve.
>
> **REVISED THESIS:**   Bright sunshine dramatically improves people's moods.

. . . .

Writing Assignment

Write a thesis statement using the narrowed topic and ideas you developed in Chapter 2 or one of the following topics (which will need to be narrowed). Use the checklist below as you work.

Friendship	Fashion or style	A good cause
Drug use	Video games	A waste of time
Exercise	Going "green"	A cultural icon

CHECKLIST

Writing a Thesis Statement

FOCUS

☐ Read your narrowed topic.

☐ Decide what you think is important about it. You may want to use a prewriting technique.

☐ Consider your audience and purpose.

ASK

☐ What is your position or your point about your topic?

☐ Why is it important to you?

☐ Do you have assumptions or biases? Does your audience?

☐ What do you want to show, explain, or prove?

☐ Can you think of additional ideas to support it?

☐ Is your position a single point?

☐ Is it a complete sentence?

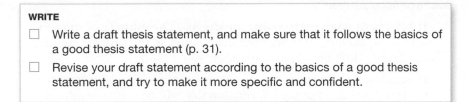

WRITE

☐ Write a draft thesis statement, and make sure that it follows the basics of a good thesis statement (p. 31).

☐ Revise your draft statement according to the basics of a good thesis statement, and try to make it more specific and confident.

Support for Your Thesis

Support consists of the evidence, examples, or facts that show, explain, or prove your main point, or thesis, so you need to keep that main point in focus. **Primary support points** are the major support for your thesis. **Supporting details** (or secondary support points) are specifics that explain your primary support points.

Key Features of Good Support

Without support, you *state* the main point, but you do not *make* the main point. Consider the following statement:

My neighborhood needs more markets.

This statement may be true, but without support it is not convincing.

Keep in mind that restating the same idea several times using different words is not support; it is just repetition of an idea that does not help you support your thesis.

REPETITION, NOT SUPPORT	I do not deserve an F on this paper. It is not a failing paper. It should get a better grade.
SUPPORT	I do not deserve an F on this paper. It not only follows the assignment, but I was careful to apply the criteria for grading that was handed out. It has a thesis and support. Even though it has many grammar errors, the paper meets other criteria and should have received a better grade.

As you develop support for your thesis, make sure that each point has the following basic features.

BASICS OF GOOD SUPPORT

▪ **It relates to your main point, or thesis.** The purpose of support is to show, explain, or prove your main point, so the support you use must relate directly to that main point.

▪ **It considers your readers.** Aim your support at the people who will read your writing. Supply information that will convince or inform them.

▪ **It is detailed and specific.** Give readers enough detail, particularly through examples, so that they can see what you mean.

▪ **It helps you achieve your purpose for writing.** Remember your reason for writing.

▪ **It is logical.** One point follows another and does not have logical fallacies (see Chapter 1).

Generating Support

A short essay usually has between three and five primary points that support the thesis statement. Longer pieces of writing require more support. Each primary support point becomes the topic sentence of its own paragraph. Each paragraph presents details that support that topic sentence.

The following sections detail the steps in supporting a thesis statement.

PREWRITE TO FIND SUPPORT

Reread your thesis and imagine your readers asking, "What do you mean?" To answer this question and generate support for your thesis, try using one or more of the prewriting techniques discussed in Chapter 2.

PRACTICE 8   Prewriting to Find Support

Complete one of the following sentences or write a sentence of your own and use one of the prewriting techniques on pages 26–29 to generate at least a dozen different ideas.

1.   Everyone in my family . . . .

2.   Although people want to "eat healthy". . . .

3.   One way my city (or town) has improved is . . . .

4.   Today, bullying is . . . .

DROP UNRELATED IDEAS

After prewriting, remind yourself of your main point. Then, review your prewriting carefully, and drop any ideas that are not directly related to your main point. If new ideas occur to you, write them down.

PRACTICE 9 Dropping Unrelated Ideas

Review the prewriting you did for Practice 8 (p. 40), and cross out any unrelated ideas.

SELECT THE BEST SUPPORT POINTS

After dropping unrelated ideas, review the ones that remain, and select those that will be clearest and most convincing to your readers. As noted earlier, short essays usually have three to five primary support points. They will become the topic sentences for your support paragraphs.

PRACTICE 10 Selecting the Best Support Points

For each remaining point from Practice 9 (above), circle the three points you would use to support the thesis statement.

Add Supporting Details

Once you have chosen your primary support points, you will need to add details to explain or demonstrate each of those points. These supporting details can be examples, facts, or evidence. As the following examples show, a supporting detail is always more specific than a primary support point.

THESIS STATEMENT More research is needed on how to treat autism, a serious disorder affecting behavior, communication, and social interaction.

PRIMARY SUPPORT POINT The disorder affects many people, their families, and communities.

SUPPORTING DETAILS Autism is now diagnosed in about 1 in every 110 children.

This rate is much higher than it was thirty years ago (was 1 in 2000).

Parents and school staffs struggle to know how best to help autistic children.

PRIMARY SUPPORT POINT	Some people go online to buy risky treatments that are not science based.
SUPPORTING DETAILS	pressurized oxygen chambers, drug and vitamin supplements, special diets and nutrition consultations, blood transfusions
PRIMARY SUPPORT POINT	More research has already started to have some good effects.
SUPPORTING DETAILS	Funding has increased 15 percent a year between 2000 and 2010, with hundreds more scientists now studying autism.
	Many of the treatments advertised online have now been scientifically proven not to work.
	Children can now be diagnosed as young as one to two years old, when behavior therapy has a better success rate.

PRACTICE 11   Adding Supporting Details

For your three primary support points from Practice 10 (p. 41), imagine your readers asking, "What do you mean?" Add specific details to answer that question.

Review Support

When you have developed support for your main point, along with supporting details, use your critical thinking and reading skills to evaluate it. Does the support make assumptions? Does it reveal a bias in your point of view? Go back to Chapter 1 and remind yourself of the common logical fallacies described on pages 6–7. It is important to review your support in this way because errors in reasoning make it difficult to make your main point effectively.

Write Topic Sentences for Your Support Points

Your primary support points will form the topic sentences of the paragraphs that support your thesis statement. Each topic sentence should clearly relate to and show, explain, or prove your thesis.

THESIS STATEMENT	Playing a team sport taught me more than how to play the game.

TOPIC SENTENCE   I learned the importance of hard practice.
(paragraph 1)

TOPIC SENTENCE   I also realized that, to succeed, I had to work with
(paragraph 2)   other people.

TOPIC SENTENCE   Most important, I learned to be responsible to others.
(paragraph 3)

Once you develop topic sentences to support your thesis, back up your topic sentences with supporting details.

PRACTICE 12 Writing Topic Sentences and Supporting Details

Using the support points you generated in Practice 10, write topic sentences that support your thesis statement. Then list the details you came up with in Practice 11. When you have completed this practice, you will have developed support for an essay.

Writing Assignment

Develop primary support points and supporting details for the thesis you wrote on page 38 or for one of the following thesis statements.

William Lowe Bryan said, "Education is one of the few things a person is willing to pay for and not get."

Elderly people in this country are not shown enough respect.

Few people know how to really listen.

Some movies have made me cry from happiness.

Before writing, read the following checklist.

CHECKLIST

Supporting Your Thesis

FOCUS

☐ Reread your thesis.

☐ Think about the people who will read your writing.

☐ Think about your purpose for writing.

ASK

☐ What support can you include that will show, explain, or prove what you mean?

☐ What do your readers need to know or understand to be convinced?

☐ What examples come to mind?

☐ What have you experienced yourself?

☐ What information can you find on the Internet, in a print source, or from people you meet and interview?

☐ What details could you use to strengthen the support?

WRITE

☐ Use a prewriting technique to find as many support points as you can.

☐ Drop ideas that are not directly related to your main thesis.

☐ Select the best primary support.

☐ Add supporting details.

☐ Review and evaluate your support.

☐ Write topic sentences for your primary support points.

☐ Make sure that all of your support points have the basics of good support (p. 40).

Arrange Your Ideas

Once you have generated support for your thesis, you need to arrange that support in a logical order. Three common ways of ordering your ideas are **chronological order** (by the time sequence in which events happened), **spatial order** (by the physical arrangement of objects or features), and **order of importance** (by the significance of the ideas or reasons).

Chronological Order

Use **chronological order** to arrange points according to when they happened. Time order works well when you are telling the story of an event or explaining how to do something. Usually, you go in sequence from what happened first to what happened last; in some cases, though, you can work back from what happened last to what happened first.

EXAMPLE USING CHRONOLOGICAL (TIME) ORDER

The cause of the fire that destroyed the apartment building was human carelessness. The couple in apartment 2F had planned a romantic dinner to celebrate the woman's raise at work. They lit candles all over the apartment and then shared a bottle of wine and ate a delicious meal. After dinner, they decided to go out to a club to continue the celebration. Unfortunately, they forgot to blow out all of the candles, and one of them was too close to a window curtain, which caught fire. The fire spread quickly throughout the apartment and then spread to others. By the time another resident smelled smoke, the fire was uncontrollable. The building was destroyed. Fortunately, rescuers were able to save everyone who was in the building. But all of the tenants lost their homes and most of their possessions. Human carelessness caused much human misery.

Spatial Order

Use **spatial order** to arrange ideas so that your readers see your topic as you do. Space order works well when you are writing about what someone or something looks like. You can move from top to bottom, bottom to top, near to far, far to near, left to right, right to left, back to front, or front to back.

EXAMPLE USING SPATIAL (SPACE) ORDER

I stood watching in horror while all-powerful flames destroyed an entire building, including my apartment and everything I owned. The first few floors looked normal, except that firefighters were racing into the front entry. A couple of floors up, windows were breaking and gray, foul-smelling smoke was billowing out. I could see shadows of the firefighters moving in and out of the apartments. My eyes were drawn to the top two floors, where flames of orange and white leapt from the windows. A dog with brown and white spots barked furiously from the rooftop until it was rescued. Until you have actually witnessed a severe fire, you cannot imagine how powerful it is and how powerless you feel in its presence.

Order of Importance

Use **order of importance** to arrange points according to their significance, interest, or surprise value. Save the most important point for last.

EXAMPLE USING ORDER OF IMPORTANCE

Fires caused by human carelessness often have disastrous effects on people's lives. In a recent incident, when an apartment building was completely destroyed by a fire, the owner and tenants had no homes to return to. They also lost all of their possessions: furniture, clothing, and irreplaceable treasured personal items. Worse than that, however, was that the owner and many of the tenants had no insurance to help them find new housing and replace their possessions. Many had to depend completely on relatives, friends, and a fund that was started for them by neighbors. The most disastrous effect of the fire, however, was that many tenants lost their beloved pets. While firefighters bravely rescued all the people, they were not able to save all the animals. Carelessness has no place around fire, which has the power to destroy.

As you arrange your ideas, consider what your purpose for writing is and what kind of organization would work best to make your main point. Some examples follow in the chart.

PURPOSE	ORGANIZATION
To describe an experience To explain how something works To explain how to do something	Chronological
To help your reader visualize whatever you are describing as you see it To create an impression using your senses—taste, touch, sight, smell, sound To re-create a scene	Spatial
To persuade or convince someone To make a case for or against something	Importance

Make a Plan

When you have decided how to order your ideas, make a written plan—an **outline**—starting with your thesis statement. Then, state each of your primary support points as a topic sentence for one of the body paragraphs of the essay. Add supporting details to develop or explain the topic sentence. Your plan should also include a possible main point for the concluding paragraph. Although your outline serves as a good guide, it can be changed as you draft your essay.

For a diagram of the relationship between paragraphs and essays, see page 18–19.

Some people find it useful to write full sentences as they plan so that their outline is a more complete guide for the essay.

Also, there is no one right order for any essay. Use the order that will help you make your main point most effectively.

OUTLINE FOR A SHORT ESSAY: The example that follows uses "standard" or "formal" outline format, in which numbers and letters distinguish between primary support points and secondary supporting details. Some instructors require this format. If you are making an outline for yourself, you might choose to write a less formal outline, simply indenting secondary supporting details under the primary support rather than using numbers and letters.

Thesis statement

   I. Topic sentence (primary support point 1)
     A. Supporting detail
     B. Supporting detail (and so on)
  II. Topic sentence (primary support point 2)
     A. Supporting detail
     B. Supporting detail (and so on)
 III. Topic sentence (primary support point 3)
     A. Supporting detail
     B. Supporting detail (and so on)

Concluding paragraph

Writing Assignment

Create an outline using the thesis statement, topic sentences, and supporting details you have developed in this chapter. Arrange your ideas according to chronological order, spatial order, or order of importance. As you work on your outline, complete the checklist below.

CHECKLIST

Making an Outline

FOCUS

☐ Reread your thesis.

☐ Review your support points and details.

☐ Think about your audience and purpose.

ASK

☐ Do you have at least three supporting points for your thesis?

☐ Does each supporting point have at least one supporting detail?

☐ What order would work best for your writing purpose: chronological order, space order, or order of importance? (Review the table on page 46.)

☐ Does your instructor require you to use a formal outline format?

WRITE

☐ Put your thesis statement at the top of the outline.

☐ List your three main support points as topic sentences, following chronological order, spatial order, or order of importance.

☐ Include supporting details in complete sentences under each topic sentence.

☐ Draft a main point for your concluding paragraph.

You now have a clear main point with support, organized in a logical way. In the next chapter, you will begin drafting your paragraph or essay.

4

Drafting and Revising

Putting Your Ideas Together

A **draft** is the first whole version of your ideas in writing. Do the best job you can in writing a draft, but remember that you will have a chance to make changes later.

BASICS OF A GOOD DRAFT

- It has a thesis statement that presents the main point.
- It has a logical organization of ideas.
- It has primary support points that are stated in topic sentences that develop or explain the thesis statement.
- It has supporting details that develop or explain each topic sentence.
- It follows standard essay form (introduction, body paragraphs, conclusion) and uses complete sentences.
- The introduction captures the readers' interest and lets them know what the essay is about.
- The conclusion reinforces the main point and makes an observation.

For advice on support and more on thesis statements, see Chapter 3.

For a diagram showing the parts of an essay, see page 19, and for a complete draft of an essay, see page 56.

Writing a Draft

The explanations and practices in this section will prepare you to write a good draft essay.

Draft the Body of the Essay

Use your plan for your essay as you begin to write your draft. The plan should include your thesis statement, the primary support points for your thesis, and supporting details for your primary support points.

✓ LearningCurve **For extra practice in the skills covered in this chapter, visit** bedfordstmartins.com/reinteractive.

49

First, draft complete paragraphs that support your thesis. Each should contain a topic sentence (usually the first sentence in the paragraph) that presents a primary support point as well as supporting details. At this point, draft the body of your essay; you will write the introduction and conclusion later. In general, essays have at least three body paragraphs, and they may have many more, depending on your assignment and purpose.

If you are having trouble with a word or sentence as you draft, make a note to come back to it and then keep going.

PRACTICE 1   Writing Topic Sentences

Writing topic sentences for primary support points is a good way to start drafting the body of an essay. Convert each of the following primary support points into a topic sentence that supports the thesis. You can make up details if you want.

> **THESIS STATEMENT:** Being a good customer service representative in a retail store requires several important skills.
>
>   I. Being pleasant and polite [Primary support point 1]
>   A. Smiling, saying hello [Supporting detail]
>   B. Looking at person [Supporting detail]
>
> **TOPIC SENTENCE I:** _____
>
>   II. Listening carefully [Primary support point 2]
>   A. Making notes [Supporting detail]
>   B. Asking questions [Supporting detail]
>
> **TOPIC SENTENCE II:** _____
>
>   III. Figuring out how to solve the problem [Primary support point 3]
>   A. Calling the right people [Supporting detail]
>   B. Filling out paperwork [Supporting detail]
>
> **TOPIC SENTENCE III:** _____

Write an Introduction

The introduction to your essay should capture your readers' interest and present the main point. Think of your introductory paragraph as a challenge. Ask yourself: How can I get my readers to want to continue reading?

BASICS OF A GOOD INTRODUCTION

- It should catch readers' attention.
- It should present the essay's thesis statement (narrowed topic + main point).
- It should give readers an idea of what the essay will cover.

The thesis statement is often either the first or the last sentence in the introductory paragraph, though you may find essays in which it is elsewhere.

Here are examples of common kinds of introductions that spark readers' interest.

START WITH A SURPRISING FACT OR IDEA

Surprises capture people's attention. The more unexpected and surprising something is, the more likely people are to take notice of it and read on.

> I was saved from sin when I was going on thirteen. But not really saved. It happened like this. There was a big revival at my Auntie Reed's church. Every night for weeks there had been much preaching, singing, praying, and shouting, and some very hardened sinners had been brought to Christ, and the membership of the church had grown by leaps and bounds. Then just before the revival ended, they held a special meeting for children, "to bring the young lambs into the fold." My aunt spoke of it for days ahead. That night I was escorted to the front row and placed on the mourners' bench with all the other young sinners, who had not yet been brought to Jesus.
>
> —Langston Hughes, "Salvation"

OPEN WITH A QUOTATION

A good short quotation can definitely get people interested. It must lead naturally into your main point, however, and not just be stuck there. If you start with a quotation, make sure that you tell the reader who the speaker or writer is (unless it is a general quote, like the proverb in the following excerpt).

> "Grow where you are planted" is an old proverb that is a metaphor for living. Although I had heard it before, it took me many years to understand and appreciate its meaning. If I had listened to that proverb earlier, I would have saved myself and others many painful experiences.
>
> —Teresa Fiori, "Appreciate What You Have"

GIVE AN EXAMPLE OR TELL A STORY

Opening an essay with a brief story or illustration often draws readers in.

> Brian Head saw only one way out. On the final day of his life, during economics class, the fifteen-year-old stood up and pointed a semi-automatic handgun at himself. Before he pulled the trigger, he said his last words: "I can't take this anymore."
>
> —Kathleen Vail, "Words That Wound"

OFFER A STRONG OPINION

The stronger the opinion, the more likely it is that people will pay attention.

> Sex sells. This truth is a boon for marketing gurus and the pornography industry but a rather unfortunate situation for women. Every issue of *Playboy,* every lewd poster, and even the Victoria's Secret catalog transform real women into ornaments, valued exclusively for their outward appearance. These publications are responsible for defining what is sexy and reinforce the belief that aesthetic appeal is a woman's highest virtue.
>
> —Amy L. Beck, "Struggling for Perfection"

ASK A QUESTION

A question needs an answer. If you start your introduction with a question, you engage your readers by inviting them to answer it.

> If you're a man, at some point a woman will ask you how she looks. "How do I look?" she'll ask.
> You must be careful how you answer this question. The best technique is to form an honest yet sensitive opinion, then collapse on the floor with some kind of fatal seizure. Trust me, this is the easiest way out. Because you will never come up with the right answer.
>
> —Dave Barry, "The Ugly Truth about Beauty"

PRACTICE 2   Identifying Strong Introductions

Find a strong introduction in a newspaper, a magazine, a catalog, an advertisement — anything written. Explain, in writing, why you think it is a strong introduction.

Write a Conclusion

Your conclusion should have energy and match the force of your thesis statement; it is your last chance to drive home your main point. In fact, you should give yourself a last push at the end because people usually remember best what they see, hear, or read last. A good conclusion creates a sense of completion: It not only brings readers back to where they started but also shows them how far they have come.

BASICS OF A GOOD CONCLUSION

- It should refer to your main point.
- It should briefly summarize the support you have developed.
- It should make a final observation.

A good way to end an essay is to refer back to something in the introduction.

- If you used a quotation, use another one—by the same person or by another person on the same topic. Or refer back to the quotation in the introduction, and make an observation.
- If you stated a surprising fact or idea, go back to it and comment on it, using what you have written in the body of the essay.
- If you asked a question, ask it again, and answer it based on what you have said in your essay.
- If you started a story, finish it.
- Remind your reader of your original point, perhaps repeating key words that you used in your introduction.

Look again at three of the introductions you read earlier, each shown here with its conclusion.

OPEN WITH A QUOTATION

INTRODUCTION A: "Grow where you are planted" is an old proverb that is a metaphor for living. Although I had heard it before, it took me many years to understand and appreciate its meaning. If I had listened to that proverb earlier, I would have saved myself and others many painful experiences.

CONCLUSION A: Finally, I have learned to grow where I am planted, to appreciate the good things in my life rather than look for the bad and be angry. I have learned to take advantage of the many opportunities

I have for personal and professional growth, right here and now. And I have vowed to help others around me grow also. My life is much richer now that I follow that old wisdom, and I will pass its lesson on to my children.

—Teresa Fiori, "Appreciate What You Have"

START WITH A STRONG OPINION OR POSITION

INTRODUCTION B: Sex sells. This truth is a boon for marketing gurus and the pornography industry but a rather unfortunate situation for women. Every issue of *Playboy*, every lewd poster, and even the Victoria's Secret catalog transform real women into ornaments, valued exclusively for their outward appearance. These publications are responsible for defining what is sexy and reinforce the belief that aesthetic appeal is a woman's highest virtue.

CONCLUSION B: Women are up against a long history of devaluation and oppression, and, unfortunately, the feminist movements have been only partially successful in purging those legacies. Sexually charged images of women in the media are not the only cause of this continuing problem, but they certainly play a central role.

—Amy L. Beck, "Struggling for Perfection"

ASK A QUESTION

INTRODUCTION C: If you're a man, at some point a woman will ask you how she looks. "How do I look?" she'll ask.

You must be careful how you answer this question. The best technique is to form an honest yet sensitive opinion, then collapse on the floor with some kind of fatal seizure. Trust me, this is the easiest way out. You will never come up with the right answer.

CONCLUSION C: To go back to my main point: If you're a man, and a woman asks you how she looks, you're in big trouble. Obviously, you can't say she looks bad. But you also can't say that she looks great, because she'll think you're lying, because she has spent countless hours, with the help of the multibillion-dollar beauty industry, obsessing about the differences between herself and Cindy Crawford. Also, she suspects that you're not qualified to judge anybody's appearance. This is because you have shaving cream in your hair.

—Dave Barry, "The Ugly Truth about Beauty"

PRACTICE 3   Analyzing Conclusions

After reading the preceding paired introductions and conclusions, indicate the techniques used in each conclusion to refer back to its introduction.

PRACTICE 4   Identifying Good Introductions and Conclusions

In a newspaper, magazine, or any other written material, find a piece of writing that has both a strong introduction and a strong conclusion. Answer the following questions about the introduction and conclusion.

1.   What method of introduction is used?

2.   What does the conclusion do? Does it restate the main idea? Sum up the points made in the piece? Make an observation?

3.   How are the introduction and the conclusion linked?

PRACTICE 5   Writing a Conclusion

Read the following introductory paragraphs, and write a possible conclusion for each one. Your conclusions can be brief, but they should each include the basics of a good conclusion (p. 53) and consist of several sentences.

1.   **INTRODUCTION:** When it comes to long-term love relationships, I very much believe Anton Chekhov's statement, "Any idiot can face a crisis; it's the day-to-day living that wears you out." When faced with a crisis, couples often pull together. A crisis is a slap in the face that reminds you of who and what is important in your life. It is the routine necessities of living that can erode a relationship as couples argue over who does the laundry, who does the cleaning, or cooking, or bill paying. The constant skirmishes over day-to-day living can do more serious damage over the long term than a crisis.

2.   **INTRODUCTION:** Why do so many people feel that they must be available at all times and in all places? Until recently, the only way you could reach someone was by telephone or by mail. Now if you do not have a smartphone for texting, Facebook and Twitter accounts, and call waiting, people trying to reach you get annoyed. I resent the loss of privacy. I do not want to be available twenty-four hours a day.

Title Your Essay

Even if your title is the *last* part of the essay you write, it is the *first* thing that readers read. Use your title to get your readers' attention and to tell them what your essay is about. Use concrete, specific words to name the topic of your essay.

BASICS OF A GOOD ESSAY TITLE

- It makes readers want to read the essay.
- It does not repeat the wording in your thesis statement.
- It may hint at the main point but does not necessarily state it outright.

One way to find a good title is to consider the type of essay you are writing. If you are writing an argument (as you will in Chapter 13), state your position in your title. If you are telling your readers how to do something (as you will in Chapter 8), try using the term *steps* or *how to* in the title. This way, your readers will know immediately both what you are writing about and how you will present it. For example, "Five Steps to Financial Independence" may be a more inviting and more accurate title for a process analysis essay than "Financial Independence."

Sample Student Essay: Draft

Following is a draft of a student essay. The revised essay appears on page 65.

Identifying
information

Deshon Briggs
Professor Riva
EN 099
October 15, 2012

Introductory
paragraph

Thesis
statement

   One day, my teacher wrote "You are the change in your life" on the board. She said that statement related to our going to college and making our lives better. She gave us a writing assignment: to explore the statement that was due in four weeks. I did not really know what she was talking about but figured I had plenty of time to think about it. <u>I learned that I really can be the change in my life.</u>

Primary
support 2

   <u>I took my son to play basketball at the park near us, and he gave me grief when I threw my Coke can off to the side.</u> He got a bag from my car and picked up my can. He started picking up others, and I helped. A guy I know came by with his kids, and we all started picking up cans and bottles. There were a lot.

I had the idea to go to the local freecycle.org and posted that we wanted a big trash can for bottles and cans for the park. I had a bunch of offers and other guys said they would help with clean-up. We set up a schedule. My son and I got the idea of returning the bottles and cans for the deposit money that we could use to get a new basketball net. We did that.

Primary support 3

After a few weeks, the local paper called me and wanted to interview my son and me about the stuff we had done at the basketball court. We got our pictures in the paper, and we got some more people interested and some people made donations. Now we have enough money to get a bench. The court looks great, we met a lot of other people, and people gave us a lot of respect. It was great. And this is my paper for my English class, how my son and I were the change in our lives, starting with just picking up a Coke can.

Concluding paragraph

Point for conclusion

Writing Assignment

1. Write an outline and a draft using the thesis statement and support you developed in Chapter 3, using one of the following thesis statements. Use the checklist below as you work.

    With the advent of so many new technologies, teenagers no longer do much traditional dating.

    Although cartoons are typically intended to entertain, they may also have important messages.

    Living with roommates requires patience.

CHECKLIST

Writing a Draft Essay

FOCUS

☐ Review your support.

ASK

☐ Is your thesis clear?

☐ Are there topic sentences for each body paragraph?

☐ Do you have supporting details for each topic sentence?

☐ Is your support arranged in a logical order?

☐ What introductory technique will get your readers' attention and make your point stand out?

☐   How can you use the conclusion for one last chance to make your point?

☐   How can you link your conclusion to your introduction? What is the strongest or most interesting part of the introduction that you might refer back to in your conclusion?

☐   Will your title make readers want to read your essay?

WRITE

☐   Write a draft essay.

Revising Your Draft

Revising is rewriting your drafts to make your ideas clearer, stronger, and more convincing. When revising, you might add, cut, move, or change whole sentences or paragraphs.

Editing is correcting problems with grammar, style, usage, and punctuation. While editing, you usually add, cut, or change words and phrases instead of whole sentences or paragraphs.

Revising (covered in this chapter) and editing (covered in Chapters 16, 17, and 18) are two different ways to improve a paper. Most writers find it difficult to do both at once. It is easier to look first at the ideas in your essay (revising) and then to look at the individual words and sentences (editing).

No one gets everything right in a draft—even professional writers need to revise. The tips below will help you with the revision process.

TIPS FOR REVISING

▪   Take a break from your draft—set it aside for a few hours or a whole day.

▪   Read your draft aloud, and listen to what you have written.

▪   Imagine yourself as one of your readers.

▪   Get feedback from a friend, a classmate, or a colleague (see the last section of this chapter).

▪   Get help from a tutor at your college writing center or lab.

Revise for Unity

Unity in writing means that all the points are related to your main point: They *unite* to support your main point.

Sometimes writers drift away from their main point, as the writer of the following paragraph did with the underlined sentences.

Online dating services have many benefits, but users should be aware of the possible negatives as well. One benefit of online dating services is that people do not have to cruise bars to meet people. The Web sites offer subscribers potential matches, and the first contact is via e-mail. Contact via e-mail or text allows users to get to know each other a little before meeting. Sometimes a couple of exchanges can reveal that meeting is not necessary, so not only do users get to avoid cruising, they save time by eliminating bad matches. The services also try to match compatible people by comparing profiles, so the likelihood of having something in common is greater than in a random encounter. With all the online dating services available, people can choose ones that appeal to people with specific interests and preferences. <u>A good place to meet is a cheap restaurant. Most people like Italian food or burgers, so those types of places are safe.</u> Also, online dating services offer many choices of screened possible dates, more than anyone could meet in a bar in months. On the negative side, online dating services can be expensive, and there are no guarantees of a good match. Also, although the companies do minor screening, nothing prevents a person from lying. People often lie about their age, weight, and appearance. Arranging a date through a dating service can put more pressure on people than meeting in a natural way because people sometimes have unreasonably high expectations. Online dating services can be successful, but people should be realistic about what to expect.

· ·

PRACTICE 6   Revising for Unity

The following essay includes four sentences that are off the main point. Underline those sentences. The main point in the essay is in boldface type.

A recent survey of the places students prefer to study revealed some strange results. We would expect the usual answers, such as a library, bedroom, desk, and kitchen, and the survey respondents did in fact name such areas. But some people prefer less traditional places.

One unusual place cited was a church. The respondent said it was a great spot to study when services were not taking place because it was always quiet and not crowded. Some churches are locked during the day because of vandalism. Other churches have had big problems with theft.

Another unusual study area was the locker room during a football game. A problem is that the person would miss the game. Except for half-time, the large area was empty. The person who studied there claimed that there was a high energy level in the locker room that, combined with the quiet, helped him concentrate. I wonder what the smell was like, though.

The most surprising preference for a place to study was the bleachers by the pool of a gym. The light was good, said the student, she loved the smell of chlorine, and the sound of water was soothing.

The results may seem strange—a church, a locker room, and a pool—but they do share some characteristics: quiet, relative solitude, and no interruptions, other than half-time. Perhaps we should all think about new places that might help us study.

Revise for Support and Detail

Support is the evidence, examples, or facts that show, explain, or prove your main point. **Primary support points** are the major ideas developed in the paragraphs that make up the body of your essay. **Supporting details** are the specifics that explain your primary support to your readers.

For more on primary support points and supporting details, see Chapter 3.

When you read your draft essay, ask yourself: Do you provide enough information for your reader to understand the main point? Do you present enough evidence to convince your reader of that point? Look for places where you could add more support and detail, and examine your writing for obvious biases or errors in logic (see pp. 6–7).

Read the two paragraphs that follow, and note the support the writer added to the second one. Notice that she did not simply add to the paragraph; she also deleted some words and rearranged others to make the story clearer to readers. The additions are underlined; the deletions are crossed out.

> This morning I learned that my local police respond quickly and thoroughly to 911 calls. I meant to dial 411 for directory assistance, but by mistake I dialed 911. I hung up after only one ring because I realized what I had done. A few seconds after I hung up, the phone rang, and it was the police dispatcher. She said that she had received a 911 call from my number and was checking. I explained what happened, and she said she had to send a cruiser over anyway. Within a minute, the cruiser pulled in, and I explained what happened. I apologized and felt stupid, but I thanked him. I am glad to know that if I ever need to call 911, the police will be there.

REVISED TO ADD SUPPORT AND DETAIL

> This morning I <u>tested the 911 emergency system and found that it worked perfectly. Unfortunately, the test was a mistake.</u> ~~learned that my local police respond quickly and thoroughly to 911 calls.~~ I meant to dial 411 for directory assistance, but <u>without thinking</u> ~~by mistake~~ I dialed 911. I <u>frantically pushed the disconnect button</u> ~~hung up~~ after only one ring because I realized <u>my error.</u> ~~what I had done.~~ <u>As I reached for the phone to dial 411,</u> ~~A few seconds after I hung up,~~ <u>it rang like an alarm.</u> ~~the phone rang, and it was the police dispatcher.~~ <u>The police dispatcher crisply announced</u> ~~She said~~ that

she had received a 911 call from my number and was checking. I
laughed weakly and explained what happened, hoping she would see
the humor or at least the innocent human error. Instead, the crispness
of her voice became brittle as ~~and~~ she said she had to send a cruiser
over anyway. I went to meet my fate. Within a minute, the cruiser
pulled in, and a police officer swaggered toward me. I explained what
had happened, apologized, and thanked him humbly. I felt guilty of
stupidity, at the least. ~~and felt very stupid, but I thanked him.~~ We learn
from our mistakes, and in this case I am glad to know that if I ever
need to call 911, the police will be there.

· ·

PRACTICE 7   Revising for Support

Read the following essay, and write in the space provided at least one
additional support point or detail for each body paragraph and for the
conclusion. Indicate where the added material should go in the paragraph by
writing in a caret (^).

For more practice
in revising for
support, visit
LearningCurve at
bedfordstmartins
.com/realessays.

    Anyone who has owned a dog knows that there is a special
bond between dogs and humans. Even without speech, dogs seem
to understand humans' words and emotions. Dogs have been
beloved family pets for a very long time, but they are also being
used effectively in new educational, workplace, and therapeutic
settings.

_____

    Dog rescue organizations often bring dogs into schools to talk
about the dogs' resilience and responsiveness to good care. For
example, Greyhound Rescue, an organization that saves dogs from
death after they are too old to race or when a track is being closed,
is active in schools. Students meet the dogs and learn about caring
for them and ways to help them. After visits, some students become
volunteers at the organization.

_____

    Dogs work hard, too. They are sometimes brought into hotels to
check for bedbugs, to airports for security checks, and to hospitals
and nursing homes for patient therapy. There are also programs
where chronically ill children are visited weekly by the same dog. The
dogs seem to sense the children's pain or weakness, and their visits
give the children something to look forward to. The dogs have the
same effect on nursing home residents.

_____

Dogs are also brought into prisons to be trained by prisoners. Sometimes inmates train these dogs as seeing-eye dogs for blind people. Other times prisoners ready abandoned puppies for adoption. Many violent prisoners have been successful trainers. The sad part is that they cannot keep the dogs they have trained.

It is said that dogs are man's best friend. They are trusting companions who love unconditionally. They are able to communicate and help where words sometimes do not.

Revise for Coherence

Coherence in writing means that all the support connects to form a whole that makes sense. In other words, even when the support is arranged in a logical order, it still needs "glue" to connect the various points.

A piece of writing that lacks coherence sounds choppy, and is hard for the reader to follow. Revising an essay for coherence helps readers see how one point leads to another. The best way to improve coherence is to add transitions.

Transitions are words, phrases, and sentences that connect ideas so that writing moves smoothly from one point to another. Transitions can connect sentences and ideas within a paragraph and also connect one paragraph to another. The following box lists some, but not all, of the most common transitions and their purpose.

The following essay shows how transitions link ideas within sentences and paragraphs and connect one paragraph to the next. It also shows another technique for achieving coherence: repeating key words and ideas related to the main point. The transitions and key words in this piece are underlined.

Common Transitional Words and Phrases

INDICATE SPACE RELATION

above	below	near	to the right
across	beside	next to	to the side
at the bottom	beyond	opposite	under
at the top	farther	over	where
behind	inside	to the left	

INDICATE TIME ORDER			
after	eventually	meanwhile	soon
as	finally	next	then
at last	first	now	when
before	last	second	while
during	later	since	

INDICATE IMPORTANCE			
above all	in fact	more important	most
best	in particular	most important	worst
especially			

SIGNAL EXAMPLES			
for example	for instance	for one thing	one reason

SIGNAL ADDITIONS			
additionally	and	as well as	in addition
also	another	furthermore	moreover

SIGNAL CONTRAST			
although	in contrast	nevertheless	still
but	instead	on the other hand	yet
however			

SIGNAL CAUSE OR CONSEQUENCE			
as a result	finally	so	therefore
because			

　　I thought I would never make it to work today. I had an important meeting, and it seemed as if everything was conspiring against me. The conspiracy started before I even woke up.
　　I had set my alarm clock, but it did not go off, and therefore I did not wake up on time. When I did wake up, I was already late, not just by a few minutes but by an hour and a half. To save time, I brushed my teeth while I showered. Also, I figured out what I was going to

wear. <u>Finally,</u> I hopped out of the shower ready to get dressed. <u>But the</u>
<u>conspiracy continued.</u>

    <u>The next act of the conspiracy</u> concerned my only clean shirt,
which was missing two buttons right in front. <u>After finding a sweater</u>
<u>that would go over it, I ran to the bus stop.</u>

    <u>When I got to the stop,</u> I discovered that the buses were running
late. <u>When one finally came,</u> it was one of the old, slow ones, and it
made stops about every ten feet. <u>In addition,</u> the heat was blasting,
and I was sweating but could not take off my sweater because my shirt
was gaping open. Now I was sweating, and perspiration was running
down my scalp and neck. <u>At least, I thought, I will dry off by the time</u>
<u>the bus gets to my work.</u>

    <u>In fact, I did dry off a little, but the conspiracy did not end there.</u>
<u>When I finally</u> got to work, the elevator was out of service, <u>so</u> I had to
walk up ten flights of stairs. I was drenched, late, and inappropriately
dressed. <u>By the time I got to my desk,</u> I knew that the hardest part of
the day was behind me.

- -

For more practice
in achieving
coherence in
writing, visit
bedfordstmartins
.com/realessays.

PRACTICE 8   Adding Transitional Sentences

Read the following essay. Then, write a transitional sentence that would link
each paragraph to the one following it. You may add your transitional sentence
at the end of a paragraph, at the beginning of the next paragraph, or in both
places.

    Many teenagers today do not date in the traditional sense — one
boy and one girl going on dates or "going steady." Instead, they
go out in groups rather than as couples. This new pattern gives
many parents a sense that their sons and daughters are safe from
premature sex and sexually transmitted diseases.

_____

_____

    Although teenagers do not pair off romantically, they are getting
plenty of sex, just not with people they care about. They care about
their friends and do not want to risk ruining friendships, so they
"hook up" with strangers they meet while out at night or online.
"Hooking up" means having sex with someone, and many teens
hook up only with people they have no other contact with, preferably
from different schools or towns.

_____

_____

Although teenagers often think that sex without emotional involvement will avoid heartbreak and breakups, many teens, both girls and boys, admit that it is difficult not to develop feelings for someone they are physically intimate with. If one person begins to feel an attachment while the other does not, a distancing occurs: That hurts. It is a breakup of a different sort.

_____

_____

Teenagers have always experimented with ways to do things differently than their parents did. Trying new ways to do things is an important stage in teenagers' development. Experimentation is normal and sometimes produces better ways of doing things. According to most teens, however, the "hook-up" is not the answer to heartbreak: It is just another road to it. Perhaps teenagers are destined to experience some pain as they try out what "love" means.

Sample Student Essay: Revised

Below is a revised version of Deshon Briggs's essay on pages 56–57. His revisions are highlighted in green.

Deshon Briggs
Professor Riva
EN 099
October 29, 2012

BE THE CHANGE ————————————————————————— Title added

On the first day of my English class last spring, my teacher wrote ———— Added detail
"You are the change in your life" on the board. She said that ~~statement related to our going to college and making our lives better.~~ we had already taken a step toward change by coming to college to improve our lives. She said that we would be revisiting the theme of "people — Details connecting to their communities" in our assignments and discussions and that we should be alert to ways that people are making a difference. She also gave us a writing assignment to explore ~~the statement that was due~~ — Transition ~~in four weeks.~~ and find ways that we could make the statement true in our own lives. The paper would not be due for four weeks, but we should start taking action now. I did not really know what she was talking about but figured I had plenty of time to think about it. In those four weeks, — Revised though, I learned that I really can be the change in my life. Thesis

Transition — The weekend after we got the assignment, I took my son to play basketball at the park near us, and he gave me grief when I threw my Coke can off to the side. He said in his school they were learning about

Detail — how litter is bad for the earth. He got a bag from my car and picked up

Transitions — my can. Then he started picking up others, and I helped. Once we started,

Detail — I was surprised how many bottles and cans there were that I just had not

Transition — noticed before. While we were working, a guy I know came by with his kids, and we all started picking up cans and bottles. ~~There were a lot.~~ We

Details — filled three big bags, just with bottles and cans. But then we kept going,

Transitions — ~~filling another bag with paper and other litter.~~ When we were done, we brought the bags home, threw away the trash, and took the cans and bottles to the supermarket to redeem the deposit money.

Transitions — That night, I had the idea to go to the local freecycle.org and post that we wanted a big trash can for bottles and cans for the park. By the next morning, I had ~~a bunch of offers~~ seven offers for free trash cans and ~~other guys~~ four other guys with sons said they would help with clean-up. We set out the trash cans and labeled one for bottles and cans, one for other trash. Then we set up a schedule. The people responsible

Details — for pick-up would take the day's collection for deposit money and get rid of the trash. ~~My son and I got the idea of returning the bottles and cans for the deposit money that we could use~~ to get a new basketball net. ~~We did that~~ With the money we collected, we got a new basketball net and a bench. We felt proud of ourselves.

Detail — After a few weeks, the local paper called me and wanted to interview my son and me about ~~the stuff we had done at~~ our "campaign to

Transition — improve" the basketball court. We got our pictures in the paper, and ~~we got some more people interested~~ some people who read about what we had done made donations. ~~Now we have enough money to get a bench.~~

Details — Since then, we have made more improvements, and the court and park around it are clean. Someone had the idea of starting a community garden in the park, and now whole families come there. There are some picnic tables, and it is a wonderful and safe family recreation area. ~~The court looks great, we met a lot of other people, and people gave us a lot of respect. It was great.~~ My son and I have met many new people as we created our own little piece of paradise from what was just a junky basketball court in a park that no one used. And this is my paper for my English class: how my son and I ~~were~~ learned that we are the change in

Revised — our lives. ~~starting~~ It all started with just picking up a Coke can.
conclusion

Writing Assignment

Revise an essay using the draft you developed earlier in this chapter. Before revising, read the following checklist.

CHECKLIST

Revising Your Essay

FOCUS

☐ After a break, reread your draft with a fresh perspective.

ASK

☐ What is your point or position? Does your thesis statement clearly state your main point?

☐ Does your essay have the following?
   — An introductory paragraph
   — Three or more body paragraphs
   — A topic sentence for each paragraph that supports the main point
   — A forceful concluding paragraph that reminds readers of the main point and makes an observation

☐ Does your essay have unity?
   — Do all of the support points relate directly to the main point?
   — Do all of the supporting details in each body paragraph relate to the paragraph's topic sentence?
   — Have you avoided drifting away from the main point?

☐ Do you have enough support?
   — Taken together, do the topic sentences of each paragraph give enough support or evidence for the main point?
   — Do individual paragraphs support their topic sentences?
   — Would more detail strengthen your support?

☐ Is your essay coherent?
   — Have you used transitional words to link ideas?
   — Have you used transitional sentences to link paragraphs?

REVISE

☐ Revise your draft, making any improvements you can. Be sure to look for bias or errors in reasoning.

Peer Reviewing

Peer review is the exchange of feedback on a piece of writing from your fellow students, colleagues, or friends. Getting comments from a peer is a good way to begin revising your essay.

Other people can look at your work and see things that you might not—parts that are good as well as parts that need more explanation or evidence. The best reviewers are honest about what could be better but also sensitive to the writer's feelings. In addition, they are specific. Reviewers who say a paper is "great" without offering further comment do not help writers improve their work.

BASICS OF USEFUL FEEDBACK

- It is given in a positive way.

- It is specific.

- It offers suggestions.

- It may be given orally or in writing.

To get useful feedback, find a partner and exchange papers. Each partner should read the other's paper and jot down a few comments. The first time someone comments on what you have written, you may feel a little embarrassed, but you will feel better about the process once you see how your writing benefits from the comments.

Peer reviewers should consider the following as they read.

Questions for Peer Reviewers

1. What is the main point?

2. After reading the introductory paragraph, do you have an idea of what the essay will cover, and why?

3. How could the introduction be more interesting?

4. Is there enough support for the main point? Where might the writer add support?

5. Are there confusing places where you have to reread something to understand it? How might the writer make the points, the organization, or the flow of ideas clearer or smoother?

6. Does the writer have assumptions or biases that weaken the writing? What are they?

7. How could the conclusion be more forceful?

8. What do you most like about the essay? Where could it be better? What would you do if it were your essay?

9. What other comments or suggestions do you have?

10. How do you think the audience for the writing will respond to the thesis, and its support?

5

Narration

Writing That Tells Stories

Understand What Narration Is

Narration is writing that tells a story of an event or experience.

Four Basics of Good Narration

1. It reveals something of importance to your reader (**main point**).
2. It includes all the major events of the story (**primary support**).
3. It uses details to bring the story to life for your audience (**secondary support**).
4. It presents the events in a clear order, usually according to when they happened.

In the following passage, each number corresponds to one of the Four Basics of Good Narration.

1 Thanksgiving is a time of repeating old traditions, such as gathering with family and friends and eating special foods like turkey, cranberry relish, and pumpkin pie. Every year, my family and I go to my older sister's and brother-in-law's house, and we enjoy the whole traditional experience. But it was there that I also learned how unexpected new traditions can enter the mix and make a holiday even more meaningful.

2 My sister's son Jacob had spent a semester in Niger, a desert country in central Africa. There he made a good friend, Ibrahim, who later moved to the United States to study science and engineering. My sister and brother-in-law invited Ibrahim to Thanksgiving every year, so gradually we all came to know this warm and friendly person.

✓ LearningCurve For extra practice in the skills covered in this chapter, visit bedfordstmartins.com/reinteractive.

69

He would ask questions about Thanksgiving traditions, which were new and unfamiliar to him. We would ask questions about his country, which was unfamiliar to us. **3** In response he would often say, "Well, where I am from, whenever we gather, we drink a strong, sweet, green tea called atai." It was as though, to him, this tea seemed strangely missing from the party.

2 One year he brought with him everything necessary to make the tea in the traditional way of his country: **3** two small metal pots with lids; tea leaves; sugar; special small glasses, like shot glasses; a tiny wire grill; and charcoal. He made the tea on my sister's back porch, though the weather was drizzly and cold. The process was complicated, and involved boiling the tea a long time, then pouring it from high up, to cool it. Patience is a necessary ingredient.

2 When the tea was finally ready, we all hesitatingly took sips from the little glasses, expecting to try it, set it aside, and think "that will be that." **3** But the tea was so pleasingly tasty—smoky and sweet—and so strikingly different that this custom quickly became an essential and beloved Thanksgiving tradition. **2** Now Ibrahim carefully makes this tea every year and serves it at the end of the big meal, and the holiday would not seem right otherwise.

1 I give thanks to Ibrahim for enlarging my world and proving that, when it comes to excellent customs, there is plenty of room at the table for one more.

You can use narration in many practical situations. Consider the following examples.

COLLEGE   In a U.S. history course, you trace, in your own words, the specific sequence of events that led the United States to enter World War II.

WORK   A customer becomes angry with you and lodges a complaint with your boss. You recount—in writing—what happened.

EVERYDAY LIFE Your wallet is stolen, and you file a written account with the police reporting exactly what happened.

Main Point in Narration

Whenever you write a narration, have a **purpose** in mind, whether that purpose is to explain what happened, to prove something, or simply to entertain someone. If you do not know the purpose of your narration, your readers will not know it either.

Also consider who your **audience** is and what they know and do not know. Finally, be clear on your **main point**—what is important about the narration. Generally, college instructors will want your main point to indicate what is important to you about a story. For clarity, state the main point in the first paragraph, and remind readers of it at the end of your narration.

Take another look at the passage under the Four Basics of Good Narration (p. 69).

> . . . I also learned how unexpected new traditions can . . . make a holiday even more meaningful.

This statement emphasizes the event's importance to the writer.

In writing a narrative, make sure your topic sentence (for paragraphs) and thesis statement (for essays) communicate your general topic and the main point you are making about the topic.

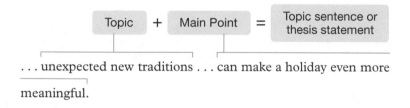

. . . unexpected new traditions . . . can make a holiday even more meaningful.

Support in Narration

To **support** your main point, you will present and explain the major events in the story and describe relevant details. As you write a narration, you will have decisions to make—what to include, what to leave out, and what perspective you will take on events. Your **point of view** determines how you will present the major events and details of the story and how you will support your main point.

The **major events** of a story are your primary support in narration, and they will usually become the topic sentences for the body paragraphs in your essay. Ask yourself what the major events are and what makes them important. To help your readers experience the events as you did, give supporting details that bring the experience to life.

For more on
supporting
a point, see
Chapter 3.

For example, one student stated the main point of an event in the following thesis: *The theft of my wallet this morning showed me how easy it is for criminals to deceive unsuspecting victims.*

For more on
listing, see
Chapter 2.

The student then did some listing to come up with the major events and details about those events.

MAJOR EVENTS (primary support)	SUPPORTING DETAILS (secondary support)
Woman bumped into me	Light bump, but she dropped her folder of papers, and they scattered
I bent down to help her collect the papers.	Wind was blowing, so I had to work fast
A man stopped and asked if he could help.	I didn't get a good look at him because I was trying to get the papers, but he stood close to me and hung around for a minute just watching us. Then, he just left without saying anything.
Woman thanked me, and I said no problem	She had her head down and walked off fast.
When I went to get coffee, I realized the wallet was gone.	I broke into a sweat at the café and had that horrible panicked feeling.
I realized that the man and woman were working together.	Looking back on the details, it was clear how carefully they had planned the theft.

For more
on using
quotation
marks, see
Chapter 18.

As you tell the story, you might want to include direct speech or dialogue, the words that you or other people said. If you report exactly what was said, use quotation marks.

> The woman said, "Oh, I'm so sorry! I'll never be able to get these papers before they blow away, and my boss will have a fit."

Using direct speech can bring a narration alive.

Organization in Narration

For more on
chronological
order, see
page 44.

Because narration tells a story of "what happened," it often uses **chronological (time) order**. Start at the beginning of the story, and describe the events in the sequence in which they occurred.

Time transitions (words and phrases like *next* and *meanwhile*) are important in narration because they make the order of events clear to readers. Writers of narration use these common transitions not only within a paragraph — to move from one detail about the event to the next — but also between paragraphs to move from one major event to the next.

For more on transitions, see pages 62–64.

Common Time Transitions

after	eventually	meanwhile	soon
as	finally	next	still
at last	first	now	then
before	last	second	when
during	later	since	while

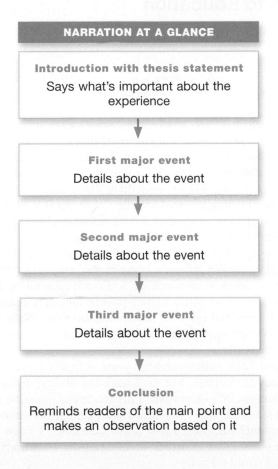

NARRATION AT A GLANCE

Introduction with thesis statement
Says what's important about the experience

↓

First major event
Details about the event

↓

Second major event
Details about the event

↓

Third major event
Details about the event

↓

Conclusion
Reminds readers of the main point and makes an observation based on it

Read and Analyze Narration

Read the following three examples of narration—from college, the workplace, and everyday life—and answer the questions that accompany them. For each essay, review the Four Basics of Good Narration (p. 69) and practice the critical reading process explained in Chapter 1 (pages 1–15).

Narration in College

A student wrote the following essay for a college writing course. The assignment was "Write an essay describing an important decision in your life."

Jordan Brown

A Return to Education

GUIDING QUESTION
How does Jordan feel about his return to college?

VOCABULARY
The following words are *italicized* in the essay: *anticipation, stamina*. If you do not know their meanings, look them up in a dictionary or online.

CRITICAL READING
■ **Preview**
■ Read
■ Pause
■ Review

(See pp. 3–8.)

PAUSE: Why did Brown join the army? Was it a good decision for him?

PAUSE: How does Brown's first sentence here relate to the first paragraph? What questions does he have?

For me, college has been an experience marked by *anticipation*, fear, and 1
pride. I sometimes find myself still surprised that I am really here. The journey to get here has been a long one, but if I can put my fears behind me, I believe I will be able to accomplish something that I can really be proud of.

Being able to go to college is something that I have been anticipating for 2
many years. Since I left high school and the California Bay Area behind, I have been on the go in one way or another. After graduation, I felt that I wasn't ready for the commitments or responsibilities of college. Instead, I enlisted in the army. The army provided me with the maturity and self-discipline that I desperately needed in my life; however, being in the army also provided me with very little time or money to go to college, so I put it off until "a later date."

After the army, I sought a higher-paying job, first becoming a truck 3
driver. This job provided me with money but no time. Now I work for the railroad, and with my apprenticeship behind me, I have some free time for the first time in my life.

What I have been anticipating for years is finally here. I now have the 4
time and money for college, but do I have the ability? It has been eleven years since I last sat in a classroom. This made me question myself: Can I do this? Will I succeed? Will I fail? Am I even capable of learning in a classroom environment? Although I had these questions, I knew that the only way to face my fears was to attack them head-on. I reminded myself that the only thing I could do is try.

5　　When I first walked into Front Range Community College, I was nervous. I couldn't help but notice how young everyone looked. I got to my study skills class, sat down, and looked around. I felt out of place. Most of the people in the class looked as if they had just graduated from high school. When we did our introductions, however, I learned that one of the women sitting across the room had graduated from high school eleven years ago. I started to feel a little younger.

PAUSE: Why was Brown nervous?

6　　When I got to my philosophy class, I watched the other students come in and noticed that not everyone looked like a kid. This class looked very much like an American melting pot, with students of many ages and cultures. As we went around the room introducing ourselves, I felt very much more confident about my decision to try college. Many students were even older than I was. A woman sitting near me, who looked about my mom's age, said she was in college because all of her kids were in college now. She told us that she wanted a college education and a better job. An older gentleman across the room said that he was a business executive from Germany. His job had become boring, and he was looking for something more challenging. By the end of the introductions, I was convinced that this "college thing" might just work.

PAUSE: How do the other students help Brown feel better?

7　　Since I have gone back to school, there has been a lot of pride surrounding me. My parents can't stop talking about me and how proud they are. My family and friends are excited for me and congratulate me on my decision. I am also proud of myself for making the tough decision to go back to school. I know that when I get my degree, I will have something to be truly proud of.

PAUSE: How does Brown's first sentence here relate back to his thesis statement?

8　　I still have fears and uncertainties. But I also have positive anticipation and hope. Now, I know that I am on the right course. I know that as long as I have *stamina* and determination, nothing can stop me from achieving my dream of getting my degree in mechanical engineering.

PAUSE: How does Brown tie his conclusion to his introduction?

1.　**Summarize.** Briefly summarize Brown's essay, including his **main point** and **purpose** and the **major events** in his story. What is his point of view?

2.　**Analyze.** Does Brown's **support** all relate to his main point? Is it logically organized? Does he give you enough details? How do the topic sentences relate specifically to the thesis statement? Did the title give you an idea of what the essay would be about?

3.　**Synthesize.** How does Brown's experience relate to your own or to other things you have thought about, read, or heard?

4.　**Evaluate.** Does Brown achieve his purpose? Does his essay have the **Four Basics of Good Narration** (see p. 69)? What do *you* think of his essay, and why?

CRITICAL THINKING
■ Summarize
■ Analyze
■ Synthesize
■ Evaluate

(More on p. 21.)

Narration at Work

The following is an excerpt from an article, published in the *Chronicle of Higher Education*, that the author wrote in her profession as a journalist.

Monique Rizer

CRITICAL
READING
■ Preview
■ Read
■ Pause
■ Review

(See pp. 3–8.)

When Students Are Parents

GUIDING QUESTION
How has being a parent and student affected Rizer's decisions?

VOCABULARY
The following words are *italicized* in the excerpt: *fidgeted, postpartum, intangible*. If you do not know their meanings, look them up in a dictionary or online.

Monique Rizer
Journalist and
Development
Associate

PAUSE: Have you felt out of place in college or other places?

Crammed behind my desk, I *fidgeted* and shifted my eyes to observe the other students in the room. I tried not to look the way I felt—like I didn't belong there with them. I couldn't help noticing that all the other women were wearing shorts, sandals, flirty summer dresses: appropriate clothes for a warm September day. I tugged at the baggy clothes hiding my *postpartum* weight. I thought of my six-week-old son and hoped I'd make it home to nurse him at the scheduled time. The thought of him reminded me that however odd I felt, I was going to stay in college this time.

1

PAUSE: How do you think Rizer found the strength to go back to school after dropping out?

It was the summer of 1998. I was a twenty-year-old new mother and wife, and it was my first day of class, though not my first day of college. I'd begun my long journey through higher education three years before, but my plans to attend full time after high school graduation were put on hold when financial difficulties forced my family of eight to move. I then found a local community college and felt prepared to start again, but instead the registration papers sat abandoned in my car, where I practically lived since home was a 32-foot trailer filled with seven other people. In the summer of 1996, I packed my bags and left to live on my own; I enrolled again the next spring and had my son in July 1998. I knew I had to stay in school and go full time. I wanted more for my son and myself, even though I wasn't sure what exactly "more" was at the time.

2

Focusing on my son helped me to persist in college during difficult times, and there were many. I did not have time to socialize with other students because when I was not in class, I had to rush to take care of the details of life as a mother. Grocery shopping, cooking, arranging for child care, taking my son to the doctor when he was sick, seemed to take every minute. I was exhausted every day, and finding the time and mental energy to study and do homework

3

PAUSE: How was being a student parent both difficult and helpful?

often seemed an overwhelming challenge. But I stuck with it, determined to finish, to do what my mother had not done. When she had me at nineteen, she quit college and never returned.

What helped me finish college, even after my marriage and the birth of my second son, was meeting other students who were also parents. I realized

4

other people were in my situation, too, and probably felt just as stretched. As I met other mothers, we offered to baby-sit for each other or to get together with our children so that they could play, and we could study. All of us wanted more for our children than we had had, and that kept us going.

5   My commitment to finish college has paid off. Now, I have a bachelor's in journalism from Gonzaga University and a master's in information management from Syracuse University. During my years in school, my son kept me focused and ignited my ambition to be a better student. In my experience, there is no better motivation to finish college and to appreciate the full experience than a child whose future depends on your decisions. I had to continue to use my education to give him a better life and to set an example for him to follow.

6   I feel a tremendous sense of accomplishment: I've learned so many *intangible* lessons about myself; I've decided that I want to help other young parents achieve their educational goals; and I see a better future for my boys (I have two now). And I keep telling my mom that she doesn't have to live vicariously through me: She can return to college any time she wants. Being a student and a parent is challenging, but nothing is more rewarding than providing a bright future for your children.

PAUSE: Do you have enough information to understand how Rizer got through college?

1.   Briefly summarize Rizer's essay, including her **main point** and **purpose** and the **major events** in her story.

2.   Carefully examine the **Four Basics of Good Narration** (p. 69) and determine specifically whether Rizer's workplace writing is a good narration. Make notes to support your opinion.

3.   What is your reaction to Rizer's essay? What would you say to her or ask her if you had the chance?

Narration in Everyday Life

The following address was originally broadcast on National Public Radio.

Howard White

The Power of Hello

GUIDING QUESTION
What is the power of hello in White's experience?

VOCABULARY
The following words are *italicized* in the essay: *gazillion, acknowledged, guidepost, foundation, humble.* If you do not know their meanings, look them up in a dictionary or online.

1   I work at a company where there are about a *gazillion* employees. I do not say that I know them all by name, but I know my fair share of them. I think that almost all of them know me. I would say that's the reason I've been able to go wherever it is I've made it to in this world. It is all based on

CRITICAL READING

■ Preview
■ Read
■ Pause
■ Review

(See pp. 3–8.)

one simple principle: I believe every single person deserves to be *acknowl-edged*, however small or simple the greeting.

PAUSE: Why does White tell this story?

When I was about 10 years old, I was walking down the street with my 2 mother. She stopped to speak to Mr. Lee. I was busy trying to bulls-eye the "O" in the stop sign with a rock. I knew I could see Mr. Lee any old time around the neighborhood, so I did not pay any attention to him. After we passed Mr. Lee, my mother stopped me and said something that has stuck with me from that day until now. She said, "You let that be the last time you ever walk by somebody and not open up your mouth to speak, because even a dog can wag its tail when it passes you on the street." That phrase sounds simple, but it has been a *guidepost* for me and the *foundation* of who I am.

PAUSE: What does the first sentence mean?

When you write an essay like this, you look in the mirror and see who 3 you are and what makes up your character. I realized mine was cemented that day when I was ten years old. Even then, I started to see that when I spoke to someone, they spoke back. And that felt good.

PAUSE: Why do you think the founder feels this way about White?

It is not just something I believe in; it's become a way of life. I believe that 4 all people deserve to feel someone acknowledge their presence, no matter how *humble* they may be or even how important. At work, I always used to say hello to the founder of the company and ask him how our business was doing. But I was also speaking to the people in the café and the people who cleaned the buildings, and asked how their children were doing. I remembered after a few years of passing by the founder, I had the courage to ask him for a meeting. We had a great talk. At a certain point, I asked him how far he thought I could go in his company. He said, "If you want to, you can get all the way to this seat."

PAUSE: How has what White learned helped him?

I have become vice president, but that has not changed the way I 5 approach people. I still follow my mother's advice. I speak to everyone I see, no matter where I am. I have learned that speaking to people creates a pathway into their world, and it lets them come into mine, too.

The day you speak to someone who has his head held down and when 6 he lifts it up and smiles, you realize how powerful it is just to open your mouth and say, "Hello."

1.   Briefly summarize White's essay.

2.   What is the author's purpose?

3.   What did you learn from reading White's essay?

4.   Does White's story reflect the **Four Basics of Good Narration** (p. 69)?

5.   Write three questions that you would ask if you were writing a quiz on White's essay (and be able to answer your own questions).

6.   Of the three essays in this chapter, which do you think is the best narration, and why? Which did you like the best? Which made you think?

Write a Narration Essay

Write your own narration essay on one of the following topics or on a topic of your own choice. Use **NARRATION AT A GLANCE** as a basic organizer (p. 73), and follow the Writing Guide: Narration checklist as you write and revise (pp. 79–80).

COLLEGE
- Explain what led you to start college.
- Summarize an interesting story you learned in one of your other classes, such as psychology or history.

WORK
- Tell the story of something positive you did at work (some achievement).
- Explain what you learned from getting or doing your first job.

EVERYDAY LIFE
- Recount a time when you took a risk.
- Write about a time when you were proud or ashamed of your behavior.

WRITING GUIDE: NARRATION

STEPS IN NARRATION	HOW TO DO THE STEPS
☐ Focus.	• Think about your audience and what is important about your story.
☐ Explore your topic. See Chapter 2.	• Narrow your topic. • Prewrite, recalling what happened. Why is the story important?
☐ Write a thesis statement. Topic + Main Point = Thesis See Chapter 3.	• Say what is important about the story — how it affected you or others.
☐ Support your thesis. See Chapter 3.	• Recall the major events. • Provide background information that your readers will need. • Describe the events with specific details.

STEPS IN NARRATION	HOW TO DO THE STEPS
☐ **Write a draft.** See Chapter 4.	• Arrange the events chronologically. • Consider using one of the introductory techniques in Chapter 4, and include your thesis statement in your introduction. • Write topic sentences for each major event. • Write a paragraph for each event giving details about them.
☐ **Revise your draft.** See Chapter 4.	• Read to make sure that all events and details show, explain, or prove what is important about the story. • Add important events or details that occur to you. • Add time transitions. • Improve your introduction, thesis, and conclusion.
☐ **Edit your revised draft.** See Chapters 16 through 18.	• Correct errors in grammar, spelling, word use, and punctuation.
☐ **Evaluate your writing.**	• Does it have the Four Basics of Good Narration (p. 69)? • Is this the best I can do?

6

Illustration

Writing That Shows Examples

Understand What Illustration Is

Illustration is writing that uses examples to show, explain, or prove a point.

Four Basics of Good Illustration

1 It has a point.

2 It gives specific examples to show, explain, or prove the point.

3 It gives details to support the examples.

4 It uses enough examples to get the point across to the reader.

In the following paragraph, each number corresponds to one of the Four Basics of Good Illustration.

What is the strongest predictor of your health? **1** It may not be your income or age but rather your literacy. **2** People with low literacy skills have four times greater annual health costs than those with high skills. Why is literacy so important? **3** Most Americans read at an eighth- or ninth-grade level, and 20 percent read at just a fifth-grade level or below. However, most health-care materials are written above the tenth-grade level. **3** As many as half of all patients fail to take medications as directed, often because they don't understand the instructions. **2** Americans can improve their health literacy by asking their doctor or pharmacist **3** three questions: (1) "What is my main problem?" (2) "What do I need to

4 Enough examples given to back the writer's main point

✓ LearningCurve **For extra practice in the skills covered in this chapter, visit**
bedfordstmartins.com/reinteractive.

4
Enough
examples
given to back
the writer's
main point

do?" and (3) "Why is it important to do this?" If you're still confused, don't hesitate to ask your doctor, nurse, or pharmacist to go over the information again.

—"Literacy and Health," *Parade,* 18 January, 2004

Whenever we explain something, we use examples to show what we mean. Here are some ways you might use illustration.

COLLEGE   In a criminal justice course, you discuss and give examples of the most common criminal violations.

WORK   Your written self-evaluation for work includes specific and measurable examples of how well (or poorly) you performed.

EVERYDAY LIFE   You take your car to a mechanic and give him or her examples that show how the car is not running properly.

Main Point in Illustration

Look at the opening sentences in the paragraph with the colored shading (p. 81).

What is the strongest predictor of your health? It may not be your income or age but rather your literacy.

For more on
thesis state-
ments, see
Chapter 3.

In this case, the topic—the strongest predictor of your health—is in the opening sentence, which is followed by a surprising **main point**: that literacy might be a predictor of health. Because the point is surprising, the reader will be interested in reading on to find out how it could be true. The writer demonstrates the main point by giving examples.

Often, a thesis statement in illustration includes the topic and your main point.

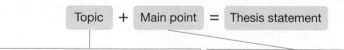

Topic + Main point = Thesis statement

Getting involved in college activities has many benefits, including some you might not expect.

Support in Illustration

In illustration, the **examples** show or prove your stated main point.

A student who had written the thesis *Homeschooling is beneficial to both the child and the parent* focused her prewriting on finding examples of benefits of homeschooling. Here are some examples from her brainstorming.

individualized to child	parent and child have control
parent and child together	more flexibility
at child's own pace	considers child's learning style
one-on-one	education is part of regular life

An illustration essay usually uses several examples as **support points**. The writer of the prewriting on homeschooling selected "individualized to child" as one support point and asked herself, "What do I mean? How? In what ways?" to find supporting details.

She also chose "parent and child have control" as another major example that would support the thesis. She then asked herself, "How do they have more control?" and listed potential supporting details.

control over materials used (what books, what computer programs, what approach)

control over time of instruction (what hours of the day, based on child's natural rhythms, vacations—not tied to a school's calendar)

Organization in Illustration

Illustration often uses **order of importance** to organize several examples, saving the most vivid, convincing example for last.

Transitions are important in illustration because they signal to readers that you are moving from one example to another. Use transitions to move between sentences within a paragraph and also to move between paragraphs.

For more on order of importance, see pages 45–46.

Common Transitions in Illustration

also	finally	for instance	in addition
another	for example	for one thing	one example . . . another example

Read and Analyze Illustration

Read the following three examples of illustration—from college, the workplace, and everyday life—and answer the questions that accompany them. For each essay, review the **Four Basics of Good Illustration** (p. 81) and practice the critical reading process explained in Chapter 1 (pages 1–15).

Illustration in College

The following is part of a report that Luz Medina wrote when she served as a student representative to the Division of Student Affairs at her college. Her job was to survey some other students and present a list of suggestions for new services that would help students.

GUIDING QUESTION
What does Luz Medina learn from her interviews?

To: Vice President, Student Affairs
Fr: Luz Medina
Re: Suggestions for student services

CRITICAL
READING
■ Preview
■ Read
■ Pause
■ Review
(See pp. 3–8.)

1   To complete this report, I interviewed twenty-five students, asking them the following questions: (1) Do you know about the student services that are available on this campus? (2) What service or organization would help your college experience and why? (3) Would you be willing to help set up this program? I have attached the complete responses to these questions, but here I will summarize what I found. The responses were both surprising and well worth considering in the future.

PAUSE: How is the first sentence linked to the thesis statement?

2   To my surprise, most of the students I interviewed were not aware of the many programs that are already available to them. For example, several of the students said that they did not know what to do if they were thinking about dropping out. I told them about our Succeeding Together program and gave them the Web site that lists the people and services that are designed just for these situations. I encouraged them to go to these sites for help, telling them that the college works hard to help keep students from dropping out.

PAUSE: What is Medina's purpose? Who is her audience?

3   Another area in which we have many services that students do not know about is in preparing for a job search. Most students knew that there is an office of career planning, but they thought it just posted job announcements. They did not know about great programs like the Virtual Job Fair or the many mini-seminars on interviewing, making a good first impression, or one-on-one counseling to match students with employers. They also did not know about the program that gives very specific career counseling that matches student interests with careers and then helps students plan what courses will best help them get started in the career.

PAUSE: What examples does Medina give of her topic sentence?

4   There were many other services students did not know about. Although they are listed online and we offer an orientation, I think we, as a committee, should figure out how to more successfully let students know what resources they have on this campus.

5   The students offered some good suggestions for new services. One is that we devise an instant-messaging system for communication with advisers. Students said that often they have to wait to see their advisers when they have a question that would take only a minute to ask and answer. One student compared it to standing in a long line to buy a package of gum: It doesn't seem worth the wait.

6   Two other good suggestions regard the problems students often have with transportation and child care. Students suggested that there be a college-sponsored online bulletin board that students can go to to find rides at various times. Students looking for transportation could find other students with cars who would be willing to give students rides for a small fee.

PAUSE: How are paragraphs 6 and 7 related to paragraph 5?

The students also suggested a similar child-care bulletin board that might help parents connect to baby-sit for each other.

A final suggestion that two students made was to have professors re- 7 cord their lectures so that they could be downloaded for students who had to miss a class. Students said that they could already get the homework assignments for a missed class, but they had no way to get the lecture material.

PAUSE: How does Medina tie paragraph 8 to the introductory paragraph?

Students were surprised that the college already has so many resources, 8 and they gave serious and thoughtful suggestions for new and needed services. I am sorry to report that only five of the twenty-five students said that they would be willing to help set up a new service, but at least those few are willing. Interviewing other students was an interesting project for me, making me think about the importance of student-affairs programs and giving me experience gathering and analyzing information.

CRITICAL THINKING
■ Summarize
■ Analyze
■ Synthesize
■ Evaluate

(More on p. 00.)

1.   **Summarize.** Briefly summarize Medina's essay (which is itself a summary), including her **main point** and purpose and the major **examples** she gives. What is her point of view?

2.   **Analyze.** Do Medina's examples all relate to her thesis statement? How do her topic sentences state what the paragraph will be about? What word does she repeat to link the thesis and support?

3.   **Synthesize.** What is Medina's conclusion? What do you know about student services at your college? Ask three other students the same question and include them in your response.

4.   **Evaluate.** Does Medina achieve her purpose? Does her essay have the **Four Basics of Good Illustration** (see p. 81)? What effect did her essay have on you, and why?

Illustration at Work

The following is from an address that a university vice president gave to a group of new students.

Juan Gonzalez

Complete Learning

GUIDING QUESTION
What is the purpose of Student Affairs?

VOCABULARY
The following words are italicized in the excerpt: *embarking, striving, encapsulates, indicators, collaborative, integrated, aspire, complementing, facilitates, foster, engendering, status quo.* If you do not know their meanings, look them up in a dictionary or online.

Juan Gonzalez
Vice President of Student Affairs, University of Texas, Austin

CRITICAL READING
■ Preview
■ Read
■ Pause
■ Review

(see pp. 3–8.)

As new students, you are *embarking* on an incredibly   1
exciting and challenging time, a time of expanding knowledge, relationships,

viewpoints, and achievements. In my role as vice president, I am constantly *striving* to match that energy level so that we can offer the highest level of service on this very diverse campus. I frequently marvel at college students who seem to have an unlimited amount of energy that allows them to attend classes, read and study, maintain a social life, run for political office, pursue a hobby, play an intramural sport, volunteer for a worthy cause, hold down a job. We in the Division of Student Affairs strongly encourage activities outside the classroom that enrich the academic experience, as we recognize that a university education is enhanced through involvement in our campus community.

PAUSE: Why is Gonzalez surprised by students?

2   Last November, a group of Student Affairs staff, students, and faculty began work on creating a strategic plan for the division. They have been laboring diligently on this document, and I am excited to share with you the fruit of that labor, our newly developed Student Affairs Strategic Plan, which has as its motto "Student Affairs: Where Life and Learning Intersect."

3   This phrase *encapsulates* the driving force behind the Division of Student Affairs. We exist, in essence, to help students succeed and grow, and we believe that growth and success must be measured in many ways. Academic success is one gauge of how well students are performing, but there are a variety of *indicators* other than grades. Those who take the most from their college experience are those who recognize that learning happens both inside and outside the classroom.

PAUSE: How does Gonzalez define success?

4   In fact, I recently had our units count the services they offer that are *collaborative* efforts with the academic side of the family, and a rough survey yielded 140 programs. This idea of *integrated* learning carries through most of what we do, whether it is a program to recruit the best students from around Texas like the Honors Colloquium, the increasingly popular "Academic Community Centers" for studying and advising on site in the residence halls, Summer Orientation, or the professor-led Freshman Reading Round-Up book discussions.

Our Vision Statement

Our vision statement lights the path we are following to where we *aspire* to be:

> The Division of Student Affairs at The University of Texas at Austin seeks to become the premier organization of its kind. We envision a network of programs and services that excels in meeting students' out-of-classroom needs, *complementing* their academic experiences, and building community on a diverse campus. In doing so, we will contribute to developing citizens and leaders who will thrive in and enrich an increasingly complex world.

Our Mission

Our mission, or the explanation of what we do, is described this way:

PAUSE: How does this paragraph relate to the introductory paragraph?

> The Division of Student Affairs *facilitates* students' discovery of self and the world in which they live. We enhance students' educational

experiences through programs and services that support academic success. We provide for fundamental needs, including shelter, nourishment, and a sense of security. We create environments that *foster* physical, emotional, and psychological wellness, and advance healthy lifestyles. Student Affairs builds communities, both real and virtual, that encourage inclusiveness, invite communication, and add to the cultural richness of the institution. We focus on personal development, including career decision making, problem solving, and group dynamics, challenging students to work both independently and as part of a team.

PAUSE: What is "complete learning"?

The work group that wrote the strategic plan also composed a defining phrase to encapsulate Student Affairs: "Our passion is complete learning." These, I hope you will agree, are stirring words. We take our responsibility for providing an environment that is inclusive and promotes a healthy lifestyle seriously. We are committed to supporting you as you achieve your goals at this university.

Our Core Values

Sharing a fundamental belief in the value of Student Affairs and its ability to transform lives, we will pursue our vision by

- Focusing on the lifelong learning and personal growth of all members of the university community;

- *Engendering* a community that is inclusive, accessible, and secure;

- Conducting ourselves and our programs with the highest integrity;

- Enhancing our services by creating opportunities to collaborate and nurture partnerships;

- Challenging ourselves to move beyond the *status quo* and pursue higher levels of excellence with determination and enthusiasm;

- Strengthening a tradition of quality, compassion, and an unwavering belief in students and ourselves;

- Demonstrating the innovation and courage to adapt to changing conditions; and

- Realizing that both action and vision are necessary for a better future.

PAUSE: What is education, according to Gonzalez?

Our society benefits by having everyone educated, and education is a process that requires everyone to be engaged in the advancement of all peoples. The well-being of our state requires the next generation of leaders and scholars to understand our new world. This understanding means looking at the process of education as more than four years in college, the material in textbooks, or the contents of a classroom lecture but as a way to improve the world.

1. Who is the audience for Gonzalez's illustration? What is his purpose?

2. Carefully reread the **Four Basics of Good Illustration** (p. 81) and determine if Gonzalez's essay is a good example of illustration. Make notes to support your opinion.

3. What do you know about the services that are offered on your campus? If you know little, find out more, and comment on whether your college offers services like those that Gonzalez refers to.

4. In your own words, state what you think Gonzalez says about what a good education is. Does he give you good examples? Do you agree with what he says?

Illustration in Everyday Life

The following is from the *New York Times*.

Rob Walker

Stuck on You

GUIDING QUESTION
What examples of bumper stickers does Walker give?

VOCABULARY
The following words are italicized in the essay: *incredulous, inferences, plausible, delve, revelatory, benign, beguiling, paradox.* If you do not know their meanings, look them up in the dictionary or online.

[1] Yankee: A Civil War term that means a person who lives in the northern United States and is assumed to have particular attitudes and beliefs

1   My friend Scott once laughed in my face when I told him I did not like driving a car with Massachusetts plates in Texas. I am from Texas, you see, and when I visit my native state in a rental car, I don't want to be mistaken for a Yankee.[1] Scott, *incredulous* and logical, pointed out that it really did not make the slightest difference what *inferences* drivers on the roads I traveled might make about my geographical roots because I would never have any real-life dealings with them. Who cares what strangers in other cars think about you? One answer is that a lot of people must care or there would be no such thing as bumper stickers.

2   That doesn't mean that my friend didn't have a point, though: How much thought do we really put into the rather extraordinary number of identity signals that zoom by on highways or inch along in commuter traffic? It's possible that from time to time a Misfits or McCain message hits its mark, and somebody, somewhere, gives a thumbs up to another driver. (It's also *plausible* that some stickers inspire fellow motorists to extend another digit as a form of acknowledgment.) But the overwhelming majority of signals sent via bumper sticker almost certainly float unnoticed

PAUSE: Why doesn't Walker want to be mistaken for a Yankee?

CRITICAL READING
■ Preview
■ Read
■ Pause
■ Review

(See pp. 3–8.)

into the ether for the simple reason that nobody much cares. It's sad, really.

PAUSE: What are tribal-affiliation stickers?

In addition to tribal-affiliation stickers — I Like This Band; I Root 3 for That Sports Team; I Graduated From the Following Institution of Higher Learning — many bumper stickers attempt the more ambitious business of broadcasting some point of view on a matter of public contention, geopolitical policy, or even a philosophical mode of being. It's even more sad to conclude that nobody thinks about those either, but it turns out that somebody does or at least has: Jack Bowen, who teaches philosophy at Menlo School in Atherton, California. In a recent book called *If You Can Read This: The Philosophy of Bumper Stickers*, he not only thinks about bumper stickers but takes them seriously, evaluating the underlying worldviews they express.

PAUSE: What political point of view does the sticker reveal?

Consider, for example, the sticker "Against Abortion? Then Don't 4 Have One!" The political point of view there is obvious enough. But, Bowen says, if we *delve* deeper, we find the suggestion that morality itself is up for grabs, resolved on a person-by-person, situation-by-situation basis. "This is not at all what we want to say morality is," he says. "It would make the idea of morality completely pointless." He says he takes issue with about 70 percent of the broader conclusions implied by the many bumper stickers he evaluates.

PAUSE: What predicts road rage?

Now, do we really need a philosopher to reveal that bumper stickers 5 are simplistic? Probably not. We know that bumper stickers are about declaration, not dialogue; designed to end conversations, not start them. Possibly the most *revelatory* research to date on the subject was a 2008 Colorado State University study concluding that drivers who put bumper stickers and other decorations on their vehicles are 16 percent more likely to engage in road rage. It wasn't the message on the "territory markers," as a researcher called bumper stickers in an interview with *Nature News*, but the number of them that "predicted road rage better than vehicle value, condition or any of the things that we normally associate with aggressive driving."

PAUSE: What questions do callers ask Bowen?

Bowen concedes all this. But when he appears on radio call-in 6 shows and the like to promote his book, he has learned that "people are really fired up about bumper stickers." Tellingly, however, the people he hears from almost never engage him with counter-interpretations of their own stickers (or even admit to having them). Instead they want explanations for messages they find baffling — or aggravating. "My Child Is an Honors Student" turns out to be one message that ticks

² Ticks off: slang for irritates, annoys

off² a surprising number of people. As it happens, that one used to vaguely annoy Bowen too, but when he reflected on it for the book, he concluded that it was a perfectly reasonable thing to have on a car and not deserving of the "My Child Beat Up Your Honor Student" response stickers it has inspired.

7   Still, the general reaction to this *benign* message suggests that when the signals we send are noticed, we might not be happy with how they are received. This brings us to the most puzzling sticker Bowen evaluates: "Don't Judge Me." He argues that passing judgment is not such a bad thing. But this sticker struck me as an even more extreme version of my own silly worries about license-plate signifiers: Why would someone go out of the way to demand neutrality from strangers? And yet this *beguiling paradox* of a message might capture what bumper stickers are really about. Probably no one thinks about the signals sent along the highway more than those sending them. And bumper stickers are all about announcing judgments, not accepting them.

PAUSE: What sentence answers a question asked in paragraph 1?

1.   Briefly summarize Walker's essay. What is his purpose?
2.   What examples does he give of bumper stickers?
3.   Write three questions that might be on a quiz of Walker's essay.
4.   What stereotype does Walker start the essay with?
5.   What is another good title for Walker's essay?
6.   What types of bumper stickers have you seen? What attitudes do they express?

Write an Illustration Essay

Write your own illustration essay on one of the following topics or on a topic of your own choice. Use ILLUSTRATION AT A GLANCE as a basic organizer (p. 84), and follow the Writing Guide: Illustration checklist as you write and revise (p. 92).

COLLEGE
• Discuss some of the activities, services, and programs offered on your campus.

• Write about what you expect to get out of college.

WORK
• Tell someone applying for a job like yours what his or her typical responsibilities might be.

• Demonstrate to an interviewer the following statement: "I am a detail-oriented employee."

EVERYDAY LIFE
• Write a letter to your landlord about how your apartment's maintenance needs to be done more regularly.

• Name the most influential person in your life, and give examples of his or her characteristics.

WRITING GUIDE: ILLUSTRATION

STEPS IN ILLUSTRATION	HOW TO DO THE STEPS
☐ Focus.	• Think about your topic and what your audience knows about it.
☐ Explore your topic. See Chapter 2.	• Prewrite to give examples of your topic.
☐ Write a thesis statement. Topic + main point = Thesis See Chapter 3.	• Write a working thesis that includes your topic and main point about it. You might also include some examples you will give in your support paragraphs.
☐ Support your thesis. See Chapter 3.	• Choose at least three examples that demonstrate your main point. • Consider what details about the examples your reader needs to know.
☐ Write a draft. See Chapter 4.	• Arrange your examples in order of importance or time. • Write topic sentences for each major example. • Write a paragraph for each example, giving details about the examples.
☐ Revise your draft. See Chapter 4.	• Make sure that your examples and details all relate to your main point. • Add transitions. • Improve your introduction, thesis, and conclusion.
☐ Edit your revised draft. See Chapters 16 through 18.	• Correct errors in grammar, spelling, word use, and punctuation.
☐ Evaluate your writing.	• Does it have the Four Basics of Good Illustration? (p. 81) • Is this the best I can do?

7

Description

Writing That Creates Pictures with Words

Understand What Description Is

Description is writing that creates a clear and vivid impression of the topic. Description translates your experience of a person, place, or thing into words, often by appealing to the senses—sight, hearing, smell, taste, and touch.

Four Basics of Good Description

1. It creates a main impression — an overall effect, feeling, or image — about the topic.
2. It uses specific examples to support the main impression.
3. It supports those examples with details that appeal to the five senses.
4. It brings a person, place, or object to life for the reader.

In the following paragraph, each number corresponds to one of the Four Basics of Good Description.

> **1** Nojoqui Falls is a special place to me because its beauty provides a break from human worries. **2** At the start of the trail leading to the falls, the smell and sound of oak trees and pine trees make visitors feel they are up for the journey. **3** The sun hitting the trees makes the air fresh with a leafy aroma. Overhead, the wind blows through the leaves, making a soft noise. **2** Closer to the waterfall, the shade from the trees creates a shielding blanket. When the sun comes out, it fills the place with light, showing the

4 All the details bring the falls to life.

✓ LearningCurve For extra practice in the skills covered in this chapter, visit
bedfordstmartins.com/reinteractive.

4
All the details bring the falls to life.

vapor coming out of the trees and plants. To the left of the trail are rocks that are positioned perfectly for viewing the waterfall. **3** Water splashes as it hits the rocks. **2** The waterfall itself is beautiful, like a transparent, sparkling window of diamonds. **3** The water is so clear that objects on the other side are visible. It is like a never-ending stream of water that splashes onto the rocks. **1** The total effect of these sights, sounds, and smells is a setting where daily cares can be set aside for a while.

— Liliana Ramirez, student

Being able to describe something or someone accurately and in detail is important both in college and in other settings. Describing something well involves using specific, concrete details. Here are some ways that you might use description:

COLLEGE   For a science lab report, you describe the physical and chemical properties of an element.

WORK   You write a letter to your office manager describing the unacceptable conditions of the office refrigerator.

EVERYDAY LIFE You describe a jacket that you left at the movies to the lost-and-found department.

Main Point in Description

In descriptive writing, your **main point** conveys the main impression you want your readers to see.

Take another look at the paragraph starting on page 93. What if the topic sentence had been

I love Nojoqui Falls.

You would not know why the writer likes the place. But the actual topic sentence conveys a main impression of the falls and lets you know why this place is important to the writer.

Nojoqui Falls is a special place to me because its beauty provides a break from human worries.

This statement provides a preview of what is to come, helping the audience read and understand the description.

The thesis statement in description essays typically includes the topic and the main impression about it that the writer wants to convey.

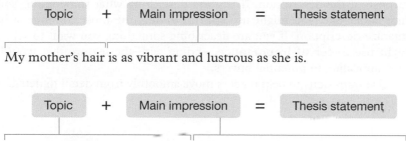

My mother's hair is as vibrant and lustrous as she is.

The Vietnam Veterans Memorial is an incredibly powerful monument.

Support in Description

Good description uses specific, concrete details to create the sights, sounds, smells, tastes, and textures that support and show your main impression.

SIGHT	SOUND	SMELL
Colors	Loud/soft	Sweet/sour
Shapes	Piercing/soothing	Sharp/mild
Sizes	Continuous/off-and-on	Good (like what?)
Patterns	Pleasant/unpleasant (how?)	Bad (rotten?)
Brightness	High/low	New (like what?)
Does it look like anything else?	Does it sound like anything else?	Does it smell like anything else?

TASTE	TOUCH
Good (What does *good* taste like?)	Hard/soft
Bad (What does *bad* taste like?)	Liquid/solid
Bitter/sugary	Rough/smooth
Metallic	Dry/oily
Burning/spicy	Textures
Does it taste like anything else?	Does it feel like anything else?

As you think about the main impression you want to convey, ask yourself: What sensory details might bring this subject to life? Add additional details to convey each sensation more accurately or vividly.

Organization in Description

For more on spatial order and order of importance, see pages 45–46.

Description may use any of the orders of organization, depending on the purpose of the description. If you are describing what someone or something looks like, you might use **spatial order**, the most common way to organize description. If you are describing something you want to sell, you might use **order of importance**, ending with the feature that would be most appealing to potential buyers.

Use transitions to help readers move smoothly from detail to detail.

Common Transitions in Description

TRANSITIONS TO SHOW SPATIAL ORDER	TRANSITIONS TO SHOW ORDER OF IMPORTANCE
above/underneath	even more
beyond	more
in front of/behind	the most
to the left/right	the most intense
	the strongest

DESCRIPTION AT A GLANCE

Introduction with thesis statement
Gives a main impression

First major sensory detail
Supporting details

Second major sensory detail
Supporting details

Most important sensory detail
Supporting details

Conclusion
Reminds readers of the main impression
Makes an observation

Read and Analyze Description

Read the following three examples of description—from college, the work-place, and everyday life—and answer the questions that accompany them. For each essay, review the Four Basics of Good Description (p. 93) and practice the critical reading process explained in Chapter 1 (pages 1–15).

Description in College

The following description essay was written by a student for a course assignment.

Florence Bagley

Photograph of My Father

CRITICAL
READING
■ Preview
■ Read
■ Pause
■ Review

(See pp. 3–8.)

GUIDING QUESTION
What does Bagley see in the photo of her father?

1   This old black-and-white photograph of my father fills me with con-flicting emotions. He died young, and this photo is one of the few that my family has of him. The picture seems to show a strong, happy man, young and smiling, but to me it also reveals his weakness.

2   Looking at this picture of my father, I feel how much I have lost. In it, my father is sitting upright in a worn plaid easy chair. It was "his" chair, and when he was at work, I'd curl up in it and smell his aftershave lotion and

PAUSE:
Underline the sensory details in this paragraph.

PAUSE: What mood has Bagley created so far?

cigarette smoke. His pitch-black hair is so dark that it blends into the background of the photo. His eyes, though indistinct in this photo, were a deep, dark brown. Although the photo is faded around my father's face, I still can make out his strong jaw and the cleft in his chin. In the photo, my father is wearing a clean white T-shirt that reveals his thick, muscular arms. Resting in the crook of his left arm is my younger brother, who was about one year old at the time. Both of them are smiling.

PAUSE: How has the mood changed and what transition signals the change?

However, when I study the photo, my eyes are drawn to the can of 3 beer that sits on the table next to him. Against my will, I begin to feel resentful. I have so many wonderful memories of my father. Whether he was carrying me on his shoulders, picking me up from school, or teaching me to draw, he always made time for me. All of these memories fade when I see that beer. From what I remember, he always made time for that beer as well. The smell of beer was always on him, the cool, sweating can always within reach.

PAUSE: What conflicting feelings does the picture create?

In this photo, my father appears to be a strong man; however, looks are 4 deceiving. My father died at the age of thirty-seven because he was an alcoholic. I was eleven when he died, and I really did not understand that his drinking was the reason for his death. I just knew that he left me without a father and the possibility of more memories. He should have been strong enough to stop drinking.

In spite of the resentment I may feel about his leaving me, this photo 5 holds many loving memories as well. It is of my father—the strong, wonderful man and the alcoholic—and it is the most precious thing I own. Although I would much rather have him here, I stay connected to him when I look at it.

CRITICAL THINKING
■ Summarize
■ Analyze
■ Synthesize
■ Evaluate

(More on pp. 9–15.)

1.   **Summarize.** Briefly summarize Bagley's essay, including her **main impression** and **major support**. What is her purpose? How does she feel about the photo and her father?

2.   **Analyze.** How do the second and third paragraphs create different impressions? How do these paragraphs and paragraph 4 support the main impression in the first paragraph?

3.   **Synthesize.** How does Bagley's essay prove the saying, "Photographs can be deceiving"? Find a photograph that deceives. How can you apply what you know about reading visuals to Bagley's essay and the photo you have found?

4.   **Evaluate.** Does Bagley achieve her purpose? Can you visualize her father? Does her essay have the **Four Basics of Good Description** (see p. 93)? What do *you* think about her essay, and why?

Description at Work

The following is a passage from the novel *Still Water Saints*. Note that there is no thesis statement because this is not an essay but rather part of a novel.

Alex Espinoza

From *Still Water Saints*

GUIDING QUESTION
What kinds of sensory details does Alex Espinoza use?

VOCABULARY
The following words are italicized in the excerpt: *bellows, padlock, massacred, lynched, opossum, dingy*. If you do not know their meanings, look them up in a dictionary or online.

Alex Espinoza
Writer and Assistant
Professor

CRITICAL
READING
■ Preview
■ Read
■ Pause
■ Review

(See pp. 3–8.)

1   The iron security gate unfolded like the *bellows* of an accordion as Perla pulled it along the rail in front of the door. She snapped the *padlock* shut, turned around the corner of the building, and headed home. Her house was close, just across the empty lot next to the shopping center. Wild sage and scrub grew beside the worn path that cut through the field. Boys sometimes rode their bikes there, doing tricks and wheelies as they bumped over mounds and breaks, falling down, laughing and scraping their knees, their faces coated with grime. Their tires left thin tracks that looped around the salt cedar trees, around the soiled mattresses and old washers and sinks that were dumped there.

PAUSE: What impression do you have of the area so far? Why?

2   People told of a curse on these grounds, a group of monks traveling through Agua Mansa in the days when California was still a part of Mexico, back before states were shapes on a map. They said a tribe of Indians *massacred* the monks; they skinned them and scattered their body parts around the lot for the crows. Still others said Mexican settlers had been *lynched* from the branches of the cedars by Anglos who stole their land for the railroads. Seeing a piece of stone, Perla wondered about the monks and those men dangling from branches. *A tooth? Part of a toe?* Empty soda cans and wrappers were caught under boulders and discarded car parts. *What would the monks think about having a tire for a headstone, a couch for a marker?* She thought of her husband, Guillermo, of his tombstone, of the thick, green lawns of the cemetery where he was buried.

PAUSE: How does this paragraph change the mood?

PAUSE: How does the impression change here? Why?

When she reached her house and stepped inside, the air was warm 3 and silent. Perla put her purse down on the rocking chair near the front door and went around, pushing the lace curtains back and cracking open the windows. She breathed in the scent of wood smoke from someone's fireplace down the street, a smell that reminded her of her father toasting garbanzo beans. She went into the kitchen and looked for something to eat.

PAUSE: How does the last sentence of this paragraph change the mood of the scene?

Dinner was a bowl of oatmeal with two slices of toast, which she took 4 out to the patio. The night was cold, and the steam from the oatmeal rose up and fogged her glasses as she spooned it in her mouth. Police sirens wailed down the street, and dogs answered, their cries lonely and beautiful. She looked up, and in the flashing lights saw a set of glowing red eyes.

PAUSE: Underline the sensory details in this paragraph.

Perla flicked on the porch light. It was an *opossum*, its fur *dingy* and 5 gray, the tips and insides of its ears bright pink. It stood motionless, behind the trunk of the organ pipe cactus, staring at her. It climbed to the top of the fence, making a low, faint jingle as it moved. Perla looked again; a small brass bell was tied to a piece of red yarn knotted around the opossum's tail. She took her spoon and threw it. When it hit the bottom of the fence, the animal darted, the clatter of the bell frantic. The opossum disappeared behind the branches of the avocado tree and down the other side of the fence into the empty lot, the ringing growing fainter and fainter.

From under the kitchen sink, behind the pile of cloths and old sponges 6 she could never bring herself to throw away, was a bottle of rum. She poured some into a cup and took a drink. Then she took another. The warmth calmed her nerves.

She imagined the ghosts of the dead monks and the lynched men ris- 7 ing up from the ground, awakened by her thoughts. Curls of gray smoke at first, they slowly took human form. They walked in a straight line, one in front of the other. A slow progression followed the opossum's tracks through the lot and back home.

PAUSE: What impression does the final paragraph create?

She took another drink and closed her eyes. That animal was a messen- 8 ger. It was letting her know that something was out there. It was coming.

1. What is Espinoza's purpose?

2. What does he assume readers know about Agua Mansa?

3. How does the final paragraph contrast with the introductory one in terms of the impressions they create?

4. How are you left feeling about the place? Why? Choose several details that give you that impression.

Description in Everyday Life

The following is a letter that Jennifer Orlando wrote for a helium.com contest.

Jennifer Orlando

Rattlesnake Canyon: A Place of Peace and Beauty

GUIDING QUESTION
What impression does Orlando create?

VOCABULARY
The following words are *italicized* in the essay: *restorative, swarms, savory, perspective, eternity, surpass, humanity.* If you do not know their meanings, look them up in a dictionary or online.

CRITICAL READING
■ Preview
■ Read
■ Pause
■ Review

(See pp. 3–8.)

1   Today I went for a hike in Rattlesnake Canyon in my hometown of Grand Junction, Colorado. I had been a little down and I just wanted to get out and forget my troubles. Instead, though, I came back happy and feeling really lucky to be alive. Rattlesnake Canyon is incredibly beautiful, peaceful, and *restorative.*

2   The hiking path is lined with gorgeous desert plants that go on for acres. There are many varieties of cactus, many with long white spines reaching out to the green "leaves." I never thought of cactus as being colorful, but there can be purple or about five shades of green. Some of them have "flowers" that look like huge, bright red radishes. Others have tiny yellow flowers growing beside the sharp spines, and still others have lavender flowers sprouting. There are all kinds of yellow flowering plants — some pale, and some darker, like an egg yolk. *Swarms* of yellow butterflies flutter around them, dancing in and out of the branches. I just started laughing when I saw them; it was so perfect. My favorite plant is sage, again lots of different kinds. Some have billions of little purple flowers, and they are about four feet tall. Others are a silvery green, and when you run your hand over the leaves, they give off this *savory* scent that is barely sweet and makes me think of my mother's stuffing at Thanksgiving. It is sage, the herb. The air just smells all herby from sage, juniper, and other smells I cannot identify. Some low bushes have bright red flowers—some scarlet, some rust, and some orangy. The desert plants are beautiful. The desert is so much more than just sand.

3   As I went along, I was surrounded by the huge rocks of the canyon, like a mini-Grand Canyon. At the base, the rocks are a dark, rusty color.

PAUSE: What do you expect the rest of the essay will be about?

PAUSE: What impression does paragraph 2 create? Underline details that contribute.

PAUSE: How
does the
geography
affect
Orlando's
sense of
time?

As they rise up, they have about ten different layers of color—from a kind of light grey, to darker grey, to pale red, and finally to a brilliant red that shines in the sunlight from flecks of mineral in them. Those layers of rock reveal the many different climates the area has experienced over billions of years, including being underwater several times. I was literally surrounded by these looming rocks, thousands of feet high.

Best of all, though, is the sky. The towering, multicolored cliffs are met by 4 the bluest sky imaginable. There were no clouds, and this blue was dark and beautiful against the red of the rock. The sun was bright, as it usually is here, and everything was so big, so colorful, so intense that I felt lucky to be alive. There is something about all this beauty that has been here for billions of years that makes you feel as if your problems are unimportant: It gives peace.

PAUSE: What
final impres-
sion does
Orlando
create?

Rattlesnake Canyon and places like it give us *perspective* on our lives. 5 The beauty and *eternity* of nature assure us that so much in our lives is small compared with our surroundings. It opens our senses if we allow it to: We see, smell, hear, and feel more closely. These places restore our faith in forces that far *surpass* us in power and endurance. I left the canyon with my spirit restored. Nature is open to everyone, and we should take the time to let it work its wonders on our *humanity*.

1. Summarize Orlando's description of Rattlesnake Canyon and its effect on her.

2. What details and impressions contribute to the effect?

3. What experience have you had of a place affecting you, either positively or negatively? What details caused your feeling?

4. Find a picture of a place and consider the effect or impression it creates.

Write a Description Essay

Write your own description essay on *one* of the following topics or on a topic of your own choice. Use **DESCRIPTION AT A GLANCE** as a basic organizer (pp. 96–97), and follow the Writing Guide: Description checklist as you write and revise (pp. 103–04).

COLLEGE

• Describe your favorite place on campus so that a reader understands why you like to be there.

• Describe an event or a setting that you learned about in one of your courses.

WORK
- Describe a product your company makes, or a service it provides.
- Describe a specific area at work that you see every day but have not really noticed. Look at it with new eyes.

EVERYDAY LIFE
- Describe a favorite food without naming it. Include how it looks, smells, tastes, and what it means to you.
- Describe a place you have lived or visited

WRITING GUIDE: DESCRIPTION

STEPS IN DESCRIPTION	HOW TO DO THE STEPS
☐ **Focus.**	• Think about what you want to describe and who your readers are.
☐ **Explore your topic.** See Chapter 2.	• Make sure your topic can be described in a short essay. • Prewrite to generate sensory images and details.
☐ **Write a thesis statement.** Topic + Main impression = Thesis See Chapter 3.	• Decide your purpose for writing a description and what picture you want to create for your readers.
☐ **Support your thesis.** See Chapter 3.	• Add images and details that will bring what you are describing to life for your audience. • Use your senses to create the images.
☐ **Write a draft.** See Chapter 4.	• Arrange your main point and the images that help create it in a logical order. • Write topic sentences for the supporting images and details that show them.

STEPS IN DESCRIPTION	HOW TO DO THE STEPS
☐ **Revise your draft.** See Chapter 4.	• Reread your essay, adding vivid details. • Add transitions to help show your reader your main impression of your topic. • Improve your introduction, thesis, and conclusion.
☐ **Edit your revised draft.** See Chapters 16 through 18.	• Correct errors in grammar, spelling, word use, and punctuation.
☐ **Evaluate your writing.**	• Does it have the Four Basics of Good Description (p. 93)? • Is this the best I can do?

8

Process Analysis

Writing That Explains How Things Happen

Understand What Process Analysis Is

Process analysis explains either how to do something (so your readers can do it) or how something works (so your readers can understand it). Both types of process analysis present the steps involved in the process.

Four Basics of Good Process Analysis

1. It helps readers either perform the steps or understand how something works.
2. It presents the essential steps in the process.
3. It explains the steps in detail.
4. It arranges the steps in a logical order (usually in chronological order).

In the following paragraph, each number corresponds to one of the Four Basics of Good Process Analysis.

> **1** Two teenagers, Robbie and Brittany Bergquist, wanted to help American soldiers in combat zones call home, so in 2004 they founded the organization Cell Phones for Soldiers, which has proved to be extremely successful. **2** First, Robbie and Brittany pooled their own money, a total of $14. Realizing that would not go far, they then decided to hold fund-raising events. **3** Next, they enlisted friends and family to help them organize a series of bake sales and car washes. As people learned about their efforts, more joined them, and they began to raise serious money to purchase phones. **2** Second, they started another fund-raising initiative:

4 Steps arranged in chron-ological order

✓ LearningCurve For extra practice in the skills covered in this chapter, visit bedfordstmartins.com/reinteractive.

105

4
Steps arranged in chronological order

recycling old cell phones. **3** They collected old phones and brought them to a recycling company. **3** With this money, they purchased minutes on phone cards for the soldiers. **3** Then, they organized volunteers to wrap and send the cards to soldiers who had heard about their work and had contacted them. **2** To date, they have provided over 60 million minutes of phone time. Robbie and Brittany continue their efforts to include not only soldiers overseas but also returning veterans who are in the hospital.

Whenever you give someone directions about how to do something or explain how something works, you are using process analysis. Here are some ways you might use process analysis.

COLLEGE
In an information technology course, you write an essay explaining the process for implementing a new data management system.

WORK
The office has a new security system, and you are asked to write a memo to employees explaining how to access their work areas during and after normal business hours.

EVERYDAY LIFE
You write directions telling your child how to operate the washing machine.

Main Point in Process Analysis

Your **purpose** in process analysis is to explain a process so that readers can either do it themselves or understand how it works. Your **main point** lets your readers know what you think about that process—for example, whether it is easy or complicated.

The Web site *MapQuest.com* can get you from where you are to where you want to go in several easy steps.

A thesis statement for a process analysis usually identifies the process and the point you want to make about it. The thesis should also suggest what you want your readers to know or learn about the process.

Process   +   Main point   =   Thesis statement

Painting a room takes careful preparation and application.

In process analysis, include your thesis statement in your introduction so that readers know from the start what the process and the purpose are.

Support in Process Analysis

A clear process analysis presents all the essential steps in the process; these steps constitute the **major support**. Each step is explained by supporting details. For example, the writer of the thesis *Successful weight loss is a challenge, but it starts with some simple steps* might use the following essential steps and details to explain the steps.

ESSENTIAL STEPS

STEP 1: Get rid of the junk food in your home and commit not to buy any.

> **SUPPORTING DETAILS**
>
> It is tempting and is not nutritional
>
> That includes chips, candy, and any other unhealthy foods you snack on
>
> Do not shop when you are hungry
>
> Stay away from the junk food aisles

STEP 2: Keep a list of everything you eat each day.

> **SUPPORTING DETAILS**
>
> When you are tempted, wait five minutes before eating
>
> Write each item just before or just after you eat it
>
> Include everything, even just tastes

STEP 3: Weigh yourself just once a week.

> **SUPPORTING DETAILS**
>
> Not daily because weight fluctuates
>
> Record your weight

STEP 4: Reward yourself, but not with food.

> **SUPPORTING DETAILS**
>
> Call a friend to share your success
>
> Go to a movie you want to see

Organization in Process Analysis

For more on chronological order, see pages 44–45.

Because process analysis explains how to do something or how something works, it usually uses **chronological (time) order.** Start with the first step, and then explain each step in the order that it should occur.

Add transitional words and sentences to your essay to help readers follow each step in the process.

Common Transitions in Process Analysis

after	eventually	meanwhile	soon
as	finally	next	then
at last	first	now	when
before	last	second	while
during	later	since	

PROCESS ANALYSIS AT A GLANCE

Introduction with thesis statement
Includes the process you are describing

First step in process
Details about the first step (how to do it or how it works)

Second step in process
Details about the second step

Third step in process
Details about the third step

Conclusion
Reminds readers of the process and makes an observation related to your main point

Read and Analyze Process Analysis

Read the following three process analysis essays—from college, work, and everyday life—and answer the questions that accompany them. For each essay, practice the critical reading process explained in Chapter 1 (pages 1–15).

Process Analysis in College

Daniel Flanagan

The Choice to Do It Over Again

GUIDING QUESTION
What did Flanagan do over?

VOCABULARY
The following words are *italicized* in the essay: *degenerate, spiral, consequence, fragile, shortcomings.* If you do not know their meanings, look them up in a dictionary or online.

CRITICAL
READING
■ Preview
■ Read
■ Pause
■ Review

(See pp. 3–8.)

1   I do not know why I came to the decision to become a loser, but I know I made the choice at a young age. Sometime in the middle of fourth grade, I stopped trying. By the time I was in seventh grade, I was your typical *degenerate*: lazy, rebellious, disrespectful. I had lost all social graces. I was terminally hip and fatally cool.

PAUSE: What does the second sentence mean?

2   Not long after that, I dropped out of school and continued my downward *spiral*. Hard physical labor was the *consequence* for the choices I made as an adolescent. At the age of twenty-one, I was hopelessly lost and using drugs as a way to deal with the fact that I was illiterate and stuck in a dead-end job carrying roof shingles up a ladder all day.

3   But now I believe in do-overs, in the chance to do it all again. And I believe that do-overs can be made at any point in your life, if you have the right motivation. Mine came from a surprising source.

PAUSE: Why did Flanagan decide to change his life?

4   It was September 21, 2002, when my son Blake was born. It's funny that after a life of avoiding responsibility, now I was in charge of something so *fragile*. Over the years, as I grew into the title of Dad, I began to learn something about myself. In a way, Blake and I were both learning to walk, talk, work, and play for the first time. I began my do-over.

PAUSE: Underline the steps in Flanagan's do-over.

5   It took me almost three years to learn how to read. I started with my son's books. Over and over, I practiced reading books to him until I remembered all the words in every one of them. I began to wonder if it were possible for me to go back to school. I knew I wanted to be a good role model, so after a year-and-a-half and a lot of hard work, I passed my GED[1] test on my son's fourth birthday. This may not sound like much, and I am not trying to get praise for doing something that should have been done in the first place, but all things considered it was one of the best days in my life. Today, I am a full-time college student, studying to become a sociologist.

[1] GED: General Education Development tests that substitute for high school graduation

Growing up, I always heard these great turn-around stories of triumph   6
over *shortcomings*. But I never thought they applied to me. Now I believe it
is a choice anyone can make: to do it all over again.

CRITICAL
THINKING
■ Summarize
■ Analyze
■ Synthesize
■ Evaluate
(More on pp. 9–15.)

1.   **Summarize.** Briefly summarize Flanagan's essay, including the
     process he describes and the major steps.

2.   **Analyze.** How does the title set up the essay? Why do you think
     Flanagan placed his thesis somewhere other than the first paragraph?
     How is his concluding sentence tied to his thesis statement?

3.   **Synthesize.** What has Flanagan learned about choices? How does
     this relate to other stories and choices you have experienced or read
     about?

4.   **Evaluate.** What is Flanagan's purpose for writing, and does he
     achieve it? Does he give enough information? Is the process he
     went through clear? Does his essay use the **Four Basics of Good
     Process Analysis**?

Process Analysis at Work

The following is from a report that a nurse prepared for a patient's file to
document the steps taken to treat her. The report shows that when a nurse
on the team and a resident disagreed as to the treatment called for, the
nurse called for another opinion. This type of communication is frequent
among medical personnel.

CRITICAL
READING
■ Preview
■ Read
■ Pause
■ Review
(See pp. 3–8.)

Patty Maloney

Patient Report

Patty Maloney
Clinical Nurse
Specialist

GUIDING QUESTION
How did Maloney and others save a child's life?

VOCABULARY
The following words are *italicized* in the excerpt: *vital signs,
pneumothorax, rupture, resident, attending physician.* If you
do not know their meanings, look them up in a dictionary or
online.

Patient: (name), female, age 8, with tumor and   1
disease progression

Symptoms at arrival: Child had not eaten much for two days and   2
was withdrawn and uncommunicative.

Treatment process: First, we needed to determine if the child was in   3
immediate danger or in need of further medications for pain control. We
took her *vital signs*, which were within the range of normal for her, with a

slightly elevated heart rate. Then we interviewed the child's mother to see if she had administered any breakthrough pain medication during the last 24 hours. We gave the child a short-term pain medication.

4   As a next step, we had a discussion with the doctor in the unit, and we then administered a breakthrough pain medication. We closely monitored the patient's vital signs, particularly noting if the heart rate came down. We were documenting the signs every hour formally but also checked on the child's status in the Intensive Care Unit every 15 minutes.

5   During one check, one of our nurses noted that the child looked pale, and her breathing was somewhat shallow. The nurse knew that the child had fragile lungs and felt that she was at risk of the *pneumothorax* collecting fluid with a possible *rupture* of the lung lining and collapse of the lung. Following procedure, the nurse immediately alerted the *resident*, who felt that the child was fine and suggested that nothing but continued observation was necessary.

6   The nurse disagreed with the resident's diagnosis and at that point sent another nurse to page the *attending physician* for another opinion. In the meantime, while waiting for the attending, the nurse called for an x-ray. She then pulled the cart over to the patient in preparation for inserting a tube into the lung cavity to reinflate the lung. When the attending physician arrived and was briefed, he agreed with the nurse's diagnosis. The tube was quickly inserted, and the collapse of the lung was avoided.

7   The child continues in observation in the ICU. Her condition is stable.

1.   Briefly summarize Maloney's report.

2.   Although a description of a treatment process, the report does not give many details. What is the purpose of the report?

3.   How would the report differ if its purpose was to teach new nurses how to do a particular procedure?

4.   Write a possible thesis statement for the report.

5.   Write a possible concluding statement.

Process Analysis in Everyday Life

Michael Gates Gill

How I Learned to Be a Barista[1]

GUIDING QUESTION
What are the steps that Gill learns, and what else does he learn during his first day?

VOCABULARY
The following words are *italicized* in the essay: *combative, module, humiliating, literally, renewed, conspicuous.* If you do not know their meanings, look them up in a dictionary or online.

COMBINING MODES: If you have already studied illustration, note that illustration is used here to give examples of steps in the process. Also, note that the report uses narration within the process.

PAUSE: What do you think will happen next?

[1] barista: Italian for "bartender." Starbucks servers are called *baristas*.

CRITICAL READING
■ Preview
■ Read
■ Pause
■ Review
(See pp. 3–8.)

For this reading, you do not need to underline the major support or circle transitions.

"**G**et out to the registers, Mike," my boss Crystal encouraged me. "And be sure to make eye contact and connect with conversation."

I had heard those words on the training video, but I was more concerned with just handling the cash so that I did not make a perfect fool of myself. Unfortunately, now the kids from school arrived.

Joann came over to me, though, and helped me put the drawer in.

"The computer will show you the correct change, and the great thing is that the Guest[2] will see the numbers, too, so they can catch you if you get it wrong. You will do fine, Mike."   5

"But I'm terrible with money."

"So were my first two husbands. Just let the register do the work."

I smiled. That was a good mantra.[3]

A guy stepped up to my register to order. He had no idea that he was dealing with a person who had never done this before.

"I want a Tall Mocha."

I called down to Tawana, an attractive but *combative* barista on the   10 espresso bar: "Tall Mocha."

"Tall Mocha," Tawana called back to me, confirming that she had gotten the order right.

I looked at the register. On the screen read the words "Tall" and "Mocha," just like on the computer training *module*. I jabbed at them with my finger. Sure enough, it worked, and the price came up on my screen.

The guy handed me five dollars.

The screen displayed the option "Five dollars" in a box, so I punched the box.

Then, the register opened, and the screen displayed the exact change I   15 should hand the guy: $2.73. I dug out the change from my drawer. The guy looked at it and stuck it in his pocket and made his way to the espresso bar to pick up his drink.

My screen, about the size of a small television, read, "Close your drawer."

I closed my drawer, and said to myself, *Hey, you can do this!*

Then, the next Guest stepped up, a young lady who was clearly pregnant.

"Just a Decaf Tall Coffee," she said.

I punched in Tall, took her money, gave her the change, closed the   20 drawer, and turned to get a cup of coffee for her. Fresh coffee was right behind me, with the cups. I gave one to her.

She gave me a big smile, as though I were already a friend. "My name's Rachel. I have another child on the way. I have to stick to Decaf for a while. Can't wait to get back on the hard stuff."

I had a sudden realization that people might treat me the way they were said to treat bartenders. . . . They wanted to engage with someone serving

[2] **Guest:** what Starbucks employees call their customers

PAUSE: Why was Gill concerned about the kids from school coming in?

[3] **mantra:** a sound, word, or group of words that when repeated is supposed to be transformative

PAUSE: So far, what steps in the process has Gill presented?

PAUSE: What steps does the register do for the barista?

PAUSE: What has Gill just realized?

them the good stuff. The afternoon went surprisingly well, despite the con-stant stream of customers.

As evening fell, it got even busier, but Joann came over a couple of times to help me out. The line moved smoothly, with people ordering Single Pump Mocha or Tall Latte. I was supposed to call out the size, name of drink, and any "customizing" such as One Tall One Pump Mocha. Often I would get the order wrong and start with One Pump Mocha, forgetting to call the size . . . or call for a Tall Latte forgetting to mention the Guest wanted it with skim milk. Sometimes, Guests would order Single Pump Mocha, or they would order a drink backward, starting with the milk, then the syrup, then the size, and I would repeat what they said and call it out to Tawana. Tawana would correct me at the top of her lungs, putting the order in the right way. It was *humiliating* for me, but I learned fast.

Also, it was a gift to me that Tawana had such a large, commanding voice. I had been worried about getting the orders straight, and I never missed Tawana's powerful calls. And I found that by leaning over the regis-ter, closer to the Guests, I could also hear them clearly.

25   "Ask if you have any questions," Joann said. "Just ask."

And I did. I found that the Guests didn't seem to mind helping me get their request just right.

That night, around 7:00 p.m., I was surprised to see the store grow really busy. I had thought coffee was something you picked up on the way to work, but it clearly was now an essential pick-me-up[4] on the way home as well. I noticed a businessman enter the store and join the growing line. When I had been on the *other* side of the bar, I had worked so hard just to get a prospective client like this well-dressed man to return a call. Now, my customers were *literally* waiting in line for my services, I thought to myself. How funny.

The businessman stepped up in line and told me, "Double Macchiato."

This was Starbucks language. I had a hard time figuring out what it translated to on the cash register screen. I started to feel flushed as I punched at various combinations incorrectly.

30   "You are new here, right?" the man asked. I looked at him. Was he going to complain to Crystal and get me fired on my first day at the register?

But he smiled at my look of panic.

"Don't worry, you'll get it."

He actually took the time to encourage me. Wow. I looked back at the screen with a *renewed* clarity of mind. Double Macchiato. Hit Tall, then Macchiato. Simple.

The businessman wasn't the only one to try to set me at ease.

35   "Welcome to the neighborhood," one lady said.

Another guy with an open shirt who looked like a hippie commented, "I'm glad to see they are hiring older people."

PAUSE: How does Tawana help Gill learn the job?

[4] **pick-me-up:** something that gives extra energy

PAUSE: What has Gill learned about people getting coffee?

5 **Partners:**
what
Starbucks
baristas are
called

Older?! Okay, so I wasn't so happy with this comment, but I appreciated his attitude. There was no denying it: I was older, at least a generation or two older than most Partners[5] so it was good to be welcomed even if it was for my *conspicuous* seniority.

Around eight o'clock, it started to get even busier. I had not realized that people had made Starbucks a part of their nightlife. Crowds of young people were piling in to share time with one another over their Lattes.

Focus, I reminded myself: You know how this works. *Punch the right button, call out the order, make the right change, smile.*

1.   Briefly summarize Gill's process.

2.   Were you surprised by anything in the essay? What and why?

3.   In addition to the critical skills needed to do his new job, what else did Gill observe and learn?

4.   Write three questions that might be on a quiz on this essay (and be prepared to answer them).

5.   Does Gill's essay have the **Four Basics of Good Process Analysis** (p. 105)? Why or why not, specifically?

6.   Of the three essays in this chapter, which do you think is the most effective model of process analysis? Is it the same one you like best? Why or why not?

Write a Process Analysis Essay

Write your own process analysis essay on *one* of the following topics or on a topic of your own choice. Use **PROCESS ANALYSIS AT A GLANCE** as a basic organizer (p. 108), and follow the Writing Guide: Process Analysis checklist as you write and revise (p. 115).

COLLEGE

- How to apply for financial aid
- How to study for a test

WORK

- How to do one of your major tasks at work
- How to get fired or how to get promoted

EVERYDAY LIFE

- How to wake up or how to get to sleep
- How to break up with someone

WRITING GUIDE: PROCESS ANALYSIS

STEPS IN PROCESS ANALYSIS	HOW TO DO THE STEPS
☐ Focus.	• Think about a process and its essential steps.
☐ Explore your topic. See Chapter 2.	• Make sure your process can be explained in a short essay. • Prewrite to decide on the steps and how you will explain them to your audience.
☐ Write a thesis statement. Process + Main point = Thesis See Chapter 3.	• Decide what you want your readers to know or learn about this process and write a thesis statement.
☐ Support your thesis. See Chapter 3.	• List all of the essential steps and details to describe them for your readers. • Imagine you are not familiar with the process. Would you understand it from the support you have listed, or do you need more explanation?
☐ Write a draft. See Chapter 4.	• Arrange the steps in a logical order (often chronological). • Write topic sentences for each essential step and paragraphs that describe them in detail.
☐ Revise your draft. See Chapter 4.	• Ask another person to read and comment on your draft. • Read to make sure that all the steps are there and relate to the topic. • Add transitions (often chronological). • Improve your introduction, thesis, and conclusion.
☐ Edit your draft. See Chapters 16 through 18.	• Correct errors in grammar, spelling, word use, and punctuation.
☐ Evaluate your writing.	• Does it have the Four Basics of Good Process Analysis (p. 105)? • Is this the best I can do?

9

Classification

Writing That Puts Things into Groups

Understand What Classification Is

Classification is writing that organizes, or sorts, people or items into categories.

The **organizing principle** for a classification is *how* you sort the people or items, not the categories themselves. The organizing principle is directly related to the **purpose** of your classification. For example, you might sort clean laundry (your purpose) using one of the following organizing principles (how you achieve your purpose) — by ownership (yours, your roommate's, and so on) or by where it goes (the bedroom, the bathroom).

Four Basics of Good Classification

1 It makes sense of a group of people or items by organizing them into useful categories.

2 It has a purpose for sorting the people or items.

3 It uses a single organizing principle.

4 It gives detailed examples or explanations of the things that fit into each category.

In the following paragraph, each number corresponds to one of the Four Basics of Good Classification.

All people do not learn in the same way, and **2** it is helpful to know what learning style you prefer. How do you naturally take in

LearningCurve **For extra practice in the skills covered in this chapter, visit** bedfordstmartins.com/reinteractive.

and absorb new information? The VARK learning styles inventory is a thirteen-item questionnaire that reveals which 3 learning style a person favors. 1 The first of its four learning styles is visual (V). 4 Visual learners absorb information best by looking at images or by drawing or diagramming a concept. For example, a visual learner may learn more by studying a flowchart of information rather than reading that same information in paragraph form. 1 The second learning style is auditory (A). 4 Auditory learners take in information most efficiently by hearing and listening. They remember information that they hear better than they remember information that they read. Even reading aloud is better than reading silently because hearing is key. Auditory learners benefit from discussion with others rather than working alone silently. 1 The third learning style is read/write (R). 4 Read/write learners learn best by reading written material. They also benefit from writing about what they have read. For example, many read/write learners study by reading and then writing a summary of what they have just read. Many people who are not naturally read/write learners have used that learning style in school because schools are oriented toward reading and writing. For example, a person whose score on the VARK is split evenly between auditory and read/write is probably an auditory learner who has learned to use a read/write learning style for school. 1 The final learning style is kinesthetic (K). 4 Kinesthetic learners learn by doing and by being active. For these learners, experiments in science may be easier to understand than reading a chapter in a book, listening to a lecture, or looking at an image. Kinesthetic learners often need to create activity in order to learn well: They may make flash cards, walk around as they study, or make a static activity interactive in some other way. All learners benefit from learning techniques such as highlighting and making notes, though different kinds of notes work for different learning styles. All learners are active learners: They learn best when they actively involve themselves in a task rather than passively observe it. 2 Taking a learning styles inventory is both fun and useful, particularly for students.

Whenever you organize or sort things to make sense of them, you are classifying them. Here are some ways that you might use classification:

COLLEGE   In a nursing course, you discuss three types of antibiotics used to treat infections.

WORK   For a report on inventory at a software store, you list the types of software carried and report how many of each type you have in stock.

EVERYDAY LIFE You look at the types of payment plans that are available for your car loan.

Main Point in Classification

The **main point** in classification uses a single **organizing principle** to sort items into useful categories that help achieve the **purpose** of the classification. The diagram below shows how movies at most rental stores or online services are classified.

The following examples show how thesis statements for classification express the organizing principle and purpose.

Several kinds of equipment are necessary for a backpacking trip.

In addition to the purpose and organizing principle, a thesis statement in a classification may also include the categories that will be explained.

Several kinds of equipment are necessary for a backpacking trip, including proper footwear, versatile outerwear, and decent cooking supplies.

Support in Classification

The **primary support** in classification consists of the **categories** that serve the purpose of the classification.

The categories in classification are the "piles" into which the writer sorts a topic (the items to be classified). These categories will become the topic sentences for the body paragraphs of the essay.

TOPIC	College costs
THESIS STATEMENT	Tuition is only one of the many costs of going to college.
ORGANIZING PRINCIPLE	Types of costs other than tuition
PURPOSE	To show the different kinds of costs and their significance
CATEGORIES/ PRIMARY SUPPORT	Fees, costs of course materials, transportation expenses

The **supporting details** in classification are **examples** or explanations of what is in each category. The examples in classification are the various items that fall within each category. These are important because readers may not be familiar with your categories.

CATEGORY: Fees

> **EXAMPLES/SUPPORTING DETAILS:** General student fee assessed to each student, lab fees, computer fees

CATEGORY: Costs of course materials

> **EXAMPLES/SUPPORTING DETAILS:** Costs of books, lab manuals, software

CATEGORY: Transportation expenses

> **EXAMPLES/SUPPORTING DETAILS:** Costs of gas, parking, train and bus fare

Organization in Classification

Classification can be organized in different ways (**time order, space order,** or **order of importance**) depending on its purpose.

PURPOSE	LIKELY ORGANIZATION
to explain changes or events over time	time
to describe the arrangement of people/items in physical space	space
to discuss parts of an issue or problem, or types of people or things	importance

As you write your classification, use **transitions** to move your readers smoothly from one category to another.

Common Transitions in Classification

another	for example
another kind	for instance
first, second, third, and so on	last
	one example/another example

CLASSIFICATION AT A GLANCE

Introduction with thesis statement
Organizing principle + purpose
OR
Organizing principle + categories + purpose

First category
Examples/explanations

Second category
Examples/explanations

Third category
Examples/explanations

Conclusion
Refers back to the classification's purpose
and makes an observation

Read and Analyze Classification

Read the following three examples of classification—from college, the workplace, and everyday life—and answer the questions that accompany them.

For each essay, review the **Four Basics of Good Classification** (p. 116) and practice the critical reading process explained in Chapter 1 (pp. 1–15).

Classification in College

The following student essay was written for an English class.

Josef Ameur

Videogame Genres

GUIDING QUESTION
What types of videogame genres does Ameur describe?

VOCABULARY
The following words are italicized in the essay: *accessible, arcade, genres, asteroids, attributes, charisma, embark, epic, quests.* If you do not know their meanings, look them up in a dictionary or online.

PAUSE: Underline the sentence where Ameur presents his categories.

CRITICAL READING
■ Preview
■ Read
■ Pause
■ Review

(See pp. 3–8.)

PAUSE: Note the detailed examples Ameur gives of each category.

Video games are an easily *accessible* way to cure the effects of boredom. 1 Ever since the late 1970s, video games have been extremely popular. They started out as *arcade* units, costing 25 cents to $1 per play. Kids would spend hundreds of dollars playing these games. The accessibility of video games has evolved over time from pay-to-play arcade units to personal home TV consoles. The *genres* of games have also evolved over time: shooter, role-playing, and strategy are just a few.

Shooters are one of the oldest genres of games. This genre was born in 2 arcade games such as *Asteroids* and *Galaga*. The early shooters were quite simple, and everything was on a two-dimensional plane. *Asteroids* consisted of a small spaceship avoiding *asteroids* by dodging and shooting at them. In *Galaga*, the players shot at enemy alien ships. Eventually, shooters evolved into third- and first-person shooters. In third-person, the player's view is from above, looking down at the character. In first-person, the player looks through the character's eyes. These shooters involve a character holding a gun shooting at enemies. Military, Sci-Fi, and Survival are a few sub-genres.

Role-playing games (RPGs) started out on paper. *Dungeons & Dragons* 3 was one of the more popular paper RPGs. Paper RPGs gave birth to computer-based ones. The benefit of computer-based RPGs is that with an Internet connection, they can be played with millions of other people. Players and their friends can create and control characters who live in a fantasy world. These characters are often class-based with classes such as thief, warrior, mage, and ranger. Players micromanage the *attributes* of their characters: *charisma*, strength, and magic, to name a few. Players *embark* on *epic quests*, slay beasts, find treasure, and fight in great battles.

Strategy games are similar to RPGs, but they are on a much larger scale. 4 In strategy games, players often control a historic civilization. The three main components of strategy games are economy, military, and politics. There are usually several types of resources that the players manage such as gold, stone, wood, and food. Players control the villagers, assigning them to gather resources. In the military aspect of this genre, players control the army and train different types of soldiers, taking into consideration the strengths and weaknesses of the different units. Politics determines allies and enemies and who wars with whom. In strategy games, there is no such thing as peace.

5   Many genres of games have been created to explore and play, but all video games offer the same core benefit: They offer a brief moment in time to escape the world around you. Video games not only cure boredom, but they also offer an experience that can rival that of books or films.

PAUSE: What sentence ties the conclusion to the thesis statement?

1.   **Summarize.** Briefly summarize Ameur's essay, including what he is classifying and what categories he uses.

2.   **Analyze.** Are the categories useful to Ameur's purpose of explaining videogame genres? Are all of the details clearly related to each category? How does Ameur's conclusion remind readers of the purpose? What system of organization does he use?

3.   **Synthesize.** What else do you know about the topic? Do you agree that the reason people play video games is to relieve boredom? What other ways are there to relieve boredom?

4.   **Evaluate.** Does Ameur achieve his purpose? Do you agree that playing video games rivals the experience of reading a book or seeing a film? Does the essay have the **Four Basics of Good Classification** (see p. 116)? What do you think of the essay?

CRITICAL THINKING
- Summarize
- Analyze
- Synthesize
- Evaluate

(More on pp. 9–15.)

Classification at Work

The following was written for a presentation at the American Institute of Certified Public Accountants.

Rebeka Mazzone

Serving on a Nonprofit Board Need Not Be Onerous

Rebeka Mazzone
Director, Rhode Island Region

GUIDING QUESTION
What kinds of practices will help nonprofits?

VOCABULARY
The following words are *italicized* in the presentation: *laudable, scrutiny, onerous, intrusion, inventoried, strategic, surplus, adequate, assets, expenditures, mandatory.* If you do not know their meanings, look them up in a dictionary or online.

CRITICAL READING
- Preview
- Read
- Pause
- Review

(See pp. 3–8.)

1   **D**oing good by serving on the board of nonprofit organizations, always *laudable*, is more demanding as public *scrutiny* of nonprofit financial management increases. But the job need not be *onerous*. A board member with a

solid financial background can help a nonprofit achieve a sounder financial footing which will in turn help maintain its independence by minimizing potential legislative *intrusion*. Several types of sound financial management practices can benefit nonprofit organizations.

Documenting accounting and financial management practices. Organizations cannot know what needs improving until they understand how they currently operate. Everything the organization does should be *inventoried* and documented, including fund-raising, accounting, generating financial reports, interactions between senior management and the board, and when these actions occur. ²

PAUSE: What is Mazzone classifying?

Budgeting as part of *strategic* planning. Budgeting provides an opportunity to link the organization's operational plans with its strategy and financial success and growth. Before plunging into the budget process and assigning costs to program activities, all program and project managers should understand and discuss the organization's strategy. The time spent educating, communicating, and planning will get everyone to agree on organizational goals and how to achieve them. ³

PAUSE: According to Mazzone, what should the budgeting process do?

Managing to the operating budget and audited financial statements. Frequently, management and the board look at cash budgets. Outsiders, including lenders, look at audited statements and can get a different picture. For example, depreciation expenses and vacation accruals can turn a $10,000 surplus on an operating budget into a $50,000 loss on an audited statement of activities. ⁴

Budget a surplus. Being around for the long term requires building reserves. Budget an annual *surplus*, even a minimal amount, to ensure that *adequate* resources exist to guard against unexpected shortfalls. ⁵

PAUSE: How does this sound business practice relate to everyone?

Project cash flow. An organization should have three to six months of current *assets* (cash, accounts receivable, and short-term investments) on hand. This policy and practice ensures enough cash to meet obligations throughout the year. It will help manage accounts receivable and accounts payable and the timing of budgeted *expenditures*. ⁶

PAUSE: How does Mazzone link the conclusion to the introduction?

With the nonprofit sector pumping more than $50 billion into the Massachusetts economy each year, solid financial management of nonprofit organizations is not simply nice to have. It is *mandatory*, and it need not be onerous for a person with financial acumen. ⁷

1. Briefly summarize Mazzone's presentation, including what she is classifying and what categories she uses.

2. What is her purpose?

3. Do you agree with her point of view?

4. Do you think Mazzone achieves her purpose? Why or why not?

Classification in Everyday Life

Dylan Marcos

Bad Roommates

GUIDING QUESTION
What kinds of bad roommates does Marcos classify?

VOCABULARY
The following words are *italicized* in the essay: *encountered, hounded, potential.* If you do not know their meanings, look them up in a dictionary or online.

1   Over the past few years, I have learned a lot about bad roommates. Although I doubt that I have *encountered* all types, I certainly know more now than I did before. I'll pass on to you some of what I have experienced, so you can try to avoid the following types of roommates—the romeos, the slugs, and the criminals.

2   The romeos are usually great guys and lots of fun, when they happen to be single—but they are usually not. They always seem to have girlfriends, who basically become nonpaying roommates. The women are mostly nice, but they change the apartment in big ways. First, we have to watch how we act. We can't walk around half-dressed in the morning, for example. Also, we have to get used to sharing: The girlfriends spend hours at a time in the bathroom, doing their hair and putting on make-up. There are always more dishes in the sink when they are around, more food disappears, and even shampoo goes faster than normal. The romeos do not seem to understand that having semipermanent guests in the apartment really changes the way we live.

3   Another type, the slug, is even harder to live with than the romeo because the slugs are slobs. They never wash the dishes or put away food, they leave a trail of dirty clothes behind them, and they completely destroy the bathroom every time they use it. Slugs pretty much live in front of the television, so you will probably never have a chance to watch what *you* want. The slug is also sloppy about paying rent and bills. Although he usually has the money, he has to be reminded—no, *hounded*—before he will actually pay what he owes.

4   The worst type of roommate is the criminal, for obvious reasons. I've had only one of these, but one was more than enough. He was a nice guy for about two weeks—clean, not around too much, but good to have a beer with when he was there. One day, though, I came home after work to find that he was gone, along with everything valuable in the apartment—our laptops, iPods, some cash, a bunch of CDs, and my favorite leather jacket. Although we called the police, I know I will never get back anything he stole.

PAUSE: What is Marcos's purpose in writing the essay?

CRITICAL READING
▪ Preview
▪ Read
▪ Pause
▪ Review

(See pp. 3–8.)

PAUSE: What categories does Marcos use?

PAUSE: What three types of roommate does Marcos identify? Which one does he like least?

PAUSE:
How does
Marcos tie the
conclusion
to the
introduction?

What I have learned from my experience is that, when I interview *poten-* 5
tial roommates, I should ask for at least two references, preferably from
former roommates, so I can weed out the romeos, slugs, and criminals.
That should keep my living situation sane—at least until I meet someone
who seems great at first but turns out to fall into another, equally bad category. I'll keep you posted.

1.   What is Marcos's topic, and what categories does he use?

2.   Does he give enough detail about each category for you to
     understand it as he does?

3.   Write three questions that might be on a quiz on Marcos's essay.

4.   Does the essay have the **Four Basics of Good Classification**
     (p. 116)?

5.   What other categories would you add based on your experience or
     that of other people you know?

Write a Classification Essay

Write your own classification essay on one of the following topics or on a
topic of your own choice. Use CLASSIFICATION AT A GLANCE as a basic
organizer (p. 121), and follow the Writing Guide: Classification checklist as
you write and revise (pp. 126–27).

COLLEGE	• Types of degree programs
	• Types of students
WORK	• Types of customers or clients
	• Types of skills needed for a particular job
EVERYDAY LIFE	• Types of drivers
	• Types of restaurants in your town

WRITING GUIDE: CLASSIFICATION

STEPS IN CLASSIFICATION	HOW TO DO THE STEPS
☐ Focus.	• Think about your topic and how you can sort it so that your audience will understand the categories.
☐ Explore your topic. See Chapter 2.	• Prewrite to find possible categories to use and examples that will explain each category.

STEPS IN CLASSIFICATION	HOW TO DO THE STEPS
☐ **Write a thesis statement.** Organizing principle + Purpose = Thesis Or Organizing principle + Categories = Thesis See Chapter 3.	• Include your topic and either the method you are using to sort (the organizing principle) or the categories you will describe.
☐ **Support your thesis.** See Chapter 3.	• Choose useful categories that will achieve your purpose. • Consider what your readers need to know to understand the categories.
☐ **Write a draft.** See Chapter 4.	• Arrange the categories logically. • Write topic sentences for each category and paragraphs giving examples of each of the categories.
☐ **Revise your draft.** See Chapter 4.	• Add any examples that will help your readers understand. • Add transitions. • Improve your introduction, thesis, and conclusion.
☐ **Edit your revised draft.** See Chapters 16 through 18.	• Correct errors in grammar, spelling, word use, and punctuation.
☐ **Evaluate your writing.**	• Does it have the Four Basics of Good Classification (p. 116)? • Is this the best I can do?

10

Definition

Writing That Tells What Something Means

Understand What Definition Is

Definition is writing that explains what a term or concept means.

Four Basics of Good Definition

1 It tells readers what term is being defined.

2 It presents a clear definition.

3 It uses examples to show what the writer means.

4 It gives details about the examples that readers will understand.

In the following paragraph, each number corresponds to one of the Four Basics of Good Definition.

1 Internet addiction is **2** chronic, compulsive use of the Internet that interferes with the addicts' lives or their relationships with others. **3** For example, addicts may spend so much time on-line that they are unable to perform as expected at home, work, or school. **4** These addicts may spend hours surfing the Web, playing games, or e-mailing friends and family. **3** In more serious cases, the Internet addiction can cause financial problems, or worse. **4** For example, online shoppers who go to extremes can find themselves in debt and, as a result, damage their credit, not to mention personal relationships. **3** Still other Internet addictions involve potentially dangerous or illegal activities. **4** These activi-

---

ties can include meeting people online, gambling, viewing pornography, and engaging in cybersex. However, for Internet addicts, the problem usually isn't *how* they use the Internet; the problem is that they cannot stop using it, even if they want to.

Many situations require you to explain the meaning of a term, particularly how you are using it.

COLLEGE   On a U.S. history exam, you define the term *carpetbagger*

WORK   You describe a coworker as a "slacker" to a human resources staffer, and the staffer asks what you mean exactly.

EVERYDAY LIFE   You explain the term *fair* to your child in the context of games or sports.

Main Point in Definition

In definition essays, your **main point** typically defines your topic. The main point is directly related to your **purpose**, which is to get your readers to understand the way that you are using a term or concept in your essay. Although writers do not always define a term or concept in a thesis statement, it helps readers if they do.

A thesis statement in definition can follow a variety of different patterns, two of which include the term and its basic definition.

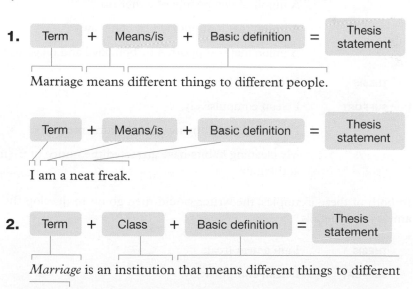

1.   Term   +   Means/is   +   Basic definition   =   Thesis statement

Marriage means different things to different people.

Term   +   Means/is   +   Basic definition   =   Thesis statement

I am a neat freak.

2.   Term   +   Class   +   Basic definition   =   Thesis statement

Marriage is an institution that means different things to different people.

Compulsive cleanliness is a condition that can sometimes indicate a problem.

In essays based on the previous thesis statements, readers would expect the italicized terms and concepts to be defined through examples that show the writer's meaning.

Support in Definition

If a friend says, "Summer in the city is awful," you do not know what she means by *awful*. Is it the weather? The people? The transportation? Until your friend explains what she means, you will not know whether you would agree that summer in the city is awful.

Support in definition provides specific examples of terms or concepts to help explain what they mean. Read the two thesis statements that follow and the lists of examples that could be used as support.

THESIS	Today, marriage means different things to different people.
SUPPORT	A union of one man and one woman
	A union of two people of either sex
	A union that is supported by state law
	A union that is supported by both civil and religious laws
THESIS	I am a neat freak.
SUPPORT	I clean compulsively.
	I am constantly buying new cleaning products.
	My cleaning habits have attracted the notice of friends and family.

In both of these examples, the writer would then go on to develop the examples with details.

THESIS	I am a neat freak.
SUPPORT	I clean compulsively.
	DETAILS: I clean in the morning and at night, and cannot let a spot on the counter go for a second.

SUPPORT	I am constantly buying new cleaning products.
	DETAILS: Every week, I buy new products, have a closet full of them, and believe every new sales pitch.
SUPPORT	My cleaning habits have attracted the notice of friends and family.
	DETAILS: Kids used to appreciate the clean house; now they complain that I am compulsive; friends tease me, but I wonder if they think I go too far.

Organization in Definition

The examples in a definition essay are often organized by **importance**, or the impact you think the examples will have on your readers. Save the most important example for last.

As you write, add transitions to connect one example to the next.

Common Transitions in Definition

another	for example
another kind	for instance
first, second, third, and so on	

DEFINITION AT A GLANCE

Introduction with thesis statement
Defines term or concept

↓

First example explaining the definition
Details about the first example

↓

Second example explaining the definition
Details about the second example

↓

> **Third example explaining the definition**
> Details about the third example

> **Conclusion**
> Refers back to the defined term/concept and makes an observation about it based on what you have written

Read and Analyze Definition

Read the following three examples of definition—from college, the workplace, and everyday life—and answer the questions that accompany them.

For each essay, review the Four Basics of Good Definition (p. 128) and practice the critical reading process explained in Chapter 1 (pp. 1–15).

Definition in College

The following essay was written for an English class. Note the use of outside sources and the documentation of them at the end.

Anna Puiia

What Is Hip?

CRITICAL READING

■ Preview
■ Read
■ Pause
■ Review

(See pp. 3–8.)

PAUSE: Can you tell who Puiia is describing?

GUIDING QUESTION
What examples does Puiia give to show her definition of *hip*?

VOCABULARY
The following words are *italicized* in the essay: *conspicuous, hodgepodge, conglomerate, dishevelment, aesthetic, amalgamated, apathy, nonchalance, ironic.* If you do not know their meanings, look them up in a dictionary or online.

You know who they are. You have seen their self-done haircuts, their   1
skinny jeans, and their oversized sweaters and sunglasses. You have seen their bright colors, and mismatches, and secondhand store hand-me-downs. You have seen that guy with the faux—or maybe real—knuckle tattoos that either make no sense, or refer to something almost no one has heard of. You may spy them riding the bus wearing obnoxiously *conspicuous* headphones, which are blaring something that can only be

described as "indie rock." You may catch them pining over some skinny boy in oxfords and a kaffiyeh.[1] Hipsters are the kids everyone loves to hate.

2   What is a hipster, anyway? Hipsterism, in general, is an to-each-his-own way of expressing oneself. Hipster fashion is a *hodgepodge* of past trends and styles; a recycled, updated *conglomerate* of former fashions. Hipsters combine elements of former subcultures to create their overall looks of *dishevelment*. Grunge's[2] flannel paired with skinny jeans and a book of Allen Ginsberg's[3] poetry, or a copy of *On The Road*[4] in your backpack could characterize a hipster. A hipster may frame his or her face in lens-less or non-prescription Buddy Holly glasses[5] or stomp around in an old pair of Converse sneakers.[6] With hipsters, it's all about seeming [effortlessly] cool, or as if they did not think or care about their outfits when they got dressed (Robie).

3   But hipsterism goes beyond just fashion. The hipster subculture is very much defined by its musical tastes as well. The music of the hipster subculture is not defined by one genre. Most of the genres popularly associated with hipsters are combinations of other styles, and sometimes carry funny names, like shoegaze — a style of music characterized by the artists' use of effect pedals, which causes them to spend all of their live performances gazing at their feet (LaRose). Some hipsters prefer music of a moodier, folksier persuasion, while others prefer pure electronica and synthesizers. Some settle in between with bands that combine the simple, pretty melodies of folk with the intricate layering of electronica, creating an offbeat, experimental sound.

4   The hipster subculture is one of the most commonly criticized groups in American youth culture. A simple Google search of the word *hipster* provides one with links to pages and articles like, "Hipster Subculture Ripe for Parody," or "Why The Hipster Must Die." Another link is to an article entitled "Hipster: The Dead End of Western Civilization." This article by Douglas Haddow discusses hipsterism as the "dead end of western civilization" (Haddow), because he claims that the hipsters are no longer producing anything new. He attacks the recycled *aesthetic* and *amalgamated* music styles of the hipsters and points to the use of past trends in new ways as a lack of creativity. This lack of creativity is reflected, he says, in today's youth culture "simply consuming cool, rather than creating it," (Haddow) as though hipsters are not making the things they buy and wear and listen to cool, but are instead being told these things are cool, and then consuming them. This criticism is founded in most of the things that hipsterism, itself, is based in: a sense of *apathy*, a projected *nonchalance* about fashion, the idea of recycling the past.

5   I do not see hipsters as a dead end. I see them as making progress for the fashion world. Hipsters are taking the trends of the past and making them cool in a new way—giving them new life. They are taking the untrends

[1] **kaffiyeh:** a triangular-shaped Arab headdress

PAUSE: Underline the details Puiia gives.

[2] **grunge:** a style of dress, usually untidy

[3] **Allen Ginsberg:** American poet and a leader of the 1950s Beat Generation

PAUSE: How does Puiia move the reader from one paragraph to the next?

[4] *On the Road:* a novel by Jack Kerouac, another leader of the Beat Generation

PAUSE: Do you agree with Haddow's opinion?

[5] **Buddy Holly glasses:** thick-rimmed glasses worn by Buddy Holly, an American musician who was one of the first rock-and-roll artists

[6] **Converse:** a brand of sneakers, particularly high tops

of the past and making them cool for the first time. They are wearing the flaws of their predecessors on their sleeves, or in the soles of their run-down boots, or in place of the lenses in their giant glasses. Their recycling is moving fashion along in a different way. So the individual items they are wearing are not new, but they have created a completely new look.

Now, as I get dressed in my skinny jeans and my oversized ugly sweater, 6 sliding on some thrift store loafers, I, a hipster, am wondering what the hippest response to being called a "dead end" would be. Maybe it was writing this paper, but I think I put in too much effort. It has to seem as if I did not care. Maybe it would be to laugh at it. Maybe I could name my band that, someday, when I have a band. Or maybe I should just make a T-shirt with the saying, "I Am the Dead End." That statement is simple, casual, and maybe even a little bit *ironic*. I like it.

Works Cited

Haddow, Douglas. "Hipster: The Dead End of Western Civilization Adbusters Culturejammer Headquarters." Adbusters Culturejammer Headquarters | Journal of the Mental Environment. 29 July 2008. Web 06 April 2011. <https://www.adbusters.org/magazine/79/hipster.html>.

LaRose, Philip. "Know Your Subgenres: Shoegazing." *The KEXP Blog.* 26 April 2009. Web 09 April 2011. <http://blog.kexp.org/blog/2009/04/26/know-your-subgenres-shoegazing/>.

Robie, Elizabeth. "Culture: Hipster Fashion: The Ultimate in Urban Cool." *Inside Vandy.* The Vanderbilt Hustler. 03 Jan. 2008. Web. 20 April 2011. <http://www.insidevandy.com/drupal/node/6260>.

For more on documenting sources using MLA style, see Chapter 14.

CRITICAL THINKING
■ Summarize
■ Analyze
■ Synthesize
■ Evaluate

(More on pp. 9–15.)

1. **Summarize.** Briefly summarize Puiia's essay, including the term she is defining, her definition, and the examples she gives.

2. **Analyze.** In what paragraph does Puiia move toward her own definition of hipsterism, in contrast to Haddow's opinions? How does she mock his piece in the last paragraph?

3. **Synthesize.** Apart from Puiia's essay, what do you know about hipsters? Read Haddow's essay at **www.adbusters.org/magazine/79/hipster.html** and use both Puiia's essay and his to determine your own definition of *hip.*

4. **Evaluate.** Does Puiia give you the reader a clear idea of how she understands the term *hip*? What is her point of view? Do you think she is biased? If so, how? Does her essay have the **Four Basics of Good Definition** (p. 128)?

Definition at Work

The following is a mission statement for a sign company.

Gary Knoblock

Customer Orientation

GUIDING QUESTION
What does customer-oriented mean to Knoblock?

VOCABULARY
The following words are *italicized* in the excerpt: *fundamental,*
orientation, prospective, installation. If you do not know their
meanings, look them up in a dictionary or online.

GARY KNOBLOCK
Business Owner

1   The *fundamental* principle of Lightning Quick (LQ) Signs is customer *orientation.* While most companies claim that they are customer-oriented, most have no idea what that really means. I tell my employees that I would like to have a customer giggle at the completion of the job, delighting in the product and service we have delivered, his every expectation met and exceeded. For all of us at LQ Signs, *customer-oriented* means that from start to finish to follow-up, the customer comes first.

2   Our customer orientation begins before the job begins. Before doing anything, we interview the customer to learn what his or her needs are and to determine the most cost-effective route to meet those needs. No job for us is "standard." Each is unique.

3   Our customer orientation means that we produce high-quality products quickly. We keep signs simple because our customers want their *prospective* customers to be able to read the sign in a glance. We use the most current digital printing processes to produce sharp, readable signs quickly. Because we have previously determined, with the customer, the most cost-effective method of producing the signs, the high quality and rapid return do not come at extra cost.

4   Our customer orientation means that our products are thoroughly checked for flaws and installed at the customer's convenience. Our signs leave our workshop in perfect condition, as the customer has ordered. Our well-trained team of installers works with the customer to determine the *installation* schedule.

5   Finally, our customer orientation means that the job is not complete when the sign is in place. We follow up every sale to make sure that the product is in top shape and that the customer is pleased.

CRITICAL READING
■ Preview
■ Read
■ Pause
■ Review

(See pp. 3–8.)

PAUSE: What are three examples of customer-oriented practices?

LQ Signs is truly customer-oriented, from start to finish to follow-up. 6 Our customers are our partners.

1.   What is Knoblock's **purpose**?

2.   Briefly summarize the essay, including the term being defined and the definition and examples.

3.   Is Knoblock likely to be biased? Why or why not?

4.   Does he do a good job of explaining the term?

Definition in Everyday Life

The following appeared originally in the *Boston Globe*.

Baxter Holmes

My Date with Fifteen Women

CRITICAL
READING
■ Preview
■ Read
■ Pause
■ Review

(See pp. 3–8.)

GUIDING QUESTION
How does the experience of judging a beauty pageant change Holmes's definition of *beauty*?

VOCABULARY
The following words are *italicized* in the essay: *innumerable, extracurricular, articulated, poise, segment.* If you do not know the meaning of these words, look them up in a dictionary or online.

PAUSE: How would you define *beauty*?

There is a lot more to a beauty pageant than meets the eye. I know, 1 after judging one myself. Beauty is a vague term often defined by first impressions. If you like what you see, it is beautiful. If not, it is not. For many people tuning in to the Miss America pageant, that will be their definition. It certainly was mine, until I judged a preliminary pageant for Miss New Hampshire last summer.

How did a twenty-one-year-old sportswriter on summer break from 2 college get to be a tiny part of this glamorous slice of Americana? Given proper guidance on the rules, pretty much anyone can become a judge, and a former journalism professor of mine who has been involved in pageantry since 1986 signed me up to be on the panel for the twenty-second annual Miss Kingston/Miss Seacoast scholarship pageant, partly because he thought it would be a good experience for me. He also thought it would be fun. So did I. It wasn't.

PAUSE: Why did seeing the contestants terrify Holmes?

As I entered the blue-gray antique home in Kingston, New Hamp- 3 shire, where a preliminary session of private interviews would take place, I saw fifteen young women, all seventeen to twenty-one years old. I walked through the crowd, knowing I would be judging which one was most deserving of a scholarship; to me, in my own common sense terms, that meant picking who was most beautiful. It seemed so cool at the out-set—there are far worse ways for a heterosexual male to spend a Sun-day—but once I saw them and they saw me, it was terrifying. I was not the only judge (there were seven of us, all men), but because communication among judges is limited to avoid bias, I felt alone.

4   They walked in one by one, and, in ten-minute segments, we asked questions. It wasn't hard to decide who was the most physically attractive, but in those first ten minutes, I began to understand just how grossly mis-understood this whole pageantry thing is. Being a role model   and a pretty one at that—is hardly enough to win and advance. (The winners of this event would go on to prepare for the 2009 Miss New Hampshire contest, which leads to the Miss America pageant.) Each of the contestants had *in-numerable* academic and *extracurricular* honors. Each had a thoroughly de-veloped plan for advancing good causes, like awareness of Lyme disease, depression, and low self-esteem; or for donating blood; helping the elderly; or volunteering at local schools. To be sure, none of them was perfect. But they were mighty impressive human beings. And yet, what most of the typi-cal observers will remember from a pageant is the swimsuit competition. If only they knew. After the interviews, the judges sat on a screened-in patio and ate lunch. I felt sick. Over and over in each interview, my definition of beauty was shattered, and I was ashamed.

> PAUSE: Why does Holmes's definition of beauty start to change?

5   That night, the pageant moved to a nearby café for the talent, swimsuit, onstage questioning, and evening-wear events. The contestants sang beauti-fully, danced gracefully, played violins and flutes, and recited poetry. They looked elegant in evening wear and *articulated* as best they could intelligent answers to the onstage questions, which were created by my former profes-sor, a charming emcee if there ever was one.

6   And then the swimsuit competition began. On my drive to Kingston, I had looked forward to this event like Christmas morning. Now, I dreaded it. After seeing the contestants' smarts, skills, *poise*, and dedication, I couldn't help but wonder: What does a swimsuit have to do with any of this? Later, after the judging, I talked to KeriAnn Lynch, a former winner of this pageant, and Lindsey Graham, who was crowned Miss Seacoast that night, about whether pageants should drop this *segment*. Lynch said she "wouldn't shed a tear," while Graham said it would be a disservice if they did, because the contestants "need to represent what healthy is."

> PAUSE: Why does Holmes dread the swimsuit segment?

7   But I guess that is a debate for another time. Each contestant crossed the stage in about fifteen seconds. I jotted a number from one to ten, and we moved on. The winners were crowned, and there was a dinner back at the blue-gray home. There, Graham told me she would not have gotten through college without the nearly $30,000 she has won in pageants. She also admitted the difficulty of presenting herself. "You walk around in life trying not to think of people's opinions," she said, "but it's really hard when they are literally in front of you with numbers, judging you."

True enough, but it is not so easy on the other side, either. Beauty is 8 not a simple matter.

1. Briefy summarize Holmes's essay including the term he is defining and how his experience affects his definition.

2. What is his purpose in writing? Do you think he achieves it?

3. What does Holmes mean by his thesis, "There is a lot more to beauty than meets the eye"? What else is there? How does he tie his conclusion to his thesis statement?

4. Do you think the swimsuit competition in beauty pageants should be eliminated? Why or why not?

5. Think of other situations where you or others are judged by "what meets the eye." What are they? What is the danger in judging by what meets the eye?

Write a Definition Essay

Write your own definition essay on *one* of the following topics or on a topic of your own choice. Use **DEFINITION AT A GLANCE** as a basic organizer (pp. 131–32), and follow the Writing Guide: Definition checklist as you write and revise (p. 139).

COLLEGE
- A term or concept from another course you have taken
- Cheating

WORK
- Any term you use at work
- A model employee

EVERYDAY LIFE
- Discrimination
- Road rage

WRITING GUIDE: DEFINITION

STEPS IN DEFINITION	HOW TO DO THE STEPS
☐ Focus.	• Think about the term you are going to define and how to get your readers to understand the term as you do.
☐ Explore your topic. See Chapter 2.	• Prewrite to get possible definitions and examples that will explain the definition.
☐ Write a thesis statement. Term + Definition = Thesis See Chapter 3.	• Include the term or concept you are defining and a basic definition of it.
☐ Support your thesis. See Chapter 3.	• Choose examples of the definition and details about the examples that will show your reader how you "see" the term.
☐ Write a draft. See Chapter 4.	• Arrange your examples. • Write topic sentences for each example and paragraphs that give details about them.
☐ Revise your draft. See Chapter 4.	• Make sure the examples explain your definition. • Think about what other details your readers might need to understand your definition. • Add transitions. • Improve your introduction, thesis, and conclusion.
☐ Edit your revised draft. See Chapters 16 through 18.	• Correct errors in grammar, spelling, word use, and punctuation.
☐ Evaluate your writing.	• Does it have the Four Basics of Good Definition (p. 128)? • Is this the best I can do?

11

Comparison and Contrast

*Writing That Shows Similarities
and Differences*

Understand What Comparison and Contrast Are

Comparison is writing that shows the similarities among subjects—people, ideas, situations, or items; **contrast** shows the differences. In conversation, we often use the word *compare* to mean either compare or contrast, but as you work through this chapter, the terms will be used separately.

Four Basics of Good Comparison and Contrast

1 It uses subjects with enough in common to be usefully compared and contrasted.

2 It serves a purpose — either to help readers make a decision or to help them understand the subjects.

3 It presents several important, parallel points of comparison and/or contrast.

4 It is organized either point by point or whole to whole (see pp. 143–44).

In the following paragraph, which contrasts the subjects, each number corresponds to one of the Four Basics of Good Comparison and Contrast.

4
Uses point-by-point organization (see pp. 143–44).

1 My current boyfriend 2 is a major improvement over 1 my ex-boyfriend 2 in terms of how he treats me. 3 One difference is that my current boyfriend opens the door when I get in the car as well as when I get out. In contrast, my ex-boyfriend never opened the door of the car or any other door. 3 My current

☑ LearningCurve For extra practice in the skills covered in this chapter, visit bedfordstmartins.com/reinteractive.

boyfriend likes to tell me that he loves me. For example, we went to the beach, and he screamed that he loved me to the four winds so everyone could hear. My ex, on the other hand, always had a ready excuse for why he couldn't say that he loved me, ever. However, he wanted me to tell him I loved him all the time. **3** Another difference between the two is that my boyfriend spends money on me. When we go out to a restaurant, he pays for the meal. My ex just never seemed to have money to pay for dinner or anything else. He would say he forgot to bring his wallet, and I would have to pay for the food. **3** To me, the most important difference between the two guys is that my current boyfriend is honest. He never lies to me about anything, and he makes me feel confident about our relationship. In contrast, I never could tell if my ex was lying or telling the truth because he often lied about his family and other things, and I never knew what to believe. **2** To sum it all up, my current boyfriend is a gentleman, and my ex was a pig.

4 Uses point-by-point organization (see pp. 143–44).

—Liliana Ramirez, student

Many situations require you to use comparison and contrast.

COLLEGE	In a business course, you compare and contrast practices in e-commerce and traditional commerce.
WORK	You compare and contrast two health insurance options offered by your company in order to select the one that is best for you.
EVERYDAY LIFE	Before choosing a telephone plan, you compare and contrast the rates, services, and options each offers.

Main Point in Comparison and Contrast

A comparison and contrast essay shows readers how two or more subjects are alike or different. The **purpose** of a comparison and contrast essay may be to have readers understand the subjects or to help them make a decision.

In comparison and contrast, your **main point** expresses similarities or differences in your subjects. For example, in the paragraph on pages 140–41, Liliana Ramirez contrasts the different ways that her two boyfriends treated her. Her purpose is to help readers understand why one became her "ex."

Typically, thesis statements in comparison and contrast essays present the central subjects and indicate whether the writer will show similarities, differences, or both.

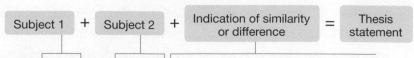

While my son and daughter both enjoy school, their educational experiences are very different.

[Purpose: To contrast educational experiences of her children.]

Leasing a vehicle and buying one are different arrangements.

[Purpose: to help readers decide whether to lease or buy]

To determine your thesis in a comparison and contrast essay, decide whether you want to show similarities, differences, or both. To make this decision, you need to think about what your purpose is—what you want your readers to understand—and what will be meaningful to those readers.

Support in Comparison and Contrast

The **support** in comparison and contrast demonstrates your main point by showing how your subjects are the same or different. To find support, many people make a list with multiple columns—one for the points that will serve as the basis of the comparison or contrast and one for each of the subjects.

For example, one student wrote the following thesis statement, which indicates that his essay will focus on the differences between the ages of twenty and forty.

The ages of twenty and forty are both enjoyable, but they represent very different stages in life.

To support this thesis, the student needs to find several points of contrast between twenty and forty. He generates the following list.

DIFFERENCES BETWEEN TWENTY AND FORTY

appearance
place in life
perspective

Then, for each point of comparison, the student lists some details that explain the differences.

	AGE TWENTY	AGE FORTY
APPEARANCE	smooth skin trendy haircut rounded features	some wrinkles classic hairstyle well-defined features
PLACE IN LIFE	just starting out single, no children living at home	established married with children own home
PERSPECTIVE	self-centered choices to make uncertainty	more thoughtful many choices made wisdom

Organization in Comparison and Contrast

A comparison and contrast essay can be organized in two basic ways: A **point-by-point** organization first compares or contrasts one point between the two subjects and then moves to the next point of comparison or contrast. A **whole-to-whole** organization first presents all the points of comparison or contrast for one subject and then all the points for the second. To decide which organization to use, consider which of the two will best serve your purpose of explaining similarities or differences to your readers. Once you choose an organization, stick with it throughout the essay.

The two organization types look like this.

Using **transitions** in comparison and contrast essays is important to move readers from one subject to another and from one point of comparison to another.

Common Transitions in Comparison and Contrast

COMPARISON	CONTRAST
one similarity	one difference
another similarity	another difference
similarly	in contrast
like	now/then
both	unlike
	while

Read and Analyze Comparison and Contrast

Read the following three examples of compare and contrast—from college, the workplace, and everyday life—and answer the questions that accompany them. For each essay, review the Four Basics of Good Comparison and Contrast (p. 140) and practice the critical reading process explained in Chapter 1 (pages 3–8).

Comparison and Contrast in College

The following is an excerpt from the textbook *Discovering Psychology*, Fifth Edition.

Don Hockenbury and Sandra Hockenbury

GUIDING QUESTION
How are anorexia nervosa and bulimia nervosa both alike and different?

VOCABULARY
The following words are *italicized* in the excerpt: *distorted, perception, emaciated, perfectionism, purging, preoccupation, compensates*. If you do not know their meanings, look them up in a dictionary or online.

1   **Anorexia nervosa** is life-threatening weight loss. Four key features define anorexia nervosa: First, the person refuses to maintain a normal body weight. With a body weight that is 15 percent or more below normal, body mass index can drop to 12 or lower. Second, despite being dangerously

CRITICAL
READING
■ Preview
■ Read
■ Pause
■ Review

(See pp. 3–8.)

PAUSE:
Underline
or highlight
the four key
features of
anorexia.

underweight, the person with anorexia is intensely afraid of gaining weight or becoming fat. Third, the anorexic has a *distorted perception* about the size of his or her body. Although *emaciated*, he or she looks in the mirror and sees someone fat or obese. And fourth, an anorexic denies the seriousness of his or her weight loss (American Psychiatric Association [APA], 2000).

Perfectionism and rigid thinking, poor peer relations, social isolation, and   2 low self-esteem are common (Halmi et al., 2000). Although estimates vary, approximately 10 percent of people with anorexia nervosa die from starvation, suicide, or physical complications accompanying extreme weight loss (APA, 2000; Kaye, Klump, Frank, and Strober, 2000).

PAUSE: How is bulimia similar to anorexia? How is it different?

Bulimia nervosa is bingeing and *purging* of food. Like people with   3 anorexia, people with bulimia nervosa fear gaining weight. Intense *preoccupation* and dissatisfaction with their bodies are also apparent. However, people with bulimia stay within a normal weight range or may even be slightly overweight. Another difference is that people with bulimia usually recognize that they have an eating disorder.

People with bulimia nervosa experience extreme episodes of binge   4 eating, consuming as many as 50,000 calories in a single binge. Binges typically occur twice a week and are often triggered by negative feelings or hunger (Agras & Apple, 1997). During the binge, the person usually consumes sweet, high-calorie foods that can be swallowed quickly, such as ice cream, cake, and candy. Binges typically occur in secrecy, leaving the person feeling ashamed, guilty, and disgusted by his or her own behavior. After bingeing, the bulimic *compensates* by purging him- or herself of the excessive food by self-induced vomiting or by misuse of laxatives or enemas. After purging, he or she often feels psychologically relieved. Some people with bulimia do not purge themselves of the excess food. Rather, they use fasting and excessive exercise to keep their body weight within the normal range (APA, 2000).

References

The documentation system used here is that of the American Psychological Association because the excerpt is from a psychology text. For English classes, use the MLA style (see Chapter 14).

Agras, W. S., & Apple, R. F. (1997). *Overcoming eating disorders: A cognitive-behavioral treatment for bulimia nervosa and binge-eating.* San Antonio, TX: Harcourt Brace.

American Psychiatric Association. (2000). Practice guidelines for the treatment of patients with eating disorders (revision). *American Journal of Psychiatry, 157* (Suppl.), 1–39.

Halmi, K. A., Sunday, S. R., Strober, M., Kaplan, A., Woodside, D. B., Fichter, M., Treasure, J., . . . Kaye, W. H. (2000). Perfectionism in anorexia nervosa: Variation by clinical subtype, obsessionality, and pathological eating behavior. *American Journal of Psychiatry, 157,* 1799–1805.

Kaye, W. H., Klump, K. L., Frank, G. K., & Strober, M. (2000). Anorexia and bulimia nervosa. *Annual Review of Medicine, 51,* 299–313.

1. **Summarize.** Briefly summarize the text excerpt, including the conditions being compared or contrasted, the authors' purpose, and some of the points of comparison or contrast.

2. **Analyze.** Is the excerpt organized point by point or whole to whole? Why do you think there is no formal introduction or conclusion? If there were an introduction, what information might it include? If you were writing a concluding paragraph, what would you say? What might a good title be?

3. **Synthesize.** Do you know anyone who has an eating disorder such as those described? What behaviors or characteristics have you noticed about the person or people?

4. **Evaluate.** Does the excerpt have the **Four Basics of Good Comparison and Contrast** (p. 140)? Do the authors achieve their purpose?

CRITICAL THINKING
- Summarize
- Analyze
- Synthesize
- Evaluate

(More on pp. 9–15.)

Comparison and Contrast at Work

The following is excerpted from an article published by a doctor on the subject of dyslexia.

Garth Vaz

Differences between Dyslexia and ADHD

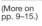

GUIDING QUESTION
How are dyslexia and ADHD different?

VOCABULARY
The following words are *italicized* in the excerpt: *dyslexics, misconceptions, misdiagnoses, abound, deficient, remediation, diligent, squirm, fidget, excessively, blurts, norms, alienates, shun, ostracism, labored, intervention, contemporary.* If you do not know their meanings, look them up in a dictionary or online.

Juan Gonzalez
Physician

1   For decades, *dyslexics* have been one of the most misunderstood groups in our society. *Misconceptions* and *misdiagnoses abound*, as when dyslexics are mislabeled stupid, retarded, or lazy and placed among the mentally *deficient*. Many dyslexics have been placed in special education programs along with the slow learners. Later, after appropriate *remediation*, these same students have gone on to become educators, lawyers, and doctors. It is therefore of

great importance that we be aware of the sensitive nature of dealing with these prize products of our society, our dyslexic students. We must be *diligent* in our efforts to help them in their struggle for success.

CRITICAL READING
■ Preview
■ Read
■ Pause
■ Review

(See pp. 3–8.)

Such misdiagnoses are due to the lack of understanding of dyslexia 2 and conditions such as attention-deficit/hyperactivity disorder (ADHD), childhood depressive disorder (CDD), central auditory processing deficit (CAPD), and many others that share some similarities with common symptoms of dyslexia. I will now list, in brief, some of the differences in behaviors that characterize ADHD and dyslexia in children, particularly children in the elementary school classroom.

A young person with ADHD cannot easily sit still, certainly a problem 3 in the classroom. He or she often leaves his assigned seat, running around and attempting to climb on shelves, desks, and the like. When told firmly to remain in his seat, the child will try to obey but will *squirm* and *fidget* almost constantly, clearly in a state of agitation. He acts as if he is driven by a motor.

PAUSE:
Summarize the charac-teristics of ADHD.

A child with ADHD often talks *excessively* and is unable to wait to be 4 called on: Instead, he *blurts* out answers and responses. He seems to just butt into games and conversations, not observing social *norms* that require a give-and-take among group members. Such behavior often *alienates* other children and frustrates teachers and others who try to maintain control. Other children may *shun* the child with ADHD. This *ostracism*, in turn, results in further negative effects, such as low self-esteem and greater isolation.

In contrast, a young person with dyslexia can sit still but has trouble 5 organizing objects, belongings, and letters. She may mix up sounds, saying, for example, "plain" for "plan" or "seal" for "soul." She may have a stutter, furthering the frustration and embarrassment she already feels.

A dyslexic child typically reads poorly, confusing the order of letters, 6 for example, in words such as "saw" and "was." Also, she may confuse words that have similar shapes or start and end with the same letters, as in "form" and "from" or the words cited in the last paragraph. While a dyslexic's reading is *labored*, his handwriting and spelling are usually worse. All of these symptoms of dyslexia, while quite different, often result in the same ostracism and loss of self-esteem. These problems then cause other behavior problems that are similar to those shown in children with ADHD and a number of other conditions. This explains why certain conditions are often confused. In addition, many children indeed have more than one condition. For example, over 40 percent of children with dyslexia have ADHD as well.

PAUSE:
Summarize the charac-teristics of dyslexia.

Unfortunately, because of budgeting restrictions, dyslexics are some- 7 times placed among the wrong group for remediation. In order for any *intervention* to succeed, it must be tailored specifically for the dyslexic. There are many improved techniques now being used successfully in reading remediation that are based on the Orton-Gillingham method. Many of these can be obtained on videocassettes and CDs. Arlene Sonday and the Scottish Rite Hospital have such programs on the market, and many other good ones can be located on the Internet (for example, **interdys.org/**, **dys.org/**, **kidshealth.org/**, and **ninds.hih.gov/disorders/ dyslexia**, among many others).

8　　There are many successful dyslexics in our society, some *contemporary* and others in the past. Albert Einstein, Benjamin Franklin, and General George Patton are a few who have made history. Athletes Bruce Jenner and Nolan Ryan and entertainers Whoopi Goldberg and Cher are among our contemporaries. Identifying with the successful dyslexic offers some hope to parents and children alike. The book *Succeeding with LD* is a collection of stories of successful dyslexics. The book was authored by Jill Lauren and published by Free Spirit Publishers. Each of these stories could make a book by itself but is short enough for the dyslexic to enjoy reading.

1.　Briefly summarize Vaz's essay, including the terms being compared or contrasted and the major similarities or differences.

2.　What organization does Vaz use?

3.　Why is dyslexia so often misunderstood, according to Vaz?

4.　Why is Vaz particularly interested in dyslexia?

Comparison and Contrast in Everyday Life

The following essay appeared in *Newsweek* in 2009.

Stephanie Lindsley

Autism and Education

GUIDING QUESTION
What are some differences between the educational resources Lindsley's son and daughter receive?

VOCABULARY
The following words are *italicized* in the essay: *intervention, attests, mandated, mediation, designated.* If you do not know their meanings, look them up in a dictionary or online.

1　　My son and my daughter are happy, active, healthy children who enjoy school and are lucky to have a solid family life, but they are very different. My autistic[1] son tests in the "severe" range in many subjects. At eight, he reads well but cannot answer basic questions about what he has read. He speaks at a three-year-old level, adores *Blue's Clues*, and is almost potty-trained.

2　　My daughter, meanwhile, tests in the 95th percentile nationwide on standardized tests. At twelve, she shows an amazing ability to process information, taking complex ideas apart and putting them back together to form

CRITICAL READING
■ Preview
■ Read
■ Pause
■ Review

(See pp. 3–8.)

[1] **autistic:** a person with autism, a developmental disorder marked by poor communication skills, difficulties with social interaction, and other behavior patterns

PAUSE: What point is Lindsley making about her daughter?

new thoughts. She reads an entire novel most Sunday afternoons, solves the Sudoku[2] puzzles in the paper, and memorizes the entire script—not just her own lines—for the school plays she loves to be in.

[2] **Sudoku:** a popular number puzzle

At school, my son spends a portion of his day in a regular classroom. 3 But primarily he learns in a group of two to six children led by an *intervention* specialist, often accompanied by an aide. Even when he is in the regular classroom, he is never without an adult by his side. His intervention specialist records everything he does in daily logs that are required to ensure funding. She often presents me with new strategies to help him learn a difficult concept, which *attests* to the volumes of time she dedicates to addressing his unique needs.

PAUSE: What point is Lindsley making about her son?

My son's teachers do their absolute best for him. I know they love him. 4 But beyond that, his government-*mandated* Individualized Education Plan legally ensures that he gets every opportunity to excel. In addition, his teachers spend countless hours each year filling out detailed quarterly reports and other government-required paperwork. If I decide that the school district should pay for something extra to improve my son's education, I can appeal to an independent board for *mediation*.

PAUSE: How is the daughter's experience different?

My daughter spends all but three hours of her school week in a regular 5 classroom, where she often hides a book in her desk and reads while the teacher talks. She complains to me when the teacher reteaches things she learned last year, and she resents being drilled over and over on something she learned in ten minutes. For three hours a week, she is pulled from her classroom for a "gifted" program with fifteen other children, where she works either on a group project with other students or independently on her own blog or a computer-based foreign-language program.

PAUSE: What does Lindsley imagine for her daughter?

I can only imagine how much my daughter would excel if she had a 6 program specifically geared to her strengths, one that challenged her creativity on a daily basis. Or if she received even half the individual attention my son receives every week. What if she had a person sitting next to her to encourage her to think of new ways of doing things? What if her teacher did not have to manage a large classroom full of kids, who did not scold her for "making things confusing for everyone else"? What would happen if she spent all day in a room with two to six other gifted children, along with a couple of adults who specialized in pushing them to realize their potential?

PAUSE: What is Lindsley's main point here?

There is no government mandate to fund gifted education. In 2008 7 there was only $7.5 million in federal grants available through the Jacob K. Javits[3] Gifted and Talented Students Education Program. All additional funding comes from states and private organizations. Compare that with the $24.5 billion allotted by No Child Left Behind, a federal program whose goal is to help every child, including the mentally disabled, meet

[3] **Jacob K. Javits:** long-time U.S. senator from New York

minimum standards. But is that a wise investment? Wouldn't some of those billions be more wisely spent on special teachers and mandated programs for gifted children, who have the potential to make advances in science, technology, and the arts that would benefit everyone?

8   It pains me to suggest taking some of the federal money *designated* for my disabled son and spending it on my overperforming daughter. My son will probably meet minimum standards, but most parents of autistic children describe goals for their kids in much more modest terms: being able to bathe themselves, get a job, or live semi-independently. My daughter has the potential for much more. If she were given even a fraction of the customized education that my son receives, she could learn the skills needed to prevent the next worldwide flu pandemic, or invent a new form of nonpolluting transportation. Perhaps she could even discover a cure for autism.

PAUSE: How does Lindsley justify her position?

1.   Briefly summarize Lindsley's essay, including what she is comparing and what major point of contrast she uses.

2.   What is Lindsley's purpose? What is her point of view?

3.   What type of comparison/contrast organization does Lindsley use?

4.   Do you agree or disagree with Lindsley? Why?

5.   Do you think this is a good contrast? Why or why not?

Write a Comparison and Contrast Essay

Write your own comparison and contrast essay on one of the following topics or on a topic of your own choice. Use the Comparison and Contrast charts on page 144 to help you with basic organization, and follow the Writing Guide: Comparison and Contrast checklist as you write and revise (p. 152).

COLLEGE	• Two professors
	• College and high school
WORK	• Two jobs you have had
	• Two companies you have worked for
EVERYDAY LIFE	• Two places you have lived
	• Good customer service and bad customer service

WRITING GUIDE: COMPARISON AND CONTRAST

STEPS IN COMPARISON AND CONTRAST	HOW TO DO THE STEPS
☐ Focus.	• Think about what you want to compare and contrast and your purpose for writing.
☐ Explore your topic. See Chapter 2.	• Make a side-by-side list of possible parallel points of comparison or contrast between your subjects.

STEPS IN COMPARISON AND CONTRAST	HOW TO DO THE STEPS
☐ Write a thesis statement. Subjects + Main point = Thesis See Chapter 3.	• Include your subjects and some indication of whether you will be comparing or contrasting them.
☐ Support your thesis. See Chapter 3.	• Choose the points of comparison or contrast that your readers will understand and that will serve your purpose.
☐ Write a draft. See Chapter 4.	• Decide whether to use point-by-point or whole-to-whole organization and how to arrange your main points (by time, space, or importance). • Write topic sentences for your support paragraphs.
☐ Revise your draft. See Chapter 4.	• Reread to add any examples that will help your readers understand. • Add transitions. • Improve your introduction, thesis, and conclusion.
☐ Edit your revised draft. See Chapters 16 through 18.	• Correct errors in grammar, spelling, word use, and punctuation.
☐ Evaluate your writing.	• Does it have the Four Basics of Good Comparison and Contrast (p. 140)? • Is this the best I can do?

12

Cause and Effect

Writing That Explains Reasons or Results

Understand What Cause and Effect Are

A **cause** is what makes an event happen. An **effect** is what happens as a result of an event.

Four Basics of Good Cause and Effect

1 The main point reflects the writer's purpose — to explain causes, effects, or both.

2 If the purpose is to explain causes, it presents real causes.

3 If the purpose is to explain effects, it presents real effects.

4 It gives clear and detailed examples or explanations of the causes and and/or effects.

In the following paragraph, each number corresponds to one of the Four Basics of Good Cause and Effect.

1 Little doubt remains that global warming is a threat to our world, but not everyone understands why it is happening and what the effects are. Many experts believe that this warming trend is largely the result of **2** greenhouse gases, including **4** carbon dioxide emissions, mainly from cars, and pollutants from industrial processes. **2** Deforestation is another significant cause. If current warming trends continue, the United States is most at risk for **1** negative consequences, although the entire world will be affected. Scientists predict that **3** sea levels will rise dangerously and

✓ LearningCurve For extra practice in the skills covered in this chapter, visit
bedfordstmartins.com/reinteractive.

4 flood coastal areas. There will also be **3** more droughts and changes in precipitation patterns, **4** such as more hurricanes and tornadoes. In addition and possibly most destructive is the **3** threat to plant and animal life and, consequently, to public health.

Analyzing causes and effects goes beyond asking "What happened?" to also ask "Why?" and "How?"

Jim Rice of Quinsigamond Community College helps his students visualize the cause-and-effect relationship by suggesting that they think of three linked rings.

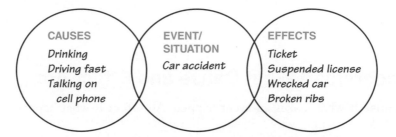

Many situations require you to determine causes or effects.

COLLEGE   In an information technology course, you must discuss the effects of a virus on a local-area computer network.

WORK   You analyze the likely effects of working five fewer hours per week.

EVERYDAY LIFE You try to figure out what is causing your phone to need a battery charge so often.

Main Point in Cause and Effect

The **main point** in a cause-and-effect essay should reflect your **purpose**. For example, if you are writing about why a certain event in history happened, your main point would be to explain the causes. If you are writing about what happened as a result of that event, your main point would be to explain the effects. Consider the following thesis from an essay on drunk driving.

Drunk driving destroys thousands of lives every year.

The main point of the essay is to discuss the effects of drunk driving—thousands of destroyed lives. The body of the essay will give examples.

Sometimes a thesis statement for a cause-and-effect essay will include both what caused the topic and what resulted from the topic. The topic sentence below follows this pattern.

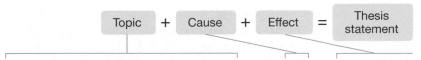

Urban wildlife populations are increasing, though why and what changes these different types of animals will bring to city life is not well understood.

Sometimes the writer does not directly indicate causes or effects in the thesis statement, as in the following example.

Until local police departments enforce restraining orders, women and children will continue to be the victims of violence.

Although the writer does not indicate a specific cause or effect, the main point of the essay is clear—to discuss how unenforced restraining orders have resulted in violence. The body of the essay will likely give examples of such situations.

As you begin to write cause-and-effect essays, you might find it helpful to include both the topic and an indicator of cause or effect in your thesis statement.

Support in Cause and Effect

In a cause-and-effect essay, **support** consists of explanations of causes and effects, and it demonstrates the main point stated in your thesis. Take, for example, the following thesis statement.

Irresponsible behavior caused my car accident.

The writer supported this thesis by presenting the causes with details that explain them.

CAUSE	Driving too fast	**CAUSE**	On my cell phone
DETAILS	Rainy and slippery	**DETAILS**	Not paying close attention
	Going too fast to control car		Hit a curve while laughing
	Could not stop		Did not react fast enough

CAUSE	Drinking
DETAILS	Not focused
	Slowed reaction time

When you are writing about causes, be careful that you do not say something caused an event or situation just because it happened beforehand. For example, many of us have gotten sick after a meal and assumed that the food caused the sickness, only to find out that we had been coming down with the flu even before the meal.

When writing about effects, do not confuse something that happened after something else with an effect. In the previous example, just as the meal did not cause the illness, the illness was not the effect of the meal.

Organization in Cause and Effect

Cause-and-effect essays are organized in different ways depending on their purpose.

MAIN POINT	PURPOSE	ORGANIZATION
Global warming is a serious threat to life as we know it.	To explain the effects of global warming	Order of importance (saving the most serious effect for last)
Global warming will flood many coastal states.	To describe how the U.S. map eventually might look	Space order
Over the next century, the effects of global warming will be dramatic.	To describe the effects of global warming over the next 100 years	Time order

As you write your essay, add transitions to show how each cause or effect relates to your main point. Here are some common transitions that are used in cause-and-effect writing.

Common Transitions in Cause and Effect

one cause, reason, effect, result	as a result
also	because
another	thus
first, second, third, and so on	

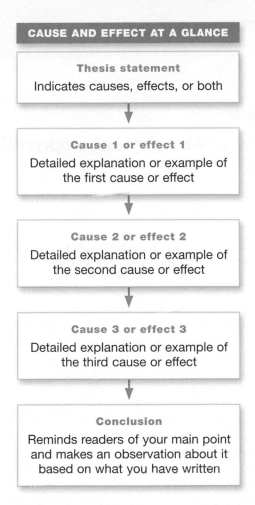

CAUSE AND EFFECT AT A GLANCE

Thesis statement
Indicates causes, effects, or both

Cause 1 or effect 1
Detailed explanation or example of the first cause or effect

Cause 2 or effect 2
Detailed explanation or example of the second cause or effect

Cause 3 or effect 3
Detailed explanation or example of the third cause or effect

Conclusion
Reminds readers of your main point and makes an observation about it based on what you have written

Read and Analyze Cause and Effect

Read the following three examples of cause and effect—from college, the workplace, and everyday life—and answer the questions that accompany them.

For each essay, review the Four Basics of Good Cause and Effect (p. 153) and practice the critical reading process explained in Chapter 1 (pages 3–8).

Cause and Effect in College

The following cause-and-effect essay was written for a child development course.

Jeanine Pepper

The Effects of Attachment Deprivation on Infants

CRITICAL
READING
■ Preview
■ Read
■ Pause
■ Review

(See pp. 3–8.)

GUIDING QUESTION
What are the effects of social deprivation on infants?

VOCABULARY
The following words are *italicized* in the essay: *instinct, deprivation, stimulation, juvenile.* If you do not know their meanings, look them up in a dictionary or online.

[1] Harlow:
Harry Harlow,
American
psychologist
famous for
his work
on social
isolation

PAUSE:
Underline
the two
effects in this
paragraph.

PAUSE: Do
any of these
effects sur-
prise you?
Why or why
not?

1   Infants are born with an *instinct* to attach themselves, to bond with, their caregivers, whether the caregiver is a parent or some other person. The instinct is so strong that experiments like Harlow's[1] have shown that infants will bond even with cloth substitutes. When infants are deprived of attachment, the effects are both immediate and long-ranging.

2   The immediate effects of attachment *deprivation* are obvious and sad. When babies are neglected or abused and deprived of any social *stimulation*, they are constantly afraid of their environment and others. Imagine being born and not being held or talked to: The world would be a pretty scary place. Another common effect is that they do not learn how to speak or communicate in any way. Because they never experience communication with others, they experience others as foreign and threatening. The infants often become totally withdrawn.

3   The effects of attachment deprivation often do not end with infancy. As the child grows older, he or she is still fearful, and that fear shows itself as anger. The child is often aggressive, defensive, and friendless. Many *juvenile* criminals have been shown to have been abused or neglected in infancy.

4   Individuals who are deprived of attachment in infancy are often depressed and more likely to develop drug and alcohol addictions, which in turn may lead to crime. The aggression they showed even as toddlers is more dangerous in adults, leading to fights, lost jobs, or unhealthy or abusive relationships.

5   The saddest long-range effect of attachment deprivation is when people carry on the pattern of abuse or neglect into another generation. Studies have shown that most child abusers were abused as children. That is the childhood they knew, and they repeat it.

6   Not all children who were abused or neglected grow up with these effects. Some are able to develop normally. However, many infants who experienced attachment deprivation grow up to be very troubled human

beings. The effects are serious and spread into all areas of their lives and the lives of others around them.

1. **Summarize.** Briefly summarize Pepper's essay, including her **audience** and **purpose** for writing and all of the major effects.

2. **Analyze.** How does Pepper organize the effects?

3. **Synthesize.** Did you know about the effects of social deprivation on children? What other kinds of negative behaviors are often carried from one generation to another? How do you know this?

4. **Evaluate.** Does Pepper clearly present the effects? What contributes to the clarity? Would an instructor reading the essay understand what Pepper has learned about the subject? Does the essay have the **Four Basics of Good Cause and Effect** (see p. 153)?

CRITICAL
THINKING
■ Summarize
■ Analyze
■ Synthesize
■ Evaluate

(More on pp. 9–15.)

PAUSE: The final question after each reading in this section makes a good essay topic.

Cause and Effect at Work

The following talk shows how a lawyer, consultant, and city councilor uses cause and effect.

Jolanda Jones

Consequences

GUIDING QUESTION
What does Jones want her audience to understand?

VOCABULARY
The following words are *italicized* in the essay: *consequences, abusive, coward, aspirations, humiliated,* and *capable.* If you do not know their meanings, look them up in a dictionary or online.

Jolanda Jones
Attorney, Houston
City Councilor, and
Consultant

1   **S**ome of the worst life situations I've seen were caused simply by people failing to consider the effects of their actions. Each of you in this room must learn for yourselves that every single decision you make has *consequences*. It is important that you think about the decisions you make **before** you make them because if you don't, then you will end up somewhere you didn't plan for.

2   My best decisions are the ones I make when I think my grandmother might find out about them. If I would be proud for her to know the decision I've made, then it's probably a good decision. If I have to sneak or would be ashamed for her to know my decision, then it is probably a bad decision. In any case, here are some examples of the thought process in good decision making. They show what happens when you don't consider consequences.

CRITICAL
READING
■ Preview
■ Read
■ Pause
■ Review

(See pp. 3–8.)

PAUSE: What do you expect the next paragraph to be about?

Some of you girls might be getting pressured by your boyfriends to 3 have sex. What should you think about? Well, you're probably wondering what he'll say if you don't sleep with him. Will he break up with you or call you "prude"? Well, don't let him define you. What if you get pregnant? What if you get a sexually transmitted disease? What if you get AIDS? What if you break up after you have sex with him? Will he tell everyone how good you were in bed? Will everyone know your business?

Single parenthood is hard. I know from personal experience. I had 4 graduated from college, was working as a minority recruiter and admissions counselor, and was training for the Olympics. I also planned to go to law school at Stanford. Then, I got pregnant without planning for it. Suddenly, I was expecting a child with a man who was both *abusive* and unsupportive. I was not married. I was disappointed in myself. I was ashamed of the shame I brought on my grandmother. I was a *coward*. I fled the United States and hid my pregnancy in Spain. I absolutely love my son, but I gave up my Olympic *aspirations* and Stanford Law School.

Some of you might be thinking about using drugs. Think long and 5 hard. I have crackheads in my family whose lives have been destroyed. Some are homeless. Some are dying of AIDS. My aunt was murdered in a drug house. My brother was murdered buying marijuana. I have an alcoholic cousin who does not take care of her children, and she is on welfare. People who do drugs come to love drugs more than they love anyone or anything else. Then, the drugs control you. You lose control of your life.

What about crime—just little stuff, like shoplifting that little pair of 6 earrings at the neighborhood Target? When I was sixteen, I'd worked to earn money to buy stuff I wanted. I wanted a pair of jeans. Instead, my mother took my check for herself. I still thought I was entitled to the jeans, so I went to Target and took a pair. I got caught. I was arrested, handcuffed, put in the back of a patrol car, and detained. I ducked my head down in the back of the patrol car. I just knew the whole world was looking at me. I was *humiliated*. I should have thought about the consequences. It wasn't right to steal from Target even if my mother took my check. You best believe I've thought about that ever since that date because I've never shoplifted again. I even told my son about it. I don't want him to make the same mistake that I did.

You have choices in life, and it's up to you to make the decisions that 7 will most positively benefit your life. We are all *capable* of thinking through stuff and making the right decision. The question is: Are you going to do it, or are you going to just take the easy road through life? My grandmother said, "If you make a bad decision, learn from it and move on; that way it's not your fault. If, however, you make the same mistake twice, you're stupid and it is your fault." I don't know about you, but I'm not stupid.

I've made good and bad decisions in my life. Thankfully, I've made 8 more good ones than bad. I hope to continue to make good decisions by considering consequences and learning from my mistakes. I hope that's your philosophy too.

1. Briefly summarize Jones's essay, including her main point and purpose.

2. Use ring diagrams to show one of the situations Jones presents, along with the causes or effects.

3. Review the **Four Basics of Good Cause and Effect** (p. 153) and determine whether Jones's writing is a good cause-and-effect essay. Make specific notes to support your opinion.

4. What is your reaction to Jones's essay? What would you ask her if you could?

Cause and Effect in Everyday Life

The following example of cause-and-effect writing appeared in a *Boston Globe* article.

Christopher Shea

In Praise of Peer Pressure

GUIDING QUESTION
How can peer pressue have positive results?

VOCABULARY
The following words are *italicized* in the essay: *peer pressure, conserve, consumption, herd, intensifying, activists, oblivion, productive, insights, quirks, psyche, immobilize, irreplaceable, heritage, symbolically, compliance, manipulate, coincidentally,* and *scrupulous.* If you do not know their meanings, look them up in a dictionary or online.

CRITICAL READING
■ Preview
■ Read
■ Pause
■ Review

(See pp. 3–8.)

1   **P**eer pressure gets bad press, but in some cases more of it might make the world a better place. In California, psychologists recently found that they could get people to *conserve* electricity with a simple notice, delivered to their doorstep, telling them how their *consumption* compared with the neighborhood average. In the weeks that followed, homeowners who were consuming more electricity than their neighbors cut back—presumably because they were embarrassed to be out of step with the *herd*.

2   The research, reported in *Psychological Science*, reflects growing interest in what's known as "social-norms marketing"—attempting to change behavior by telling people what their peers do. The basic concept is about two decades old, but psychologists have been *intensifying* efforts to find more effective ways of using it. And now, with a growing recognition of the limits of browbeating, a wide range of groups—from climate-change *activists*

PAUSE:
What is social-norms marketing?

to college deans trying to keep students from drinking themselves to *oblivion*—have been making peer pressure their ally.

"The norm is like a magnet," says Robert Cialdini, a professor at Arizona State University who is an author of the new study. "What's appropriate to do, in most people's minds, is what other people like them do." 3

The social-norms approach is part of a general movement to make *productive* use of *insights* into the *quirks* of the human *psyche*. For example, psychologists have found that presenting people with a wide range of choices (about almost anything) can frustrate and *immobilize* them, so that they end up making no choice at all or a bad choice. Supermarket managers and policy experts designing health plans have taken note. 4

PAUSE:
Why would supermarket managers want to think about this?

Cialdini's work tends to focus on the environment. In a paper from 2003, he identified a problem with signs in the Petrified Forest National Park, in Arizona, intended to discourage the theft of ancient, *irreplaceable* wood. The signs sternly warned that America's *"heritage"* was being "vandalized" by "theft losses of petrified wood of 14 tons a year." 5

That sent the message that pocketing souvenirs was the norm for tourists, Cialdini argues. In an on-site experiment, he and his coauthors demonstrated that by making use of new signs that stressed how few people removed items from the park and that by *symbolically* isolating those who do (on the sign, thieving stick figures had red slashes through them), the park could cut vandalism substantially. 6

In another experiment, Cialdini has shown that hotels will have more success encouraging their clients to reuse towels if they alter the wording of their appeals. "Join your fellow guests in helping to save the environment: A majority of our guests use their towels more than once" works better than any other approach. 7

PAUSE: Can you think of an example of a positive effect of peer pressure?

In Minnesota, a study by the Department of Revenue found that informing taxpayers that most people don't cheat on their taxes improved tax *compliance* more than stressing the link between taxes and popular public programs. 8

The field is still in flux: The effects of peer pressure remain hard to measure and hard to *manipulate*—yet the tug of the herd mindset is everywhere. *Coincidentally*, I recently came across a survey that found that 80 percent of adult males in the United States have six or fewer drinks in a week. I was taken aback, assuming the average was higher. I skipped wine with dinner a few times that week. 9

Later that same week, I read in an economics journal that freelance businessmen—I'm a freelancer—report only about 60 percent of their income, according to IRS estimates. Yet I'm *scrupulous* to the penny. Do I want to remain abnormal? Does anyone? I filed for an extension, so I've got some time to think about it. 10

PAUSE: What is he going to think about?

1. In your own words, describe the effects of peer pressure that Shea presents.

2. Describe some effects of peer pressure that you have experienced or observed.

3. Do you think peer pressure is a good thing? How can it be negative?

4. Does Shea's essay have the **Four Basics of Good Cause and Effect** (p. 153)? Why or why not?

5. Which of the essays in this chapter do you think is the best model of cause-and-effect writing? Why?

Write a Cause and Effect Essay

Write your own cause-and-effect essay on *one* of the following topics or on a topic of your own choice. Use Cause and Effect at a glance as a basic organizer (p. 157), and follow the Writing Guide: Cause and Effect checklist as you write and revise (pp. 163–64).

COLLEGE
- The immediate effects of being in college or the desired long-term effects on your life of going to college
- Causes of a legitimate absence that resulted in your missing a test (directed to your professor)

WORK
- Causes of low employee morale
- Effects of juggling work, school, and family

EVERYDAY LIFE
- Causes of an argument with a friend or a member of your family
- A good decision or a bad one, and its possible effects on your life

WRITING GUIDE: CAUSE AND EFFECT

STEPS IN CAUSE AND EFFECT	HOW TO DO THE STEPS
☐ Focus.	• Think about an event or a situation that had concrete causes and/or effects.
☐ Explore your topic. See Chapter 2.	• With your purpose in mind, prewrite or use the ring diagram to get ideas about causes and effects.
☐ Write a thesis statement. Topic + Indication of cause or effect = Thesis See Chapter 3.	• Write a thesis statement that includes your topic and an indication of whether you will be showing causes, effects, or both.

STEPS IN CAUSE AND EFFECT	HOW TO DO THE STEPS
☐ **Support your thesis.** See Chapter 3.	• List the major causes and/or effects. • For each cause or effect, give details that will help your readers understand how they caused or affected an event.
☐ **Write a draft.** See Chapter 4.	• Arrange the causes and/or effects in a logical order (often chronological or by importance). • Write topic sentences for each major cause and/or effect and paragraphs that describe them in detail.
☐ **Revise your draft.** See Chapter 4.	• Ask another person to read and comment on your draft. • With your purpose and audience in mind, read to make sure the causes and effects are real, and if you have explained them adequately. • Add transitions. • Improve your introduction, thesis, and conclusion.
☐ **Edit your draft.** See Chapters 16 through 18.	• Correct errors in grammar, spelling, word use, and punctuation.
☐ **Evaluate your writing.**	• Does it have the Four Basics of Good Cause and Effect (p. 153)? • Is this the best I can do?

13

Argument

Writing That Persuades

Understand What Argument Is

Argument is writing that takes a position on an issue and offers reasons and supporting evidence to convince someone else to accept, or at least consider, that position. Argument is also used to persuade someone to take an action (or not to take an action).

Four Basics of Good Argument

1 It takes a strong, definite position on an issue or advises a particular action.

2 It gives good supporting evidence to defend the position or recommended action.

3 It considers opposing views.

4 It has enthusiasm and energy from start to finish.

In the following paragraph, each number corresponds to one of the Four Basics of Good Argument.

1 The drinking age should be lowered from twenty-one to eighteen. 2 The government gives eighteen-year-olds the right to vote. If they are adult enough to vote for the people and policies that run this country, they should be mature enough to have a drink. 2 The U.S. penal system also regards eighteen-year-olds as adults. If an eighteen-year-old commits a crime and goes to trial, he or she is tried and sentenced as an adult, not as a minor. That

4 Writing is enthusiastic and energetic.

✓ LearningCurve For extra practice in the skills covered in this chapter, visit bedfordstmartins.com/reinstructive.

165

means that if the crime is murder, an eighteen-year-old could receive the death penalty. Eighteen-year-olds are not given special treatment. Most important is the fact that at eighteen, individuals can enlist in the armed forces and go to war. The government considers them old enough to die for their country but not old enough to have a drink? This makes no sense. **3** Opponents to lowering the drinking age justify their position by saying that if the age is lowered, teenagers will start drinking even earlier. However, there is no evidence to show that legal age is a major influence on teenage drinking. Other factors involved, such as peer pressure and the availability of fake IDs, have more impact on whether teenagers drink. While the government does need to address the issue of teenage drinking, forbidding eighteen-year-olds to drink while granting them other, more important rights and responsibilities at the same age is neither consistent nor reasonable.

4
Writing is
enthusias-
tic and
energetic.

Argument is the method you use to persuade people to see things your way or at least to understand your position. Argument helps you to take action in problem situations rather than to stand by, silent and frustrated. Although knowing how to argue will not eliminate all such situations, it will help you to defend your position.

Many situations require good argument skills.

COLLEGE   An exit essay from a writing course contains the following instruction: "Develop a well-balanced argument on the subject of free speech on the Internet."

WORK   You present reasons why you should get a promotion.

EVERYDAY LIFE   You convince a large company that it has made a mistake on your bill.

Main Point in Argument

Your **main point** in an argument is the position you take on the issue you are writing about. When you are free to choose an issue, choose something you care about. When you are assigned an issue, find something about it that you feel strongly about and take a definite position.

Take a few minutes to think about the issue, talk it over with a partner, or jot down ideas related to it. Once you have decided on your position, write a thesis statement that includes the issue and your position on it.

Today's minimum wage is not enough to live on.

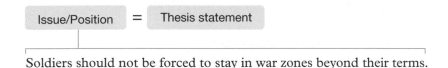

The important thing about a marriage is that two people love and

respect each other, not what sex they are.

Sometimes the thesis combines the issue and the position, as in the following statement.

Issue/Position   =   Thesis statement

Soldiers should not be forced to stay in war zones beyond their terms.

Make the thesis statement for any argument as specific as possible to help guide your writing and your readers.

VAGUE	Our health-care system is disgraceful.
MORE SPECIFIC	Two key reforms would make health care more affordable for all.
	[The paper would detail the two reforms.]

Many thesis statements for arguments use words such as the following because they clearly express a position.

could (not)	ought (not)
must (not)	requires
must have	should (not)
needs	would

Support in Argument

However strongly you may feel about an issue, if you do not provide solid **support** for your position, you will not convince anyone to see it your way. As you develop support for your position, think carefully about your readers and the kind of information that will be most convincing to them.

REASONS AND EVIDENCE

The major support for your position consists of the **reasons** that you give for that position. These reasons must be backed up with **evidence**, such as facts, examples, and expert opinions. The success of your argument depends on the quality of the reasons and evidence that you present to support your position.

Facts are statements or observations that can be proved true. **Statistics**—numerical facts based on research—can be persuasive evidence to back up your position. **Examples** are specific experiences or pieces of information that support your position. **Expert opinion** is the opinion of someone who is considered an expert in the area you are writing about. *Note:* The fact that a person's opinion appears on a Web site does not necessarily mean that he or she has any expertise. When in doubt about a source's authority, consult your instructor or a research librarian.

For more on finding sources, using quotations, and citing sources, see Chapter 14.

POSITION	It pays to stay in college.
REASON	College graduates earn more than high school graduates.
EVIDENCE/ FACT	College graduates earn 55 percent more than high school graduates.
REASON	Students learn up-to-date skills that they will need to find a job.
EVIDENCE/ EXAMPLE	Understanding how to use technology in your field may make the difference between getting a job and coming in second.
REASON	Many jobs require college degrees.
EVIDENCE/ EXPERT OPINION	John Sterling, president of one of the largest recruiting agencies, said recently, "Ten years ago, a college degree was perceived as an advantage. Today, the college degree is the basic ticket of entry for the majority of jobs." [*Note:* When you use expert opinion, you need to identify the source of the quote.]

As you choose reasons and evidence to support your position, consider your readers. Are they likely to agree with you, to be uncommitted, or to be hostile? Choose the support that is most likely to convince them, drawing on outside sources (such as the library or Internet) as needed.

OPPOSING POSITIONS

Part of your support for your position involves the opposing position: Acknowledge it, and present some evidence against it. If, for example, you are arguing in favor of lowering the drinking age to eighteen, you should not ignore the position that it should be kept at age twenty-one. If you do not say anything about the other position, you are leaving your argument unprotected. To defend your own position, show some weakness in the opposing position.

The writer of the paragraph on pages 165–66 might consider the opposing position as follows.

POSITION	The drinking age should be lowered from twenty-one to eighteen.
OPPOSING POSITION	The drinking age should not be lowered because people begin drinking before the legal age. If the age were lowered to eighteen, more sixteen-year-olds would drink.

ACKNOWLEDGING THE OPPOSING POSITION: First, laws should not be based on the extent to which they are likely to be abused or broken. They should be based on what's right. Even so, there is no evidence to show that legal age is a major influence on teenage drinking. Other factors involved, such as peer pressure and the availability of fake IDs, have more impact on whether teenagers drink.

As you gather support for your position, keep the opposing position in mind.

FAULTY REASONING

As you write and review the support for your position, be sure that your evidence is good and your reasoning is logical. Unfortunately, we are exposed to **faulty reasoning** all the time, especially in advertising. Certain kinds of errors in logic are so common that there is a name for them — **logical fallacies**. Be aware of the common fallacies so you can avoid them. For a review of logical fallacies, see pages 6–7.

Organization in Argument

Argument most often uses **order of importance** to organize reasons for the writer's position on the issue. Consider what you think your readers will find your most convincing reason. Arrange your reasons and evidence so that they build the strongest case for your position, and save the most convincing reason for last. Do not forget to acknowledge and address the opposing position somewhere in your argument.

As you write your argument, use transitions such as those in the box below to move your readers from one reason or point to the next.

Common Transitions in Argument

FROM ONE POINT TO ANOTHER	TO ADD EMPHASIS
also	above all
another fact to consider	best of all
another reason	especially
another thing	in fact
consider that	in particular
for example	more important
in addition	most important
in the first place	remember
	the last point to consider
	worst of all

ARGUMENT AT A GLANCE

Thesis statement
Includes the issue (topic) and your position on it

Reason 1
Supporting examples, facts, and expert opinions

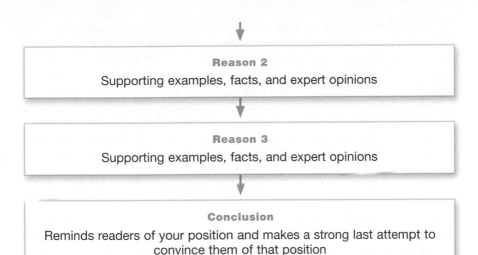

Reason 2
Supporting examples, facts, and expert opinions

Reason 3
Supporting examples, facts, and expert opinions

Conclusion
Reminds readers of your position and makes a strong last attempt to convince them of that position

Read and Analyze Argument

Read the following three examples of argument—from college, the workplace, and everyday life—and answer the questions that accompany them. As you read, notice that argument uses many of the other kinds of writing you have studied to support a position. It may tell a story, give examples, describe something, explain how something works, break a large point into categories, define a term, compare two or more things, or show cause and effect.

For each essay, review the Four Basics of Good Argument (p. 165) and practice the critical reading process explained in Chapter 1 (pages 3–8).

Argument in College

The following essay was written in response to this assignment: *Take a position on some aspect of college life, and write a short essay defending that position.*

Donnie Ney

Attendance in College Classes

GUIDING QUESTION
What reasons does Ney give in support of his position?

VOCABULARY
The following words are *italicized* in Ney's essay: *mandatory, ratio, jeopardize, correspond,* and *penalized.* If you do not know their meanings, look them up in a dictionary or online.

CRITICAL
READING
■ Preview
■ Read
■ Pause
■ Review

(See pp. 3–8.)

PAUSE: What reasons has Ney included in this paragraph?

PAUSE: Note that Ney briefly uses narration here.

PAUSE: Do you agree that paying for the course should give students the right to attend or not without a penalty?

PAUSE: Where does Ney acknowledge the opposition?

PAUSE: Note that this benefit is an effect of Ney's position.

PAUSE: What, to you, is the most persuasive reason Ney gives?

Attendance in college classes should be optional, not *mandatory*. Students pay a lot of money for their courses, so they should be able to decide whether and how to take advantage of them. Also, although class participation can help many students, not all students learn through class participation. If they learn better on their own or if they already know the content of a course that is required for graduation, they should be able to decide for themselves whether to sit in class hearing about things they already have learned. Finally, optional attendance would benefit the students who want to go to class because the student-to-instructor *ratio* would be lower, and students would get more personal attention.

First, students pay tuition, fees, and the cost of books and materials to enroll in a class. Because they have paid for the class, they should have the choice about whether to attend. Isn't it a basic right of a consumer to decide how to use the things he's bought and paid for? Also, students' lives are complicated, and there are many good reasons that they may have to miss classes, even if they want to attend. For example, this semester I have missed several classes because of my child's ongoing battle with severe asthma. I cannot *jeopardize* her health in order to get to a class. On the other hand, I do not want to fail because I have missed more than the allowed number of classes. Such a policy does not seem fair.

Also, it seems unfair to require students who already know the course content or who learn it on their own to waste their time hearing about it again. Although most students attend classes because they want to learn, there are some required courses that students have to take whether they want to or not. For example, I have had to attend basic computer classes to teach me procedures such as how to turn on a computer, what e-mail is, and how to access the Internet. I have known these things for years. Why should I sit through classes that repeat what I know when I could be spending my time doing the many things I really need to do? Why should I fail if I miss too many of these classes? Such policies do not benefit me or anyone else. In addition, although colleges do not like to admit this, attendance does not always *correspond* to grades. For example, some students can read and understand the materials assigned without any help from the teacher. If the goal of a college course is to learn, and a student can learn without attending class, why should that student need to attend lectures?

The best reason for making attendance optional is that students who do choose to attend could benefit from smaller classes and more personal attention. Classes could include more one-on-one instruction, which might improve students' grades and their ability to understand and retain course content. Many students struggle with course content and really need more of the instructor's time. However, with large classes, instructors do not have much chance to spend lots of time with individual students.

For all of these reasons, I believe that attendance should be optional in college courses. Students do not all learn in the same way. Some students learn best by studying a lot rather than sitting in class. With more study time and less class time, some students will achieve better results on tests. Attendance should be the students' choice. If they need to go to class to pass, they will attend; if they do not need to go to class to learn, they should not be *penalized*.

1. **Summarize.** Briefly summarize Ney's essay, including the topic, his position on it, and the main **support** he gives.

2. **Analyze.** How does Ney use **transitions** in his essay? How does he connect his concluding paragraph to his thesis statement? Is Ney biased or objective?

3. **Synthesize.** Read the attendance policy on the syllabus for this course. How would Ney respond to it? Have you had discussions about this topic with other students?

4. **Evaluate.** Does Ney make a good argument? Do you agree with him? Does his essay have the **Four Basics of Good Argument** (p. 165)? Are there any logical fallacies?

CRITICAL THINKING
■ Summarize
■ Analyze
■ Synthesize
■ Evaluate

(More on pp. 9–15.)

Argument at Work

The director of a nonprofit organization wrote this letter to support the parole request of a young man he had worked with.

Shawn Brown

Letter to a Parole Board

GUIDING QUESTION
What is Brown's purpose, and what is his overall point?

VOCABULARY
The following words are *italicized* in the letter: *parole, mentor, multicultural, adverse, cope, invaluable, dedication, mentees, transform, jeopardize, essential,* and *incarcerated.* If you do not know their meanings, look them up in a dictionary or online.

Shawn Brown
Founder, Diamond Educators

CRITICAL READING
■ Preview
■ Read
■ Pause
■ Review

(See pp. 3–8.)

1   To Whom It May Concern:

2   It is with enthusiasm that I am writing to support *parole* for Rodney Strong. In his work for Diamond Educators as a *mentor* to young men, he has made a positive contribution to the at-risk youth in the city of Boston.

3   Diamond Educators is a nonprofit mentoring program that serves at-risk young males who attend Boston public schools or who live in the inner-city neighborhoods of Boston. The mentors of the Diamond Educators program are *multicultural* male educators and professionals who grew up in the city of Boston and who dealt with *adverse* conditions that the majority

PAUSE: What do you think the next paragraph will be about?

PAUSE: What
conditions
does Brown
list as causes
of bad life
choices?

of our young minority males face every day, conditions that often result in bad life choices. The adverse conditions I refer to are living in an environment where young men *cope* with peer pressure to join a gang and involve themselves with drugs, crime, and violence; single-parent homes; and a lack of positive male role models. Our mentors help young men chart a course through their difficult situations. These mentors are an *invaluable* resource for our young, urban, minority males.

PAUSE: Why
does Brown
write about
Diamond
Educators
here rather
than talking
about
Rodney?

As a mentor, Rodney demonstrated commitment and *dedication* to our 4 program and to our students. Rodney worked long hours, but he found time to meet and counsel his *mentees*. He showed his mentees the importance of meeting commitments, taking responsibility, and having a positive purpose in life. He was a good example of how positive peer relationships can *transform* lives.

Rodney gave these young boys hope. He showed his mentees that by 5 applying themselves and taking advantage of the resources available to them, they could achieve success in life. Many of the boys otherwise live without hope of any kind and choose paths that *jeopardize* their own well-being and that of others in the community. That hope is *essential* to becoming a productive member of the human community. Rodney is a leader with a strong will to achieve his own success and to help others find theirs.

The path to success for urban minority males is extremely difficult, and, 6 as with many difficult courses, progress is not always direct and uninterrupted. Rodney stepped off course and made a poor decision when he committed a crime. However, he has demonstrated that he has learned from his mistake and is ready to return to his community as a positive force. He is ready to contribute to society, and to keep him *incarcerated* deprives us of a

PAUSE: Why
is the last
sentence here
important
to Brown's
argument?

good man, a good leader, and a good role model for young men. His release will show his mentees that there is hope of a good, lawful life after jail.

PAUSE: Note
that Brown
uses narration
to suggest
Rodney's
future story.

Rodney is dedicated to being a good father and a good community 7 influence. Unlike many who return to the community after incarceration, Rodney will not persist in a life of crime; he will return to his path of success and contribution. Keeping him from that serves no purpose.

I support Rodney Strong and will continue to support him after his 8 return to the community. I urge you to consider his good work and to allow him to continue it.

Sincerely,
Shawn Brown, Cofounder
Diamond Educators

1. Briefly summarize Brown's essay, including the topic, his position on it, and the main reasons he gives.

2. In what paragraph does Brown acknowledge and respond to an opposing view?

3. If you were an officer of the court, would Brown's letter alone persuade you to support parole for Rodney Strong? Why or why not? What else would you want or need to know?

4. How might Brown's point of view differ from a member of the criminal justice system's?

5. What, to you, is the strongest reason Brown presents? Why?

Argument in Everyday Life

After a class discussion and assignment on the unfairness of federal financial aid regulations, student John Around Him wrote the following letter to Senator John Kerry. Senator Kerry not only responded to the letter, promising to work to change the federal financial aid system, but he also visited Around Him's college class. Because of this contact, John Around Him was hired to work as a policy intern in Kerry's Massachusetts office.

NOTE: Partly as a result of this letter and his internship, Around Him received a full scholarship to Dartmouth College.

GUIDING QUESTION
Why does the author think the financial aid system is not fair to many students?

VOCABULARY
The following words are *italicized* in the letter: *chaos, eligibility,* and *criteria.* If you do not know their meanings, look them up in a dictionary or online.

Dear Senator Kerry:

1   My name is John Around Him, and I am a student at Bunker Hill Community College in Boston, Massachusetts. I am Native American and a veteran of the war in Iraq. I know that you, as a veteran of the Vietnam War, can relate to putting your life on the line in an environment of gunfire, explosions, *chaos*, and confusion, wondering if the next second might be your last. For most young people, being in the middle of a dangerous war—being shot at and surrounded by death and violence—is not an appealing way to earn money for college. However, for students like me who do not qualify for federal financial aid, it may be the only way to go to college, and this is why I am writing to you. The federal financial aid system needs to be changed because it is not effective in helping students, especially low-income and minority students, pay for college.

CRITICAL READING
■ Preview
■ Read
■ Pause
■ Review
(See pp. 3–8.)

PAUSE: How does Around Him appeal to his audience here?

2   I grew up on the Pine Ridge Reservation in South Dakota and graduated from Little Wound High School in 2001. I was an average student, with a grade-point average of just under 3.0. I always wanted to go to college, but I asked myself, "How would I pay for it?" I lived with a single-parent father and with two other families, and my father would often help others who needed it. My father was a language teacher, not highly paid, so for me family financial support for college was out of the question. I had to find another answer.

PAUSE: Note that Around Him uses narration in this paragraph.

When I turned to the federal financial aid system, I found that there 3 is money to help some students pay for college, but none for a student like me. According to the College Board's report, "Trends in College Pricing, 2006," the average tuition, room, and board costs for public universities is $12,796 (though many are much more, as is the case here in Massachusetts) — way out of line for my family's finances. Yet according to the financial aid formula, my father made too much money.

The formulas used to determine a student's financial need are not real- 4 istic: They do not represent the average student's situation. For example, according to the formula, to be considered independent (which largely determines *eligibility*) a student must meet one of the following *criteria:* He or she must be either twenty-four years of age or older, married, a veteran, or an orphan or ward of the court. Many students today, however, are financially independent as soon as they graduate from high school. In 2005, according to the National Center for Education Statistics, 64 percent of students at community colleges and 37 percent at public colleges and universities were financially independent. Fifty-eight percent of those students worked at least thirty-five hours per week, and 67 percent delayed entering college to earn money to help pay for it. Still, those under age twenty-four are not considered to be independent, and their family income is taken into consideration, even when the student receives no family support. As a result, many students have to try to meet one of the other eligibility requirements. For too many, the answer is joining the military, going to war.

PAUSE: Summarize what Around Him says about the criteria for eligibility. What kind of evidence does he use in this paragraph?

I am not saying that students should not enlist in the military. Would I 5 have signed on if I had received financial aid? I don't know. I support our troops and enjoyed my time in the service. The military's values and discipline and my experiences there have contributed to who I am today, and I am thankful for that. However, I don't believe that students should have to risk their lives to qualify for financial aid.

I am writing to you not only on my own behalf but for the well-being of 6 my family and my country. The federal financial aid system ignores a majority of students in need of aid. Despite rising tuition costs, our financial aid options are slim, and more and more students are not able to achieve a college education, our path to success. This problem is like a cancer; unless treated, it will spread and will hurt our nation's future.

PAUSE: Why is this conclusion effective?

Sincerely yours,
John Around Him

1. Briefly summarize John Around Him's argument, including his main point and reasons.

2. Where does Around Him acknowledge the opposing view?

3. Write three questions you would ask for a quiz on this essay (and be able to answer your own questions).

4. Is the argument a strong one? Why?

5. Which of the essays in this chapter is the best example of a good argument? Why?

Write an Argument Essay

Write your own argument essay on one of the following topics or on a topic of your own choice. Use **Argument at a glance** as a basic organizer (pp 170 71), and follow the Writing Guide: Argument checklist as you write and revise (pp. 177–78). Select an issue that you care about so that you can argue powerfully.

COLLEGE	• Present your instructor with reasons why you should be able to make up a test that you missed.
	• Write a letter to the Student Affairs office proposing a student service that does not currently exist.
WORK	• Argue that you should get a promotion.
	• Argue that employers should or should not monitor employee e-mail use.
EVERYDAY LIFE	• Argue against a rent increase.
	• Take a stand on a local issue or policy that you believe is unfair.

WRITING GUIDE: ARGUMENT

STEPS IN ARGUMENT	HOW TO DO THE STEPS
☐ **Focus.**	• Think about your position on an issue and how you can persuade your readers of that position.
☐ **Explore your topic.** See Chapter 2.	• Think about why you have taken the position you have. • Prewrite to find good support for your argument.
☐ **Write a thesis statement.** Topic + Position = Thesis See Chapter 3.	• Write a thesis statement that includes your topic and your position. • Make sure it is a strong statement with a clear position.

STEPS IN ARGUMENT	HOW TO DO THE STEPS
☐ **Support your thesis.** See Chapter 3.	• Provide facts, examples, and expert opinions to support your position. • Examine your reasons to make sure they are not faulty reasoning (see p. 169). • Consider the opposing view. • Give details to strengthen each of your main points.
☐ **Write a draft.** See Chapter 4.	• Arrange your points by order of importance, leaving the one that will have the most impact until last. • Write topic sentences for each major point and paragraphs that demonstrate and prove them. • Write a conclusion that has energy and reminds your readers of your position and main support for it.
☐ **Revise your draft.** See Chapter 4.	• With your audience in mind, read to make sure your supporting points are persuasive and complete. • Add transitions. • Improve your introduction, thesis, and conclusion.
☐ **Edit your draft.** See Chapters 16 through 18.	• Correct errors in grammar, spelling, word use, and punctuation.
☐ **Evaluate your writing.**	• Does it have the Four Basics of Good Argument (p. 165)? • Is this the best I can do?

14

Research Essays

Using Outside Sources

This chapter will guide you through the process of writing a research essay. Throughout the chapter, we show how one student, Michael McQuiston, worked through key steps in the process. Michael's completed research essay appears on pages 202–06.

Make a Schedule

After you receive your assignment, make a schedule that divides your research assignment into small, manageable tasks. There is no way that you can do every step the day (or even a few days) before the assignment is due, so give yourself a reasonable amount of time.

You can use the following schedule as a model for making your own.

SAMPLE RESEARCH ESSAY SCHEDULE

Assignment: _____
                 (Write out what your instructor has assigned.)

   Length: _____

   Draft due date: _____

   Final due date: _____

   My general topic: _____

   My narrowed topic: _____

For more information on research papers, visit bedfordstmartins.com /researchroom.

✓ **LearningCurve** For extra practice in the skills covered in this chapter, visit **bedfordstmartins.com/reinteractive.**

179

STEP	DO BY
Choose a topic.	_____
Find and evaluate sources.	_____
Take notes, keeping publication information for each source.	_____
Write a working thesis statement by answering a research question.	_____
Review all notes; choose the best support for your working thesis.	_____
Make an outline that includes your thesis and support.	_____
Write a draft, including a title.	_____
Review the draft; get feedback; add more support if needed.	_____
Revise the draft.	_____
Prepare a works cited list using correct documentation form.	_____
Edit the revised draft.	_____
Submit the final copy.	_____

Choose a Topic

Your instructor may assign a topic, or you might be expected to think of your own. If you are free to choose your own topic, find a subject that you are personally interested in or curious about.

For more on finding and exploring a topic, see Chapter 2.

POSSIBLE TOPICS FOR A RESEARCH ESSAY	
Assisted suicide	The minimum wage
Banning texting (in class, while driving)	Music downloading
	Patients' rights
Causes of stress	Presidential campaigns
Dieting/eating disorders	Reality television programs
Environmental issues	Rights of children of illegal immigrants
Gambling	
Gay/lesbian marriage/adoption	Road rage
Gun control	Sexual harassment
Healthy eating	Standardized testing
Identity theft	Veterans' issues
Mandatory drug testing	Violence in the media
Marijuana for medical purposes	Women in military combat

When you have chosen a general topic, you will need to narrow it using the same process you learned about in Chapter 2. Although a research essay may be longer than some of the other essays you have written, the topic still needs to be narrow enough to write about in the assigned length.

Before moving ahead with a narrowed topic, check its appropriateness with your instructor if you have any doubt. You might also check library resources to see if information is available on your planned topic. You do not need to actually look at the sources at this point, but you should assure yourself that a reasonable number of sources exist on your topic.

Before writing a working thesis statement, choose a **guiding research question** about your narrowed topic. For example, Michael McQuiston's paper on green landscaping began with the question, "What are the benefits of green landscaping?"

After choosing and narrowing a topic and developing a guiding research question, you are ready to find and evaluate sources that you will use.

Find Sources

Library Resources

Turn first to your college's library. Before visiting the library in person, review its Web site to get general information. You may be able to do some initial research from the Web site, but you will need to visit the library in person to access books and other print materials.

Librarians

Librarians are essential resources to help you find appropriate information in both print and electronic forms. If your library allows it, make an appointment with a librarian to discuss your project and information needs. Or, you and some other students might arrange to go together for a helpful orientation. Before your appointment, make a list of questions you would like to ask, either based on what you have seen on the library Web site or some of the following questions.

QUESTIONS FOR THE LIBRARIAN

- Can you show me how to use the library catalog? How do I use the information I find there?

- What are databases? How does database information differ from what I can find in the library catalog?

- Can I access the library catalog and article databases when I'm not on campus?

- Based on my topic, what other reference tools would you recommend that I use for my research?

- Once I identify a potentially useful source in the catalog or a database, how can I find the material?

- Can you recommend some keywords that I can use for my particular topic?

- Can you recommend an Internet search engine that will help me find information on my topic? Can you recommend some useful reference sites for my topic?

- How can I tell whether an online source is reliable?

- I have already found some online articles related to my topic. Can you suggest some other places to look? How can I find good print sources on my topic?

BOOKS

To find books on your topic, use the library catalog, which is likely to be online. By typing the keywords *green landscaping* into the library catalog, student Michael McQuiston found the following item:

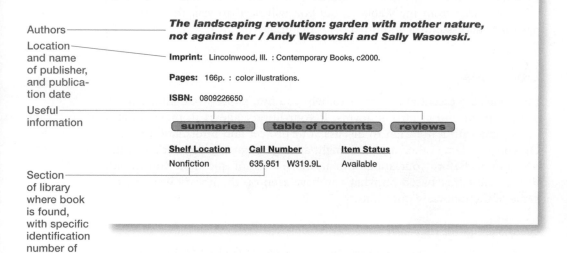

Authors

Location and name of publisher, and publication date

The landscaping revolution: garden with mother nature, not against her / Andy Wasowski and Sally Wasowski.

Imprint: Lincolnwood, Ill. : Contemporary Books, c2000.

Pages: 166p. : color illustrations.

ISBN: 0809226650

Useful information

(summaries) (table of contents) (reviews)

Shelf Location	Call Number	Item Status
Nonfiction	635.951 W319.9L	Available

Section of library where book is found, with specific identification number of book

ONLINE DATABASES/PERIODICAL INDEXES

Most libraries subscribe to online **databases,** which are lists of all **periodical** (journal, newspaper, and magazine) articles on different topics. Because the library pays a subscription fee for these databases, only library members may use them. By entering your student number on the college library Web site, you can access all these helpful reference sources, which have already been checked for reliability. Some databases are general; some are more specialized with a focus on, for example, psychology or education. Some databases have the full texts of the periodicals online, which is handy.

Most college libraries subscribe to the most popular and comprehensive subscription databases: **Academic Search Premier**, **LexisNexis Academic**, **ProQuest Research Library**, and **InfoTrac**. These databases are excellent places to start looking for sources because they cover the widest range of periodicals.

ENCYCLOPEDIAS

Encyclopedias give brief, basic information on a wide range of subjects. Like databases, encyclopedias can be general or specialized. A reliable general encyclopedia, the *Encyclopedia Britannica*, is usually available in print in the reference section of the library and online (**www.britannica .com**). Specialized encyclopedias exist for almost any subject you can imagine; you can find them in the reference section or in the online catalog. Encyclopedias might be a good place to get an overview of your topic, but many instructors want students to use more specialized sources in their writing.

Other Resources

Although your library is the best place to find good sources, other ways can work well too. But you should always make sure these types of sources are reliable.

OPEN DATABASES

Many databases, both general and specialized, are free and open. Some particularly good ones are InfoPlease (**www.infoplease.com**), the Librarian's Internet Index (**www.ipl.org**), the Library of Congress Online (**www .catalog.loc.gov/**), and Martindale's Reference Desk (**www.martindale center.com**).

SEARCH ENGINES

Using a general search engine to search the Web will bring you more sources on your topic, some reliable and some not. Some of the most popular search engines are

- Google (**www.google.com**)
- Bing (**www.bing.com**)

NOTE For a complete online research guide, visit bedfordstmartins .com/ researchroom.

NOTE Most resources referred to here can be accessed through a print reference guide as well as online. A librarian can direct you to the right area of the library and help you find good sources to start your research.

NOTE Do not rely on Wikipedia for accurate information.

- Ask.com (**www.ask.com**)
- AltaVista (**www.altavista.com**)

To use a search engine, enter your keywords in the subject box. Michael McQuiston used Google and tried several variations on his search keywords, which netted the following results.

KEYWORDS	SEARCH RETURNS
green landscaping	More than 19 million results
"green landscaping"	More than 500,000 results
"green landscaping in dry areas"	0 results
green landscaping in dry areas	More than 3 million results

Finding good sources among the countless sites online can take a long time. Therefore, using library sources is often a better strategy than using general sources.

STATISTICAL SOURCES

Statistical data are facts and figures. When they are directly related to the thesis of your research essay and are from a reliable source, they can provide very strong support. One good source of statistical data is the *Statistical Abstract of the United States,* published annually by the U.S. Census Bureau. It can help you find useful statistics related to social trends, social issues, population trends, economics, demographics, and other topics.

ONLINE RESEARCH SITES

Online research sites constitute another valuable source of information on how to do research. At **bedfordstmartins.com/researchroom**, the publisher of this book hosts the *Bedford Research Room,* which includes guided tutorials on research processes; advice on finding, evaluating, and documenting sources; tips on avoiding plagiarism; and more. Other useful sites include Purdue University's Online Writing Lab (OWL) at **http://owl.english.purdue.edu**. This site offers a variety of materials and resources for writers, including research information.

Interviews

Personal interviews can be excellent sources of information. Before interviewing anyone, however, plan carefully. First, consider what kind of person to interview. Do you want information from an expert on the subject or from someone directly affected by the issue? How would the experience or comments of each person help support your points? The person should be knowledgeable about the subject and have firsthand experience. When you have decided whom to interview, schedule an appointment.

Next, to get ready for the interview, prepare a list of five to ten questions. Ask open-ended questions (What is your position on regulating cell-phone use by drivers?) rather than questions that require only a simple yes-or-no response (Do you favor regulating cell-phone use by drivers?). Leave space for notes about the person's responses and for additional questions that may occur to you during the interview. Include in your notes the person's full name and qualifications and the date of the interview.

As you conduct the interview, listen carefully, and write down any important ideas. If you plan to use any of the interviewee's exact words, put them in quotation marks in your notes. Confirm the wording with the interviewee to be sure you have it correctly in your notes. (For more on using direct quotations, see pages 189–91 and 265–66.)

NOTE: If you plan to record an interview (whether on tape, or using a digital recorder), get your subject's permission first. Recording what a person says without being granted permission is unethical and, in some states, against the law.

Evaluate Sources

Evaluating sources means judging them to determine how reliable and appropriate they are for your topic, your assignment, your purpose, and your audience. To evaluate sources, use the critical thinking and reading skills you have learned and used in earlier chapters. Before using a source for your paper, apply the following questions to all sources: print, electronic, and open access Web.

Questions for Evaluating All Sources

WHO IS THE AUTHOR?

Is the author actually an expert on the topic? Many celebrities, for example, are involved in worthwhile charitable causes that they learn a great deal about. But just because Matt Damon, George Clooney, or Angelina Jolie writes a statement or an article about a cause does not make him or her an expert.

Most sources provide some information about authors. Books have an "About the Author" section, usually at the end or on the book jacket. Periodicals have biographical headnotes or notes about the author at the end of the article. Read this information to make sure that the author has the authority and knowledge to make the source reliable.

IS THE SOURCE WELL KNOWN AND RESPECTED?

Certain sources are generally agreed to be reliable, though not always unbiased. National magazines such as *Time, Newsweek, National Geographic,* and others verify information before publishing it. Periodicals that you find on a subscription database are also usually reliable. Newspapers too usually verify information before using it, though the tabloids (like the ones sold in the supermarket checkout lines) are not reliable. Their purpose is to shock and entertain, not necessarily to tell the truth.

IS THE SOURCE UP-TO-DATE?

Look to see when a source was published. If your topic is in a rapidly changing field (for example, science or medicine), your source should be as recent as possible to include the most current knowledge. On the other hand, if you learn about a person or a work that is considered classic (something that has been respected for a long time), the publication date is not as important. For example, Michael McQuiston's topic, green landscaping, is a relatively new practice, so he should be looking for works that have been published recently. In his reading, however, if he learns of a practice that changed the whole direction of landscaping, that would be considered classic work. Depending on his purpose, he might want to include a reference to that work, in addition to new findings. Whatever your topic is, judge each possible source for how current the information is.

IS THE SOURCE UNBIASED?

Every writer reflects some personal opinion on the subject he or she writes about. However, a good source balances those opinions with reasonable evidence. But facts and numbers can be used differently by people with different biases. For example, a researcher who believes in strict gun control may cite statistics about how many children are killed each year in gun accidents. A researcher who believes in the individual right to own guns may use statistics about how many people are killed in robberies or burglaries. Both writers use accurate numbers to argue different positions.

Consider the author's background to determine if he or she is likely to be biased in a way that interferes with reliability. In the gun issue, if an author is president of an organization named CeaseFire, he has a bias toward gun control. If an author is president of the National Rifle Association, he has a bias toward gun ownership. If you think an author is strongly advocating one side of an issue without addressing the other side, move on to another source, or include both sides in your essay.

Questions for Evaluating Web Sites

The Web is open to anyone with Internet access, which is one of the great things about it. Anyone can develop a Web site to promote anything he or she wants. That very openness means, though, that you have to be even more critical in evaluating information that you find on a Web site, especially if you are using a general search engine such as Google, Bing, or others.

The extension to the Uniform Resource Locator (URL) is the letters after the first period (or "dot"). Different extensions convey information about the site's sponsor.

EXTENSION	INDICATES
.com	a commercial or personal site
.edu	an educational institution's site
.gov	a government agency's site
.net	a commercial or personal site
.org	a nonprofit group's site

As a general rule, educational (.edu) and government (.gov) sites are likely to be reliable. The commercial and personal sites (.com, .net) may be good sources, but they may also be promoting the opinions of a biased person or group of people. A nonprofit group's site (.org) also may present either good or biased information. When a search brings you to Web sites with *.com*, *.net*, or *.org* extensions, find out about the sponsors of the sites and examine the sites for evidence of strong bias.

In addition to the questions that you would ask to evaluate any source, add the following, which use your critical reading and thinking skills.

QUESTIONS TO ASK IN EVALUATING A WEB SITE

- What is the URL extension?
- Who sponsors the site?
- Is there an "About" link? What does it tell me when I click on it?
- What is the purpose of the site?
- What kind of information is on the site?
- Does the site material indicate a bias? What is it?
- Based on the answers to the above, do I think information on the site is reliable and appropriate for my research essay?

Take Careful Notes

As you find information for your research essay, do not rely on your memory to recall details about your sources; take good notes from the start.

Students sometimes plagiarize by mistake because they have taken notes that do not distinguish a source's ideas from their own or that do not fully record source information, including publication data. For more on how to avoid plagiarism, see page 16, and visit the Bedford Research Room at **bedfordstmartins.com/researchroom**.

NOTE: This section's advice on recording, citing, and documenting sources reflects Modern Language Association (MLA) style, the preferred style for the humanities.

Keep a Running Bibliography

A **bibliography** is a complete list, alphabetized by author, of the outside sources you *consult*. A **list of works cited** is a complete list, alphabetized by author, of the outside sources that you *actually use* in your essay.

You can keep information for your bibliography and list of works cited on notecards or on your computer. Whatever method you use, be sure to record complete publication information for each source at the time you consult it; this will save you from having to look up this information again when you are preparing your list of works cited.

The following is a list of information to record for each source.

BOOKS	ARTICLES	WEB PAGES/OTHER ELECTRONIC SOURCES
Author name(s)	Author name(s)	Author name(s)
Title and subtitle	Title of article	Title of Web page/online material
—	Title of magazine, journal, or newspaper	Title of site/larger work (e.g., online periodical)
City of publication and publisher	—	Name of sponsoring organization OR name of database
Year of publication	Date of publication	Date of publication or latest update
—	Page number(s)	Page, section, or paragraph numbers (if provided)
—	Volume number	Date you accessed the site
Medium (print)	Medium (print or Web)	Medium (Web/URL, CD)

Create Clear, Complete Records of Source Information

For each source that you take notes on, create an individual notecard or file on your computer. It should include the source's author(s) and title, the page number(s) where you found the specific information, and what method you are using to present it: summary or paraphrase (which are called **indirect quotations**) or **direct quotation** (which is word for word what the source says). A sample card or entry might look like this.

Welsh, Welch, Duble ——
Water Conservation ————
"In urban areas of Texas about 25 percent of the water supply is used
 for landscape and garden watering."
"Landscape Water Conservation: Xeriscape." *Aggie Horticulture.*
http://aggie-horticulture.tamu.edu/extension/xeriscape/xeriscope.html.
Direct Quotation ————

Last name(s) of author(s): List as in works cited list.

Category of information: McQuiston is sorting information into categories, each a benefit of green landscaping.

Information: Fact or idea to include in his paper.

Information source

Method used to record information: Direct quotation, summary, or paraphrase.

Indirect Quotation: Summary

As you learned in Chapter 1, a summary is your condensed version of a longer piece of writing, which should include the main point of what you are summarizing. It should also be written as much as possible in your own words, and not by using many of the same words or phrases from the longer source.

One way to include outside source material as evidence or support in your own writing is to summarize. Look back at "Attendance in College Classes" on page 171, and then read the two summaries that follow here. The first is unacceptable because it uses too many words and phrases from the original. The second is an acceptable summary.

Direct quotation should be in quotation marks.

Phrase is a common expression, though it is from the original; here, however, it is part of a pattern of using exact phrases from the original, and so should be in quotation marks.

Exact wording of original; should be in quotation marks.

UNACCEPTABLE SUMMARY

In his essay "Attendance in College Classes" (171), Donnie Ney argues that attendance in college classes should be optional, not mandatory. One reason he gives is that because students have paid for the class, they should have the right to decide whether to attend or not, particularly since their lives are often complicated. He also says that many students already know the course content and should not have to waste time hearing about it again. He also argues that optional attendance would result in smaller classes with more personal attention, which would be good for students who do choose to attend class.

ACCEPTABLE SUMMARY

> In his essay "Attendance in College Classes" (171), Donnie Ney argues that college students should not be required to attend classes because since they have paid for the course, like a consumer purchase, it should be up to the purchaser to use or not use it. He goes on to give other reasons that expand on his basic assumption that students have the right to choose if and when they should attend a class.

The acceptable summary does not use the language of the original, other than those words that refer to the topic. It also focuses on the main point of the piece rather than including all the specific support points. This summary gives the "big picture" of the essay in a condensed form.

Indirect Quotation: Paraphrase

A paraphrase restates another person's idea in your own words. Unlike a summary, a paraphrase is not necessarily a condensed version of the original; it is the idea expressed in your own words. You cannot paraphrase a whole essay or article. Again, you should not use the same wording or phrasing that is in the original.

Because paraphrasing is a bit tricky, it may be easier for you to quote directly from the original piece. When you are taking notes from a source and find an idea that you might want to use, try writing the idea in your own words, and then look back at the original piece. If what you have written is too close to the words or phrases in the original, either try again or use a direct quotation.

Look back at the essay comparing anorexia and bulimia on page 145. The unacceptable and acceptable paraphrases are of information in the first paragraph.

Each of the shaded words and phrases are too close to the original. Though not direct quotes, the wording is close enough and the pattern of the phrases is the same as in the original.

UNACCEPTABLE PARAPHRASE

> According to the authors (Hockenbury, 593–94), anorexia nervosa is weight loss that makes a person dangerously underweight. It is characterized by four key features that include a person refusing to keep a normal weight, having an intense fear of getting fat, being unable to see how she really looks, and denying how much weight she has lost.

ACCEPTABLE PARAPHRASE

> According to the authors (Hockenbury, 593–94), the behaviors that characterize anorexics are an unwillingness to eat enough to be healthy because they believe they will get fat, and a lack of understanding that they are endangering themselves.

The ideas in this paraphrase are the authors', but the wording is very different from the original.

Direct Quotation

A direct quotation uses information from an outside source word for word, enclosing it in quotation marks (" "). Use a direct quotation when it is the best way to support your thesis. Avoid using long direct quotations in a short research essay, however, since most of what you write should be your own words. If you do use a direct quotation that is more than about forty words or four typed lines, indent the whole quotation, and do not use quotation marks.

SHORT DIRECT QUOTATION

> According to psychologists Don Hockenbury and Sandra Hockenbury, "four key features define anorexia nervosa" (593).

LONGER DIRECT QUOTATION

> Psychologists Don Hockenbury and Sandra Hockenbury explain the disorder of anorexia nervosa this way:
>
> > Four key features define anorexia nervosa. First, the person refuses to maintain a minimally normal body weight. With a body weight that is 15 percent or more below normal, body mass index can drop to 12 or lower. Second, despite being dangerously underweight, the person with anorexia is intensely afraid of gaining weight or becoming fat. Third, she has a distorted perception about the size of her body. Although emaciated, she looks in the mirror and sees herself as fat or obese. And fourth, she denies the seriousness of her weight loss. (593–94)

Again, be certain to include how the information on your notecards is recorded (summary, paraphrase, or direct quotation) and the page number. You may think you will remember, but honestly, you will not. No one does. Rather than preparing good paraphrases, it may be easier to record the idea as a direct quotation. As you draft your essay, you will see that the material is a direct quotation, and you can then take the time to paraphrase carefully.

For more on using quotations correctly, see pages 265–67.

Write a Thesis Statement

For more on writing a thesis statement, see Chapter 3.

After you have taken notes on the sources you gathered, you should be ready to write a thesis statement, which states the main idea of your research essay. You can start by turning your guiding research question into a statement that answers the question, as Michael McQuiston does below. Note how he revises his thesis to make it more forceful and concrete.

> **MICHAEL MCQUISTON'S GUIDING RESEARCH QUESTION:** *What are the benefits of green landscaping?*
>
> **DRAFT THESIS STATEMENT:** *There are many clear benefits of green landscaping.*
>
> **REVISED AFTER TAKING NOTES FROM SOURCES:** *Landscaping with drought-tolerant native plants conserves water, reduces the use of toxic soil conditioners, and makes maintenance easier.*

As you write and revise your essay, your thesis statement may change, but having a good working one helps you focus your writing and see where you might need to do additional research.

For more on outlining, see Chapter 3.

Make an Outline

To organize your notes, you need to make an outline that shows how you will support your thesis. First, write down your thesis statement. Then, review your notes to decide what your three or four major support points will be. Write these under your thesis statement and number them. Under each of your major support points, write two or three supporting details, and number them.

As you read McQuiston's outline, note that although he started with four benefits of green landscaping (*water conservation, fertilizers/safety, effect on wildlife, maintenance*), as he read and took notes, he decided to put "effect on wildlife" into the "fertilizers/safety" category. Note also that he is reviewing his organized notes and sources and trying to fit them into appropriate places in his essay (the names in parentheses and **boldface**).

MICHAEL MCQUISTON'S OUTLINE

I. **Thesis Statement (introductory paragraph):** Landscaping with drought-tolerant native plants conserves water, reduces the use of toxic soil conditioners, and makes maintenance easier.

First support point —— II. **Water Use**

Supporting details ——
- A. A limited natural resource already strained
- B. Landscaping uses lots of water **(Welsh?)**
- C. Native plants **(Tufts?)**
  1. use less water, drought-tolerant
  2. many kinds
  3. lower water bills/save money and water

Second support point —— III. **Fertilizers/Pest Control/Safety**

Supporting details ——
- A. Poisonous, kids, pets **(Native Plant, Texas Wildscapes?)**
- B. Good bugs/wildlife
- C. Native plants use little or none

IV. Maintenance
  A. Foreign plants, lots of water, lots of time and money
  B. Native plants, not much maintenance **(Lueck?)**

V. Conclusion ─────────────────────────────────────── Third support point
  A. Review benefits ⎤
                       ⎥ ─────────────────────── Supporting details
  B. Observation   ⎦

Write Your Essay

Using your outline, write a draft of your research essay. (For more information on writing a draft, see Chapter 4.)

Your **introduction** should include your thesis statement and a preview
of the support you will provide in the body of the essay. If you are taking a
stand on an issue, the introduction should let your readers know what your
position is. The **body** of the essay will present your major support points for
your thesis backed by supporting details from your research. The **conclusion** will remind readers of your main point and make a further observation based on the information you have presented.

As you write, incorporate your sources into your paper with **introductory phrases**. Most often, you will state the name of the source or author
before adding the information you are using. Use a comma after the introductory phrases.

INTRODUCTORY PHRASE IDENTIFYING SOURCE

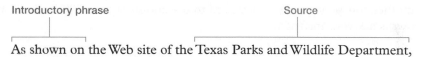

Introductory phrase   Source

As shown on the Web site of the Texas Parks and Wildlife Department,

INTRODUCTORY PHRASE IDENTIFYING AUTHOR AND SOURCE

In his article "Sustaining Mother Nature with Native Plants," Bill
Ward states,

Common Introductory Phrases

according to [source]

as [source] claims   says

          explains   shows

          notes   states

          points out   writes

When you have finished writing your draft essay, take a break from it. Then, definitely allow time to reread, revise, and edit it. At this point, you might read the draft essay and see that you need a bit more support from outside sources. Perhaps you can find more in the sources you have already been using, or you may want to find another source to support your thesis statement.

All the sources that you use must be cited correctly where you use them in your paper, as well as at the end of the paper, in the Works Cited list. The sections that follow give you the correct format for documenting in-text citation and works cited. If you are using a type of source that you do not find in these sections, visit **bedfordstmartins.com/researchroom** where you will find the documentation format for every kind of source imaginable.

For more information on documenting sources, visit bedfordstmartins.com/researchroom.

Cite and Document Your Sources

You need to include **in-text citations** of sources as you use them in the essay. You also need to document, or give credit to, your sources at the end of your research essay in a **list of works cited**.

Few people can remember the specifics of correct citation and documentation, so be sure to refer to this section or the reference text that your instructor prefers. Be sure to include all of the correct information, and pay attention to where punctuation marks such as commas, periods, and quotation marks should go.

There are several different systems of documentation. Most English professors prefer the Modern Language Association (MLA) system, which is used in this chapter. However, when you are writing a research paper in another course, you may be required to use another system. When in doubt, always ask your instructor.

Use In-Text Citations within Your Essay

Along with an introductory phrase that smoothly incorporates information from an outside source into your writing, your sources need to be cited where they are used and according to correct documentation format. In-text citations are shorter than Works Cited citations, but each must correspond to an entry in the Works Cited list.

The following section shows you what you need to include in an in-text citation for various kinds of sources. Use this format for any source material you are using: a summary, a paraphrase, or a direct quotation. In every case, insert the citation after the material you have used. If you use a direct quotation, the citation comes after the end quote and before the period ending the sentence.

DIRECTORY OF MLA IN-TEXT CITATIONS

NOTE: The formats given below are for print sources. When you cite a Web source, use page numbers if available. If the source is not paged, use the paragraph number instead. If there are no paragraphs, cite the author, title of the part of the Web site, or the Web site's sponsor.

The series of dots (called ellipses) in the following examples indicate that words have been left out.

Two examples are provided for each citation:

1. The author is named in an introductory phrase, with the page or paragraph number in parentheses.

2. The author is not named in the introductory phrase, and the author's name and page or paragraph number appear in parentheses.

One Author

As David Shipler states, ". . ." (16).

The number of people who work and fall below the poverty line has increased dramatically (Shipler 16).

Two or Three Authors   Use all authors' last names.

Quigley and Morrison found that . . . (243).

Banks and credit card companies are charging many more fees . . . (Quigley and Morrison 243).

Four or More Authors   Use the first author's last name and the words *et al.* (*et al.* means "and others").

According to Sen et al., . . . (659).

The overuse of antibiotics can result in . . . (Sen et al. 659).

Group, Corporation, or Government Agency Use the name of the group, corporation, or government agency. The source can be abbreviated in the parentheses, as shown in the second example.

> The Texas Parks and Wildlife Department offers guidelines for landscaping . . . (26).

> Texas has more native plants than any other . . . (Texas Parks and Wildlife Dept. 26).

Author Not Named Use the article title in quotations, shortened if it is a long title.

> In the article "Texas Wildscapes," . . . (7).

> Many areas of Texas are filled with drought-tolerant native . . . ("Texas Wildscapes" 7).

Encyclopedia or Other Reference Work Use the name of the entry you are using as a source.

> In its entry on xeriscaping, the *Landscape Encyclopedia* claims that . . . ("Xeriscaping").

> Xeriscaping is often used in . . . ("Xeriscaping").

Work in an Anthology Use the name of the author(s) of the piece you are using as a source.

> As Rich Chiappone believes, . . . (200).

> Fly fishing is as much a spiritual . . . (Chiappone 200).

Interview, E-mail, Speech Use the name of the person interviewed or the author of an e-mail.

> As University of Texas Vice President of Student Affairs Juan Gonzalez said in an interview. . . .

> Students have many resources available to . . . (Gonzalez).

Use a Works Cited List at the End of Your Essay

NOTE: Works cited entries that have a month and day as part of the publication date are formatted so that the date appears before the month; the month is abbreviated (Jan., Apr., Sept.); and there is no comma between the month and year:

WORKS CITED DATE STYLE: 14 Mar. 2011

For each set of entries, the first example shows the format; the second is an example of the format.

Books

One Author

Author's Last Name, First Name. *Title of Book.* Publisher Location: Name of Publisher, Publication Date. Medium of Publication.

Shipler, David K. *The Working Poor: Invisible in America.* New York: Knopf, 2004. Print.

Note that titles of books are in *italics*.

Two or Three Authors

Author's Last Name, First Name, and Other Authors' First and Last Names. *Title of Book.* Publisher Location: Name of Publisher, Publication Date. Medium of Publication.

Picciotto, Richard, and Daniel Paisner. *Last Man Down: A New York City Fire Chief and the Collapse of the World Trade Center.* New York: Berkeley, 2002. Print.

Four or More Authors

Author's Last Name, First Name, et al. *Title of Book.* Publisher Location: Name of Publisher, Publication Date. Medium of Publication.

Roark, James L., et al. *The American Promise: A History of the United States.* 4th ed. Boston: Bedford, 2009. Print.

Group, Corporation, or Government Agency

Name of Group, Corporation, or Agency. *Title of Book.* Publisher Location: Name of Publisher, Publication Date. Medium of Publication.

American Cancer Society. *The American Cancer Society's Guide to Pain Control.* New York: McGraw, 2004. Print.

Editor

> Editor's Last Name, First Name, ed. *Title of Book.* Publisher Location: Name of Publisher, Publication Date. Medium of Publication.

> Canellos, Peter S., ed. *The Last Lion.* New York: Simon, 2009. Print.

Work in an Anthology

> Selection Author's Last Name, First Name. "Title of Selection in the Anthology." *Anthology Title.* Ed. First and Last Name of Anthology Editor. Publisher Location: Name of Publisher, Publication Date. Pages of Selection. Medium of Publication.

> Brown, Sterling A. "Riverbank Blues." *250 Poems: A Portable Anthology.* 2nd ed. Boston: Bedford/St. Martin's, 2009. 141-42. Print.

Encyclopedia

> Entry Author's Last Name, First Name. "Title of Entry." *Title of Encyclopedia.* Edition Number [2nd, 3rd] ed. Date of publication. Medium of Publication.

NOTE The citation here is for an online encyclopedia. Note that the entry includes the date the article was accessed (4 Apr. 2010).

> Araya, Yoseph. "Ecology of Water Relations in Plants." *Encyclopedia of Life Sciences.* Apr. 2007. Web. 4 Apr. 2010.

Periodicals

Magazine Article

Note that titles of periodicals are in italics.

> Author's Last Name, First Name. "Title of Article." *Title of Magazine* Day Month Year of Publication: Page Numbers. Medium of Publication.

> Kluger, Jeffrey. "One Weird Dinosaur." *Time* 11 Oct. 2010: 44–45. Print.

Newspaper Article

> Author's Last Name, First Name. "Title of Article." *Title of Newspaper* Day Month Year of Publication: Page Number [if Print]. Medium of Publication.

> Barringer, Felicity. "Indians Join Fight for an Oklahoma Lake's Flow." *New York Times* 12 Apr. 2011: A1+. Print.

Editorial in a Magazine or Newspaper, Author Known

Author's Last Name, First Name. "Title of Editorial." *Title of Newspaper* Day Month Year of Publication: Page Number [if Print]. Medium of Publication.

Udall, Don. "When Someone Is Alive but Not Living." Editorial. *Newsweek* 14 June 1999: 12. Print.

Editorial in a Magazine or Newspaper, Author Unknown

"Title of Editorial." Editorial. *Title of Magazine or Newspaper* Day Month Year of Publication: Page Number [if Print]. Medium of Publication.

"Growing Smart." Editorial. *Miami Herald* 29 Apr. 2010. Web. 20 May 2010.

Article, Scholarly Journal with Numbered Volumes

Author's Last Name, First Name. "Title of Article." *Title of Journal* Volume Number. Issue Number (Year of Publication): Page Number [if Print]. Medium of Publication.

Fountain, Glinda H. "Inverting the Southern Belle: Romance Writers Redefine Gender Myths." *Journal of Popular Culture* Volume 41.1 (2008): 37–55. Print.

Article, Scholarly Journal without Numbered Volumes

Author's Last Name, First Name. "Title of Article." *Title of Journal* Issue Number (Year of Publication): Page Number [if Print]. Medium of Publication.

Thiel, Peter. "The Optimistic Though Experiment." *Policy Review* 147 (2008): 17–37. Print.

Electronic Sources

The format for citing electronic periodicals follows much of the same format as for print periodicals, so refer to the entries in the previous section for journals with numbered volumes.

Work from a Library Subscription Database (such as InfoTrac)

> Author's Last Name, First Name. "Title of Article." *Title of Periodical* Volume number. Issue number (Year of Publication): Page Numbers. *Name of Database.* Web. Date of access.

> McManus, John F. "Global Warming Skeptic Remains Adamant." *New American* 27.2 (2011): 9. *InfoTrac.* Web. 31 Mar. 2011.

Online Periodical

> Author's Last Name, First Name. "Title of Article." *Title of Online Periodical.* Name of Periodical Publisher, Day Month Year of Article Publication. Web. Day Month Year of Access.

> Manjoo, Farhad. "Is Something Rotten at Apple?" *Slate.* Slate Group, 25 Aug. 2008. Web. 14 Feb. 2011.

NOTE that titles of Web sites are in italics.

Short Work from a Web site   If no author is given, omit this information. If no site sponsor is listed, use N.p. If no date of publication is available, use n.d.

> Author's Last Name, First Name. "Title of Work." *Title of Web Site.* Name of Site Sponsor, Day Month Year of Publication. Web. Day Month Year of Access.

> "In Her Own Words." *Lady Bird Johnson Wildflower Center.* Univ. of Texas at Austin, 2010. Web. 4 Apr. 2011.

Other Sources

For citation examples for other electronic sources, visit bedfordstmartins .com/ researchroom.

Personal Interview

> Last Name, First Name of Person Interviewed. Personal interview. Day Month Year of Interview.

> Okayo, Margaret. Personal interview. 16 Apr. 2009.

E-mail

> Last Name, First Name of Author of E-mail Message. "Subject of E-mail." Name of Person Who Received E-mail. Day Month Year E-mail Received. E-mail.

> Willey, Liz. "Happy Holidays from Paraguay." Message to Susan Anker. 4 Jan. 2011. E-mail.

Revise and Edit Your Essay

After a break, reread your draft with fresh eyes and an open mind. Then, ask yourself these questions.

- Does my introduction state my thesis?
- Does each of the body paragraphs contain a topic sentence that directly supports my thesis? Do the supporting details in each paragraph relate to and explain the topic sentence?
- Do I provide a conclusion that reminds readers of my main point and makes a further observation?
- Have I included enough support for the thesis that readers are likely to see my topic the way I do? Is there anything else I could add to make my point?
- Do transitions help readers move from one idea to the next?
- Have I integrated source material smoothly into the essay? Do I need to smooth out anything that seems to be just dumped in?
- Have I reread the essay carefully, looking for errors in grammar, spelling, and punctuation?
- Have I cited and documented my sources?
- Are all of my citations and Works Cited entries in correct form (MLA or whatever style the instructor specifies)?
- Is this the best I can do?

For more on revising, see Chapter 4. When checking for grammar, spelling, and punctuation errors, consult Chapters 16 through 18 of this book.

After reading the annotated student essay that follows, use the Writing Guide on pages 207–08 to write your research essay.

Sample Student Research Essay

The student essay that follows is annotated to show both typical features of research essays (such as references to sources) and elements of good writing (such as the thesis statement and topic sentences). The paper also shows formatting (such as margins, spacing between lines, and placement of the title). Your instructor may specify different or additional formatting in class or in your syllabus.

Student's last name and page number at top of each page.

Course

Date

Title centered

Introductory phrase

Direct quotation

Introduction

Thesis statement

Body paragraphs

Michael McQuiston

Professor Bicknell

Composition 1

21 April 2010

To Be Green or Not to Be Green

When people make landscaping decisions, many do not realize that the choices they make affect not just the immediate appearance of their yard, but also the present and future environment. Lady Bird Johnson, a champion of native landscaping, once said, "My special cause, the one that alerts my interest and quickens the pace of my life, is to preserve the wildflowers and native plants that define the regions of our land—to encourage and promote their use in appropriate areas" ("In Her Own"). Many people share her feelings and might want to know how landscaping can accomplish such preservation. When planning your landscaping, it is important to choose plants that will not only be aesthetically pleasing, but low-maintenance and cost-effective as well. After owning a lawn care and landscape business in Texas for six years, I am a firm believer in green landscaping. Landscaping with drought-tolerant native plants conserves water, reduces the use of toxic soil conditioners, and requires little maintenance.

As the world's population grows, it strains our earth's limited supply of natural resources. One resource essential to both plants and animals is water. Many cities and towns already restrict watering during the hot summer months to certain days of the week or certain times of day. In an online article written for Texas A&M University, Welsh, Welch, and Duble state that "in urban areas of Texas about 25 percent of the water supply is used for landscape and garden watering." Some homeowners argue that water is necessary to ensure the survival of the plants in their yards.

However, part of the problem lies with the types of flowering plants, trees, and grass used in urban and suburban landscaping, many of them to achieve a certain "look." But these plants can require a great deal of water, as they often originate in areas with much higher rainfall per year or a more constant amount of rain

McQuiston 2

throughout the year. In order to sustain plants native to a climate zone that gets more rain, many homeowners not only see their water bills double during the arid summer months, but also contribute to the overall potential environmental water-shortage problem.

Fortunately, there is a way to have a beautiful yard in Texas without depleting our water supply: use plants that are drought-tolerant or native to the area. The nonprofit organization Wild Ones Natural Landscapers defines *native plants* as "those that were growing naturally in the area before humans introduced plants from a distant place" ("Landscaping"). Plants native to a certain area can survive with the amount of water available through local bodies of water and rainfall. Some native Texas plants that will still look beautiful in the midsummer after two weeks of record-high temperatures and drought include flowers such as the Bluebonnet, Indian Blanket, Indian Paintbrush, Lantana, and many others, as well as many shrubs and trees. Homeowners need only ask at their local nursery or ask a landscape professional to find out what plants, grass, and trees are native and drought-tolerant. Many respected Web sites also provide similar advice. Green landscaping significantly reduces people's water bills and at the same time conserves water, a limited natural resource.

On a typical Saturday in suburbia, one might hear, "Don't let the kids go in the yard today. I put down fertilizer." But, wait — aren't the pets and other wildlife out there too? Although many homeowners and landscape services recognize the harmful effects of fertilizer and pesticides, they think having the "best-looking yard on the block" is worth the risk. According to the California Department of Pesticide Regulation's "Community Guide to Recognizing and Reporting Pesticide Problems," pesticides are safest if used properly, but they are still dangerous. Children and people with asthma or other chronic diseases are much more likely to get sick from pesticides than healthy adults, and "some individuals are also more sensitive to the odor or other irritant effects of certain pesticides" (29).

Using native plants and grasses instead of turf grass in the landscape eliminates the need for fertilizers and pesticides, making

First support point

In-text citation

Body paragraphs

Support point

In-text citation

Paraphrase

the yard a safer place for both people and beneficial insects. Jane
Scott, a gardener and naturalist, argues in her book *Field and Forest*
that although the creation of a landscape of any kind causes some
disturbance of land and soil, not all the harm landscaping and
gardening does is necessary, and native plants would help reduce
our environmental impact (4). Native plants do not need fertilizer
to condition the soil because it is the soil they will naturally grow
best in; there is no need to worry about the correct Ph balance or the
perfect balance of nitrogen-potash-iron in the fertilizer. The need for
pesticides is also diminished because plants that grow naturally in an
area have developed defenses against harmful local insects.

Green landscaping also saves local wildlife, which can have a
hard time finding food and water in the hot, dry summer months.
Natural vegetation not only provides a safe haven for these creatures,
but also nourishes them. Planting native and drought-tolerant
vegetation in the yard transforms it into an extension of these
creatures' homes, and in exchange for food, water, and shelter, the
creatures offer homeowners an exclusive peek into the wild world
around them. The Texas Parks and Wildlife Department recognizes
the importance of native plants in providing food for native species
of animals, birds, and butterflies, even going so far as to offer a
"habitat restoration and conservation plan for rural and urban
areas" ("Texas Wildscapes"). Bill Ward's article "Sustaining Mother
Nature with Native Plants" illustrates the necessity of native plants
for insect life. Monarch butterfly larvae depend on the milkweed
for their survival, but as can be gathered from its name, this Texas
native is often eradicated because it is considered a weed. "Bugs
in native plant gardens," Ward states, "are helping to sustain the
ecosystem by supporting a diverse and balanced food web. The same
cannot be said about yards landscaped with predominantly exotic
plants."

**Body
paragraphs**

In addition to the environmental effects of nonnative landscape
plantings, the regular upkeep of a nonnative lawn can prove too
much for busy homeowners. What began as the best-looking yard on
the block can quickly deteriorate into the neighborhood eyesore

McQuiston 4

without the necessary maintenance and regular application of extra
water and pesticides. While all plants require some care, native plants
require far less than the transplanted ones, and Jane Scott argues that
native plants are just as attractive as common exotics: "The more we
know about the native plant communities that surround us, the more
we will come to appreciate their inherent beauty and diversity and the
more effectively we can accommodate them in the places where we
live" (4). So, native plants offer peace of mind that the yard will look
good season after season without constant daily care.

Body paragraphs

In this time of growing environmental awareness, planting
nonnative, high-maintenance plants is irresponsible. Native plants
do not strain the environment, and they provide food and shelter for
various species of wildlife. The low-maintenance nature of native
plants makes them friendly to the busy homeowner concerned about
the environment. With less fertilizer and pesticide on the lawn, the
yard will be a healthier place for families to spend their time and
enjoy the outdoors. Green landscaping makes sense for everyone, for
now and for the future. Be green.

Observation

Review of support

McQuiston 5

Works Cited

"Community Guide to Recognizing and Reporting Pesticide Problems." *California Department of Pesticide Regulation.* State of California, Apr. 2008. Web. 11 Apr. 2011. <http://www.cdpr.ca.gov/docs/dept/comguide/index.htm>.

"In Her Own Words." *Lady Bird Johnson Wildflower Center.* Univ. of Texas at Austin, 2010. Web. 4 Apr. 2011. <http://www.wildflower.org/herownwords/>.

"Landscaping with Native Plants." *Wild Ones.* Wild Ones Natural Landscapers, May 2008. Web. 3 Apr. 2011. <http://www.for-wild.org/landscap.html>.

Scott, Jane. *Field and Forest.* New York: Walker, 1992. Print.

"Texas Wildscapes: Gardening for Wildlife in Backyards, Schoolyards, and Corporate Parks." *Texas Parks and Wildlife.* Texas Parks & Wildlife Dept., Feb. 2010. Web. 2 Apr. 2011. <http://www.tpwd.state.tx.us/huntwild/wild/wildscapes/>.

Ward, Bill. "Sustaining Mother Nature with Native Plants." *Native Plant Society of Texas.* Native Plant Soc. of Texas, 29 May 2010. Web. 11 Apr. 2011. <http://npsot.org/wp/story/2010/436/>.

Welsh, Douglas F., William C. Welch, and Richard L. Duble. "Landscape Water Conservation: Xeriscape." *Aggie Horticulture.* Texas A&M U. Dept. of Horticultural Science, 26 Oct. 2000. Web. 3 April 2011. <http://aggie-horticulture.tamu.edu/extension/xeriscape/xeriscape.html>.

After you have taken notes, found outside sources, and written a draft thesis statement, use the writing guide that follows to help you write your research essay.

WRITING GUIDE: RESEARCH ESSAY

STEPS	HOW TO DO THE STEPS
☐ **Make a schedule.** See pages 179–80.	• Include the due date and dates for doing research, finishing a draft, revising, documenting sources, and editing.
☐ **Choose a topic.** See pages 180–81.	• Choose a topic that interests you. • Make sure the topic is narrow enough to cover in the assigned length of the paper.
☐ **Ask a guiding question.** See page 181.	• Ask a question that will guide your research.
☐ **Find and evaluate sources.** See pages 181–87.	• Use library resources. • Consider the reliability of each source.
☐ **Take notes to avoid plagiarism.** See pages 188–91.	• Note the publication information. • Make an entry for each piece of information (p. 188).
☐ **Write a thesis statement.** See Chapter 3.	• Based on what you have read, write a thesis statement that includes the main point of your essay. • Turn your research question into a statement: **RESEARCH QUESTION:** What are the benefits of green landscaping? **THESIS STATEMENT:** There are many clear benefits of green landscaping. **REVISED AFTER TAKING NOTES FROM SOURCES:** Landscaping with drought-tolerant native plants conserves water, reduces the use of toxic soil conditioners, and requires little maintenance.

STEPS	HOW TO DO THE STEPS
☐ **Support your thesis.** See Chapter 3.	• Review all notes to choose the best points. • Do further research if you do not have enough support to convince your readers of your main point.
☐ **Write a draft essay.** See Chapter 4.	• Make an outline that organizes your support. • Write an introduction that includes your thesis statement. • Write topic sentences and paragraphs that give support and supporting details. • Work in your outside sources using introductory phrases (see p. 193). • Write a conclusion that reminds your readers of your main point and support and makes an observation. • Title your essay.
☐ **Revise your draft.** See Chapter 4.	• Is the thesis clear? • Do I have enough support? • Do I end strongly? • Have I integrated outside sources smoothly in the essay (and cited them)? • Are all sources documented correctly?
☐ **Cite and document your sources.** For in-text citations, see pages 194–96. For works cited entries, see pages 197–200.	
☐ **Edit your essay.** See Chapters 16 through 18.	• Reread your essay, looking for errors in grammar, spelling, and punctuation.

15

Basic Grammar

An Overview

This chapter will review the basic elements of the sentence.

The Parts of Speech

In the examples in this chapter, <u>subjects</u> are underlined once and <u>verbs</u> are underlined twice.

There are seven basic parts of speech in English:

1. A **noun** names a person, place, or thing.

    Heroin is a drug.

2. A **pronoun** replaces a noun in a sentence. A pronoun can be the subject of a sentence (*I, you, he, she, it, we, they*), or it can be the object of a sentence (*me, you, him, her, us, them*). A pronoun can also show possession (*mine, yours, his, her, its, our, their*).

    It causes addiction.

3. A **verb** tells what the subject does, or it links a subject to another word that describes it.

    Heroin *causes* addiction.   [The verb *causes* is what the subject *Heroin* does.]

    It *is* dangerous.   [The verb *is* links the subject *It* to a word that describes it: *dangerous*.]

✓ LearningCurve **For extra practice in the skills covered in this chapter, visit** **bedfordstmartins.com/reinteractive.**

209

4.   An **adjective** describes a noun or pronoun.

Heroin is *dangerous*.   [The adjective *dangerous* describes the noun *Heroin*.]

It is *lethal*.   [The adjective *lethal* describes the pronoun *It*.]

5.   An **adverb** describes an adjective, a verb, or another adverb. Many adverbs end in *-ly*.

Heroin is *very* dangerous.   [The adverb *very* describes the adjective *dangerous*.]

Addiction occurs *quickly*.   [The adverb *quickly* describes the verb *occurs*.]

Addiction occurs *very* quickly.   [The adverb *very* describes the adverb *quickly*.]

6.   A **preposition** connects a noun, pronoun, or verb with some other information about it (*across, at, in, of, on, around, over,* and *to* are some prepositions).

Dealers often sell drugs *around* schools.   [The preposition *around* connects the noun *drugs* with the noun *school*.]

7.   A **conjunction** (*for, and, nor, but, or, yet, so*) connects words.

The Basic Sentence

A **sentence** is the basic unit of written communication. A complete sentence written in standard English must have three elements:

- A **subject**
- A **verb**
- A **complete thought**

Subjects

For a list of pronoun types, see page 209.

The **subject** of a sentence is the person, place, or thing that the sentence is about. The subject of the sentence can be a noun (a word that names the person, place, or thing) or a pronoun (a word that replaces the noun, such as *I, you, she,* or *they*).

To find the subject, ask yourself, "Who or what is the sentence about?"

PERSON AS SUBJECT
Vivian works for the police department.
[*Who* is the sentence about? *Vivian*]

THING AS SUBJECT
The tickets cost $65 apiece.
[*What* is the sentence about? The *tickets*]

A **compound subject** consists of two (or more) subjects joined by *and, or,* or *nor.*

TWO SUBJECTS   Nick and Chelsea have a new baby girl.

SEVERAL SUBJECTS   The jacket, pants, and sweater match perfectly.

SEVERAL SUBJECTS   Kim, Juan, or Melba will bring dessert.

A **prepositional phrase** is a word group that begins with a preposition and ends with a noun or pronoun. A **preposition** is a word that connects a noun, pronoun, or verb with some other information about it.
The subject of a sentence is *never* in a prepositional phrase.

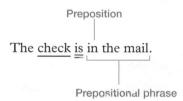

Preposition

The check is in the mail.

Prepositional phrase

The subject of the sentence is *check*. The subject cannot be the word *mail*, which is in the prepositional phrase *in the mail*.

Preposition

One of my best friends is a circus clown.

Prepositional phrase

Although the word *friends* may seem to be the subject of the sentence, it is not. *One* is the subject. The word *friends* is not the subject because it is in the prepositional phrase *of my best friends*.

When you are looking for the subject of a sentence in your writing, it may help to cross out any prepositional phrases, as in the following sentences.

The rules ~~about smoking~~ are posted everywhere.

The sound ~~of lightning striking a tree~~ is like gunfire.

Many ~~of the students~~ work part-time.

Common Prepositions

about	beneath	like	to
above	beside	near	toward
across	between	next to	under
after	by	of	until
against	down	off	up
along	during	on	upon
among	except	out	with
around	for	outside	within
at	from	over	without
before	in	past	
behind	inside	since	
below	into	through	

Verbs

Every sentence has a **main verb**, the word or words that tell what the subject does or that link the subject to another word that describes it. Verbs do not always immediately follow the subject: Other words may come between the subject and the verb.

There are three kinds of verbs—action verbs, linking verbs, and helping verbs.

ACTION VERBS

An **action verb** tells what action the subject performs.

To find the main action verb in a sentence, ask yourself, "What action does the subject perform?"

ACTION VERBS

The baby cried all night.

The building collapsed around midnight.

After work, we often go to Tallie's.

My aunt and uncle train service dogs.

LINKING VERBS

A **linking verb** connects (links) the subject to a word or group of words that describes the subject. Linking verbs show no action. The most common linking verb is *be,* along with all its forms (*am, is, are,* and so on). Other linking verbs, such as *seem* and *become,* can usually be replaced by the corresponding form of *be,* and the sentence will still make sense.

To find linking verbs, ask yourself, "What word joins the subject and the words that describe the subject?"

LINKING VERBS

The dinner is delicious.

I felt great this morning.

This lasagna tastes just like my mother's.

The doctor looks extremely tired.

Some words can be either action verbs or linking verbs, depending on how they are used in a particular sentence.

ACTION VERB   The <u>dog</u> <u>smelled</u> Jake's shoes.

LINKING VERB   The <u>dog</u> <u>smelled</u> terrible.

Common Linking Verbs

FORMS OF *BE*	FORMS OF *BECOME* AND *SEEM*	FORMS OF SENSE VERBS
am	become, becomes	appear, appears
are	became	appeared
is	seem, seems	feel, feels, felt
was	seemed	look, looks
were		looked
		smell, smells
		smelled
		taste, tastes, tasted

HELPING VERBS

A **helping verb** joins with the main verb in the sentence to form the **complete verb**. The helping verb is often a form of the verb *be, have,* or *do.* A sentence may have more than one helping verb along with the main verb.

Helping verb **+** Main verb **=** Complete verb

HELPING VERBS + MAIN VERBS

Sunil <u>was talking</u> on his cell phone.

[The helping verb is *was*, and the main verb is *talking*. The complete verb is *was talking*.]

Charisse <u>is taking</u> three courses this semester.

Tomas <u>has missed</u> the last four meetings.

My brother <u>might have passed</u> the test.

Common Helping Verbs

FORMS OF *BE*	FORMS OF *HAVE*	FORMS OF *DO*	OTHER
am	have	do	can
are	has	does	could
been	had	did	may
being			might
is			must
was			should
were			will
			would

Complete Thoughts

A **complete thought** is an idea that is expressed in a sentence and that makes sense by itself, without other sentences. An incomplete thought leaves readers wondering what is going on.

INCOMPLETE THOUGHT   as I was leaving [*What is going on?*]

COMPLETE THOUGHT   The <u>phone</u> <u>rang</u> as I was leaving.

INCOMPLETE THOUGHT   the <u>people</u> selling the car [*What is going on?*]

COMPLETE THOUGHT   The <u>people</u> selling the car <u>placed</u> the ad.

To identify a complete thought, ask yourself, "Do I know what is going on, or do I have to ask a question to understand?"

INCOMPLETE THOUGHT   in the apartment next door

[Do I know what is going on, or do I have to ask a question to understand? *You would have to ask a question, so this is not a complete thought.*]

COMPLETE THOUGHT   <u>Carlos</u> <u>lives</u> in the apartment next door.

Six Basic Sentence Patterns

In English, there are six basic sentence patterns, some of which you have already worked with in this chapter. Although there are other patterns, they build on these six.

1. Subject-Verb (S-V)

This is the most basic pattern, as you have already seen.

    S   V

<u>Airplanes</u> <u>pollute</u>.

2. Subject-Linking Verb-Noun (S-LV-N)

  S LV   N

<u>Fuel</u> <u>is</u> a pollutant.

3. Subject-Linking Verb-Adjective (S-LV-ADJ)

   S   LV   ADJ

<u>Travel</u> <u>seems</u> cheap.

4. Subject-Verb-Adverb (S-V-ADV)

    S   V   ADV

<u>Pollution</u> <u>costs</u> dearly.

5. **Subject-Verb-Direct Object (S-V-DO)**

    A *direct object* directly receives the action of the verb.

    S   V   DO
    It degrades ozone.

6. **Subject-Verb-Indirect Object-Direct Object**

    An *indirect object* does not directly receive the action of the verb.

    S   V   IO   DO
    Biofuels offer us hope.

16

The Four Most Serious Errors

This chapter emphasizes four major grammar errors that people most often notice.

These four errors may make your meaning harder to understand, and they definitely give readers a bad impression of you. It is like going for a job interview in pajamas. People *will* notice. Learning how to correct these errors will make a big difference in your writing.

In the examples in this chapter, subjects are underlined once and verbs are underlined twice.

1. Fragments
2. Run-ons: fused sentences
3. Problems with subject-verb agreement
4. Problems with verb form and tense

Fragments

A **fragment** is a group of words that is missing a subject or a verb or that does not express a complete thought.

SENTENCE   <u>I</u> <u>am going</u> to a concert on Friday at Memorial Arena.

FRAGMENT   <u>I</u> <u>am going</u> to a concert on Friday. *At Memorial Arena.*

                 [*At Memorial Arena* does not have a subject or a verb.]

✓ **LearningCurve** For extra practice in the skills covered in this chapter, visit bedfordstmartins.com/reinteractive.

To find fragments in your own writing, look for the five kinds of fragments discussed in this chapter. When you find a fragment, you can usually correct it in one of two ways.

WAYS TO CORRECT FRAGMENTS

- Add what is missing (a subject, a verb, or both).
- Attach the fragment to the sentence before or after it.

Fragments That Start with Prepositions

Whenever a preposition starts what you think is a sentence, check for a subject, a verb, and a complete thought. If any one of those is missing, you have a fragment.

For a list of common prepositions, see page 212.

FRAGMENT   The plane crashed into the house. *With a deafening roar.*

[*With a deafening roar* is a prepositional phrase that starts with the preposition *with*. The phrase has neither a subject nor a verb. It is a fragment.]

Correct the fragment by connecting it to the sentence either before or after it. If you connect the fragment to the sentence after it, put a comma after the fragment to join it to the sentence.

FRAGMENT   The plane crashed into the house. *From a height of eight hundred feet.*

CORRECTED   The plane crashed into the house, From a height of eight hundred feet.

CORRECTED   From a height of eight hundred feet, the plane crashed into the house.

Fragments That Start with Dependent Words

A **dependent word** (also called a **subordinating conjunction**) is the first word in a dependent clause, which does not express a complete thought even though it has a subject and a verb. Whenever a dependent word starts what you think is a sentence, look for a subject, a verb, and, especially, a complete thought.

FRAGMENT   Leila is still out of work. *Even though the economy is recovering.*

[*Even though* introduces the dependent clause *even though the economy is recovering*. The clause has a subject, *economy,* and a verb, *is recovering,* but it does not express a complete thought.]

Correct the fragment by connecting it to the sentence either before or after it. If you connect the fragment to the sentence after it, put a comma after the fragment to join it to the sentence.

FRAGMENT	I took the bus. *Because* I missed my ride.
CORRECTED	I took the bus because I missed my ride.
CORRECTED	Because I missed my ride, I took the bus.

Common Dependent Words

after	if	what(ever)
although	since	when(ever)
as	so that	where
because	that	whether
before	though	which(ever)
even though	unless	while
how	until	who/whose

Fragments That Start with *-ing* Verb Forms

An *-ing* **verb form** (also called a **gerund**) is the form of a verb that ends in -ing: *walking, writing, swimming.* Unless it has a helping verb (*was walking, was writing, was swimming*), it is not a complete verb in a sentence. Sometimes an *-ing* verb form is used as a subject at the beginning of a complete sentence.

-ING FORM USED AS A SUBJECT

Swimming is a wonderful form of exercise.

[In this sentence, *swimming* is the subject and *is* is the verb.]

-ING FORM USED WITH A HELPING VERB AS A VERB

I *am working* full-time this semester.

[In this sentence, *am* is the helping verb; *am working* is the complete verb.]

Whenever a word group begins with a word in *-ing* form, look carefully to see if the word group contains a subject and a verb and if it expresses a complete thought.

FRAGMENT   Snoring so loudly I couldn't sleep.

[If *snoring* is the main verb, what is the subject? There isn't one. Is there a helping verb used with *snoring*? No. It is a fragment.]

Correct a fragment that starts with an *-ing* verb form either by adding whatever sentence elements are missing (usually a subject and a helping verb) or by connecting the fragment to the sentence before or after it. Usually, you will need to put a comma before or after the fragment to join it to the complete sentence.

-*ING* FRAGMENT   *Working two jobs and going to school.* I am tired all the time.

CORRECTED   Working two jobs and going to school, I am tired all the time.

CORRECTED   *I am working*
~~Working~~ two jobs and going to school. I am tired all the time.

Fragments That Start with *to* and a Verb

An **infinitive** is the word *to* plus a verb — *to hire, to eat, to study*. Although they contain verbs, infinitive forms function as nouns, adjectives, or adverbs.

If a word group begins with *to* and a verb, it must have another verb or it is not a complete sentence.

FRAGMENT   Last week, a couple in New York fulfilled their wedding fantasy. *To get married on the top of the Empire State Building.*

[The first word group is a sentence, with *couple* as the subject, and *fulfilled* as the verb. In the second word group, there is no subject or verb outside of the infinitive.]

Correct a fragment that starts with *to* and a verb by connecting it to the sentence before or after it or by adding the missing sentence elements (a subject and a verb).

FRAGMENT   *To save on her monthly gas bills.* Tammy sold her SUV and got a hybrid car.

CORRECTED   To save on her monthly gas bills, Tammy sold her SUV and got a hybrid car.

CORRECTED   *Tammy wanted to*   *She*
~~To~~ save on her monthly gas bills. ~~Tammy~~ sold her SUV and got a hybrid car.

Fragments That Are Examples or Explanations

As you edit your writing, pay special attention to groups of words that are examples or explanations of information you presented in the previous sentences. These word groups may be fragments.

> **FRAGMENT**   <u>Parking</u> on this campus <u>is</u> a real nightmare. *Especially between 8:00 and 8:30 a.m.*
>
> [The second word group has no subject and no verb.]

Finding fragments that start with examples or explanations can be difficult, because there is no single kind of word to look for. The following are a few starting words that may signal an example or explanation, but fragments that are examples or explanations do not always start with these words:

especially   for example   like   such as

When a group of words that you think is a sentence gives an example or explanation of information in the previous sentence, stop to see if it has a subject and a verb and if it expresses a complete thought. If it is missing any of these elements, it is a fragment.

> **FRAGMENT**   The <u>Web</u> <u>has</u> many job search sites. *Such as Monster.com.*
>
> [Does the second word group have a subject? No. A verb? No. It is a fragment.]

To correct a fragment that starts with an example or an explanation, connect it either to the previous sentence or to the next one. Sometimes, you can add the missing sentence elements (a subject, a verb, or both) instead. When you connect the fragment to a sentence, you may need to reword or to change some punctuation. For example, fragments that are examples and fragments that are negatives are often set off by commas.

> **FRAGMENT**   <u>I</u> <u>pushed</u> seven different voice-mail buttons before I spoke to a real person. *Not a helpful one, though.*

> **CORRECTED**   <u>I</u> <u>pushed</u> seven different voice-mail buttons before I spoke to a real person. ~~Not a helpful one, though.~~ *, though not a helpful one.*

> **CORRECTED**   <u>I</u> <u>pushed</u> seven different voice-mail buttons before I spoke to a real person. ~~Not a~~ *He was not* helpful ~~one~~, though.

Run-Ons

A sentence is also called an **independent clause**, a group of words with a subject and a verb that expresses a complete thought. Sometimes, two independent clauses can be joined correctly in one sentence.

SENTENCES WITH TWO INDEPENDENT CLAUSES

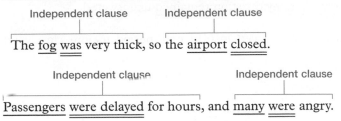

A **run-on** is two complete sentences (independent clauses) that are joined incorrectly and written as one sentence. There are two kinds of run-ons—fused sentences and comma splices.

A **fused sentence** is two complete sentences joined without any punctuation.

Independent clause   Independent clause

FUSED SENTENCE   Anger is a dangerous emotion it has many bad effects.

No punctuation

A **comma splice** is two complete sentences joined by only a comma instead of a comma and one of these words: *and, but, for, nor, or, so, yet.*

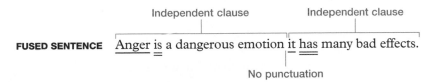

COMMA SPLICE   Anger is a dangerous emotion, it has many bad effects.

Comma

These words are known as coordinating conjunctions. They are discussed on page 224.

When you find a run-on in your writing, you can correct it in one of three ways.

WAYS TO CORRECT A RUN-ON

- Add a period or a semicolon.
- Add a comma and a coordinating conjunction.
- Add a dependent word.

Add a Period or a Semicolon

You can correct a run-on by adding a period to make two separate sentences.

> **RUN-ONS (corrected)**
>
> I called about my bill. I got four useless recorded messages.
>
> . M
> I finally hung up, my question remained unanswered.

A semicolon (;) can be used instead of a period to join closely related sentences.

> **RUN-ONS (corrected)**
>
> ;
> My father had a heart attack he is in the hospital.
>
> ;
> My mother called 911, the ambulance was there in just under four minutes.

A semicolon is sometimes used before a transition from one independent clause to another, and the transition word is followed by a comma.

> **TRANSITION BETWEEN SENTENCES**
>
>   Transition
>
> I tried to visit my father; however, I had no ride.
>
>   Semicolon   Comma

Add a Comma and a Coordinating Conjunction

TIP Note that there is no comma *after* a coordinating conjunction.

Another way to correct a run-on is to add a comma and a **coordinating conjunction**: a link that joins independent clauses to form one sentence. Some people remember the seven coordinating conjunctions (*and, but, for, nor, or, so, yet*) by using the memory device of *fanboys*, for **f**or, **a**nd, **n**or, **b**ut, **o**r, **y**et, **s**o.

To correct a fused sentence, add both a comma and a coordinating conjunction. A comma splice already has a comma, so just add a coordinating conjunction that makes sense in the sentence.

> **FUSED SENTENCE (corrected)**
>
> , and
> Tim hit another car he went through the windshield.

> **COMMA SPLICE (corrected)**
>
> but
> He is driving again, he always wears his seat belt.

Add a Dependent Word

A final way to correct a run-on is to make one of the complete sentences a dependent clause by adding a dependent word (a **subordinating conjunction** or a **relative pronoun**), such as *after, because, before, even though, if, though, unless,* or *when.* Choose the dependent word that best expresses the relationship between the two clauses.

RUN-ONS (corrected)

Dependent clause

When I got to the ice cream shop it was crowded.

Dependent word

Dependent clause

The ice cream melted fast, *because* it was really hot out.

Dependent word

When the dependent clause starts off the sentence, you need to add a comma after it, as in the first example above. When the dependent clause is after the independent clause, there is no comma, as in the second example.

Common Dependent Words

after	if	what(ever)
although	since	when(ever)
as	so that	where
because	that	whether
before	though	which(ever)
even though	unless	while
how	until	who/whose

A Word That Can Cause Run-Ons: *Then*

Many run-ons are caused by the word *then.* You can use *then* to join two sentences, but if you add it without the correct punctuation and/or joining word, the resulting sentence will be a run-on. To correct a run-on caused by the word *then,* you can use any of the four methods presented in this chapter.

COMMA SPLICE	I grabbed the remote, then I ate my pizza.
CORRECTED	I grabbed the remote. then I ate my pizza.
	[period added]
CORRECTED	I grabbed the remote; then I ate my pizza.
	[semicolon added]
CORRECTED	I grabbed the remote, *and* then I ate my pizza.
	[coordinating conjunction *and* added]
CORRECTED	I grabbed the remote, *before* then I ate my pizza.
	[dependent word *before* added to make a dependent clause]

Problems with Subject-Verb Agreement

In any sentence, **the subject and the verb must match—or agree—in number**. If the subject is singular (one person, place, or thing), then the verb must also be singular. If the subject is plural (more than one), the verb must also be plural.

SINGULAR	The phone rings constantly at work.
	[The subject, *phone,* is singular—just one phone—so the verb must take the singular form: *rings.*]
PLURAL	The phones ring constantly at work.
	[The subject, *phones,* is plural—more than one phone—so the verb must take the plural form: *ring.*]

For more on regular verbs and how they differ from irregular verbs, see pages 231–32.

Regular verbs follow standard English patterns. For regular verbs in the present tense, only third-person singular verbs take an ending, and that ending is -*s*.

Regular Verbs, Present Tense

	SINGULAR FORM	PLURAL FORM
First person	I walk.	We walk.
Second person	You walk.	You walk.

	SINGULAR FORM	PLURAL FORM
Third person	He/she/it walks.	They walk.
	Percy walks.	Percy and Don walk.
	The dog walks.	The dogs walk.

To find problems with subject-verb agreement in your own writing, look for the five trouble spots that follow.

The Verb Is a Form of *Be, Have,* or *Do*

The verbs *be, have,* and *do* do not follow the regular patterns for forming singular and plural forms; they are **irregular verbs**.

These verbs cause problems for people who use only one form of the verb in casual conversation: *You be the richest* (incorrect). *You are the richest* (correct). In college and at work, use the correct form of the verbs *be, have,* and *do* as shown in the charts on the next page.

> *are*
> You ~~is~~ the craziest person I have ever known.
>   ∧
>   *has*
> Johnson ~~have~~ the best car in the lot.
>   *does*∧
> Valery ~~do~~ the bill paying on the first of every month.
>   ∧

Forms of the Verb *Be*

PRESENT TENSE	SINGULAR	PLURAL
First person	I am	we are
Second person	you are	you are
Third person	she/he/it is	they are
	the student/Joe is	the students are

PAST TENSE	SINGULAR	PLURAL
First person	I was	we were
Second person	you were	you were
Third person	she/he/it was	they were
	the student/Joe was	the students were

Forms of the Verb *Have*, Present Tense

	SINGULAR	PLURAL
First person	I have	we have
Second person	you have	you have
Third person	she/he/it has	they have
	the student/Joe has	the students have

Forms of the Verb *Do*, Present Tense

	SINGULAR	PLURAL
First person	I do	we do
Second person	you do	you do
Third person	she/he/it does	they do
	the student/Joe does	the students do

Words Come between the Subject and the Verb

When the subject and the verb are not right next to each other, it can be difficult to make sure that they agree. Most often, what comes between the subject and the verb is either a prepositional phrase or a dependent clause.

PREPOSITIONAL PHRASE BETWEEN THE SUBJECT AND THE VERB

A **prepositional phrase** starts with a preposition and ends with a noun or pronoun: The line *for the movie* went *around the corner.*

For a list of common prepositions, see page 212.

Remember, the subject of a sentence is never in a prepositional phrase. When you are looking for the subject, you can cross out any prepositional phrases. This strategy should help you find the real subject and decide whether it agrees with the verb.

DEPENDENT CLAUSE BETWEEN THE SUBJECT AND THE VERB

A **dependent clause** has a subject and a verb, but it does not express a complete thought. When a dependent clause comes between the subject and the verb, it usually starts with the word *who, whose, whom, that,* or *which.*

The subject of a sentence is never in the dependent clause. When you are looking for the subject, you can cross out any dependent clauses.

The Sentence Has a Compound Subject

A **compound subject** consists of two (or more) subjects connected by *and, or,* or *nor* (as in *neither/nor* expressions). If two subjects are joined by *and,* they combine to become a plural subject, and the verb must take a plural form as well.

If two subjects are connected by *or* or *nor,* they are considered separate, and the verb should agree with the subject closest to it.

Subject *nor* Singular subject Singular form of verb

Neither the director *nor* the producer wants to give up control.

Subject *or* Plural subject Plural form of verb

The director *or* his assistants decide how the film will be made.

Subject *nor* Plural subject Plural form of verb

Neither the director *nor* his assistants want to give up control.

The Subject Is an Indefinite Pronoun

Indefinite pronouns, which refer to unspecified people or objects, are often singular, although there are exceptions.

When you find an indefinite pronoun in your writing, use the following to help you determine the correct verb form, singular or plural. If the pronoun may be singular or plural, you will need to check whether the word it refers to is singular or plural to determine what verb form to use.

Indefinite Pronouns

ALWAYS SINGULAR (USE THE *IS* FORM OF *BE*)

anybody	everyone	nothing
anyone	everything	one (of)
anything	much	somebody
each (of)	neither (of)	someone
either (of)	nobody	something
everybody	no one	

ALWAYS PLURAL (USE THE *ARE* FORM OF *BE*)

both	many

MAY BE SINGULAR OR PLURAL (USE THE *IS* OR *ARE* FORM)

all	none
any	some

Everyone loves vacations.

[*Everyone* is always singular, so it takes the singular verb *loves*.]

Some of the wreckage <u>was recovered</u> after the crash.

[In this case, *some* is singular, referring to *wreckage,* so it takes the singular verb *was recovered.*]

Some of the workers <u>were delayed</u> by the storm.

[In this case, *some* is plural, referring to *workers,* so it takes the plural verb *were delayed.*]

The Verb Comes before the Subject

In most sentences, the subject comes before the verb. Two kinds of sentences reverse that order—questions and sentences that begin with *here* or *there*.

To find the subject and verb in these types of sentences, you can turn them around.

<u>Are</u> the <u>keys</u> in the car? The <u>keys</u> <u>are</u> in the car.

Here <u>are</u> the <u>hot dog rolls</u>. The <u>hot dog rolls</u> <u>are</u> here.

Problems with Verb Tense

Verb tense tells *when* the action of a sentence occurs—in the present, in the past, or in the future. Verbs change their form and use the helping verbs *have* or *be* to indicate different tenses.

PRESENT TENSE	<u>Teresa</u> and <u>I</u> <u>talk</u> every day.
PAST TENSE	Yesterday, <u>we</u> <u>talked</u> for two hours.
FUTURE TENSE	Tomorrow, <u>we</u> <u>will talk</u> again.
PRESENT TENSE	<u>Krystal</u> <u>plays</u> varsity basketball.
PAST TENSE	<u>Alicia</u> <u>washed</u> dirty dishes all night.

Regular Verbs

To avoid mistakes with regular verbs, understand the basic patterns for forming the present, past, and future tenses.

PRESENT-TENSE ENDINGS

The **simple present tense** is used for actions that are happening at the same time that you are writing about them and about actions that are ongoing. There are two forms for the simple present tense of regular verbs——*-s* **ending** or **no added ending**. Use the -*s* ending when the subject is *she, he,* or *it,* or the name of one person or thing. Do not add any ending for other subjects.

Regular Verbs in the Simple Present Tense

	SINGULAR	PLURAL
First person	I laugh.	We laugh.
Second person	You laugh.	You laugh.
Third person	She/he/it laughs.	They laugh.
	The baby laughs.	The babies laugh.

PAST-TENSE ENDINGS

The **simple past tense** is used for actions that have already happened. An -*ed* or -*d* **ending** is needed for all regular verbs in the past tense.

	SIMPLE PRESENT	SIMPLE PAST
First person	I rush to work.	I rushed to work.
Second person	You lock the door.	You locked the door.
Third person	Rufus lives nearby.	Rufus lived nearby.

The past-tense form of regular verbs can also serve as the past participle, which can be paired with a helping verb such as *have.* (To learn about when past participles are used, see pages 236–37.)

PAST TENSE   My car stalled.

PAST PARTICIPLE   My car has stalled often.

Irregular Verbs

Unlike regular verbs, which have past-tense forms that end in -*ed* or -*d,* **irregular verbs** change spelling or sometimes do not change at all from the present-tense form.

The most common irregular verbs are *be, have,* and *do.* (see pages 233–36).

As you write and edit, consult the following chart to make sure that you use the correct form of irregular verbs.

NOTE: What is called "Present Tense" in the chart below is sometimes called the base form of the verb.

Irregular Verb Forms

PRESENT TENSE	PAST TENSE	PAST PARTICIPLE (used with helping verb)
be (am/are/is)	was/were	been
become	became	become
begin	began	begun
bite	bit	bitten
blow	blew	blown
break	broke	broken
bring	brought	brought
build	built	built
buy	bought	bought
catch	caught	caught
choose	chose	chosen
come	came	come
cost	cost	cost
dive	dived, dove	dived
do	did	done
draw	drew	drawn
drink	drank	drunk
drive	drove	driven
eat	ate	eaten
fall	fell	fallen
feed	fed	fed
feel	felt	felt

PRESENT TENSE	PAST TENSE	PAST PARTICIPLE (used with helping verb)
fight	fought	fought
find	found	found
fly	flew	flown
forget	forgot	forgotten
freeze	froze	frozen
get	got	gotten
give	gave	given
go	went	gone
grow	grew	grown
have/has	had	had
hear	heard	heard
hide	hid	hidden
hit	hit	hit
hold	held	held
hurt	hurt	hurt
keep	kept	kept
know	knew	known
lay	laid	laid
leave	left	left
let	let	let
lie	lay	lain
light	lit	lit
lose	lost	lost
make	made	made
mean	meant	meant
meet	met	met
pay	paid	paid

PRESENT TENSE	PAST TENSE	PAST PARTICIPLE (used with helping verb)
put	put	put
quit	quit	quit
read	read	read
ride	rode	ridden
ring	rang	rung
rise	rose	risen
run	ran	run
say	said	said
see	saw	seen
sell	sold	sold
send	sent	sent
set (to place)	set	set
shake	shook	shaken
show	showed	shown
shrink	shrank	shrunk
shut	shut	shut
sing	sang	sung
sink	sank	sunk
sit (to be seated)	sat	sat
sleep	slept	slept
speak	spoke	spoken
spend	spent	spent
stand	stood	stood
steal	stole	stolen
stick	stuck	stuck
sting	stung	stung
strike	struck	struck, stricken

PRESENT TENSE	PAST TENSE	PAST PARTICIPLE (used with helping verb)
swim	swam	swum
take	took	taken
teach	taught	taught
tear	tore	torn
tell	told	told
think	thought	thought
throw	threw	thrown
understand	understood	understood
wake	woke	woken
wear	wore	worn
win	won	won
write	wrote	written

Past Participles

A **past participle**, by itself, cannot be the main verb of a sentence. When a past participle is combined with another verb, called a **helping verb**, however, it can be used to make the present perfect tense and the past perfect tense.

The **present perfect tense** is used for an action that began in the past and either continues into the present or was completed at some unknown time in the past.

My <u>car</u> <u>has stalled</u> several times recently.

The **past perfect tense** is used for an action that began and ended in the past before some other past action took place. It is formed as follows.

My <u>head</u> <u>had ached</u> for a week before <u>I</u> <u>called</u> a doctor.

[Both of the actions (*head ached* and *I called*) happened in the past, but the ache happened before the calling.]

Be careful not to confuse the simple past tense with the past perfect tense.

SIMPLE PAST TENSE   My daughter left.

[One action (the daughter leaving) occurred in the past.]

PAST PERFECT TENSE   By the time Jill arrived, my daughter had left.

[Two actions (Jill's arrival and the daughter leaving) occurred in the past, but the daughter left before Jill's arrival.]

Passive Voice

A sentence that is written in the **passive voice** has a subject that performs no action. Instead, the subject is acted upon. To create the passive voice, combine a form of the verb *be* with a past participle.

PASSIVE   The memo was written by an employee.

[The subject, *memo,* did not write itself. An employee wrote the memo, but the subject in the sentence, *memo,* performs no action.]

In sentences that use the **active voice**, the subject performs the action.

ACTIVE   An employee wrote the memo.

Use the passive voice when no one person performed the action, when you don't know who performed the action, or when you want to emphasize the receiver of the action. Use the active voice whenever possible, and use passive voice sparingly.

PASSIVE   The dog was hit by a passing car.

[If the writer wants to focus on the dog as the receiver of the action, the passive voice is acceptable.]

ACTIVE   A passing car hit the dog.

17

Other Grammar
and Style Concerns

In addition to checking your writing for the four most serious errors covered in Chapter 16, you will want to be aware of common trouble spots in other areas of grammar and style: pronouns, adjectives and adverbs, modifiers, co-ordination and subordination, parallelism, sentence variety, and word choice. Matters of punctuation and capitalization are covered in Chapter 18.

Pronouns

Pronouns replace nouns (or other pronouns) in a sentence so that you do not have to repeat the nouns.

> *her*
> Tessa let me borrow ~~Tessa's~~ jacket.
> ⌃

> *He*
> You have met Carl. ~~Carl~~ is my cousin.
> ⌃

The noun (or pronoun) that a pronoun replaces is called the **antecedent**. The word *antecedent* means "something that comes before." In most cases, a pronoun refers to a specific antecedent nearby. In the second example above, "Carl" is the antecedent and "He" is the pronoun that replaces "Carl."

There are three basic types of pronouns — **subject** pronouns, **object** pronouns, and **possessive** pronouns. Note the pronouns in the following sentences.

> Object   Subject
> | |
> The linebacker tackled him, and he went down hard.

> Possessive
> |
> His shoulder was injured.

✓ **LearningCurve** For extra practice in the skills covered in this chapter, visit
bedfordstmartins.com/reinteractive.

Pronoun Types

	SUBJECT	OBJECT	POSSESSIVE
First person (singular/plural)	I/we	me/us	my, mine/our, ours
Second person (singular/plural)	you/you	you/you	your, yours/your, yours
Third person (singular)	he, she, it who	him, her, it whom	his, her, hers, ito whose
Third person (plural)	they	them	their, theirs

Check for Pronoun Agreement

A pronoun must agree with (match) the noun or pronoun it refers to in number: It must be singular (one) or plural (more than one). If it is singular, it must also match its noun or pronoun in gender (*he, she,* or *it*).

CONSISTENT   Sherry talked to *her* aunt.

[*Her* agrees with *Sherry* because both are singular and feminine.]

CONSISTENT   The Romanos sold *their* restaurant.

[*Their* agrees with *Romanos* because both are plural.]

Watch out for singular nouns that are not specific. If a noun is singular, the pronoun must be singular as well.

INCONSISTENT   An athlete can tell you about *their* commitment to practice.

[*Athlete* is singular, but the pronoun *their* is plural.]

CONSISTENT   An athlete can tell you about *his* or *her* commitment to practice.

[*Athlete* is singular, and so are the pronouns *his* and *her*.]

As an alternative to using the phrase *his or her,* make the subject plural if you can. (For more on this, see the note below.)

CONSISTENT   All athletes can tell you about *their* commitment to practice.

Two types of words often cause errors in pronoun agreement—indefinite pronouns and collective nouns.

INDEFINITE PRONOUNS

An **indefinite pronoun** does not refer to a specific person, place, or thing; it is general. Indefinite pronouns often take singular verbs. Whenever a pronoun refers to an indefinite person, place, or thing, check for agreement.

TIP Focus on the "significant seven" indefinite pronouns: *any, each, either, neither,* and words ending in *-one, -thing,* or *-body.*

>   *his*
> Someone forgot ~~their~~ coat.

>   *his or her*
> Everybody practiced ~~their~~ lines.

NOTE: Although it is grammatically correct, using a masculine pronoun (*he, his,* or *him*) alone to refer to a singular indefinite pronoun such as *everyone* is now considered sexist. Here are two ways to avoid this problem:

1.   Use *his or her.*

> Someone forgot his or her coat.

2.   Change the sentence so that the pronoun refers to a plural noun or pronoun.

> The children forgot their coats.

Indefinite Pronouns

ALWAYS SINGULAR (USE THE *IS* FORM OF *BE*)		
anybody	everyone	nothing
anyone	everything	one (of)
anything	much	somebody
each (of)	neither (of)	someone
either (of)	nobody	something
everybody	no one	

ALWAYS PLURAL (USE THE *ARE* FORM OF *BE*)	
both	many

MAY BE SINGULAR OR PLURAL (USE THE *IS* OR *ARE* FORM OF *BE*)	
all	none
any	some

COLLECTIVE NOUNS

A **collective noun** names a group that acts as a single unit. Some common collective nouns are *audience, class, company, crowd, family, government, group,* and *society.*

Collective nouns are usually singular, so when you use a pronoun to refer to a collective noun, it too must usually be singular.

The class had ~~their~~ *its* final exam at 8:00 a.m.

The group turned in ~~their~~ *its* report.

If the people in a group are acting as individuals, however, the noun is plural and should be used with a plural pronoun.

The audience took *their* seats.

The drenched crowd huddled under *their* umbrellas.

Make Pronoun Reference Clear

If the reader isn't sure what a pronoun refers to, the sentence may be confusing.

AVOID AMBIGUOUS OR VAGUE PRONOUN REFERENCES

In an **ambiguous pronoun reference**, the pronoun could refer to more than one noun.

AMBIGUOUS	Michelle told Carla that she needed new shoes.
	[Did Michelle tell Carla that Michelle herself needed new shoes? Or did Michelle tell Carla that Carla needed new shoes?]
EDITED	Michelle needed new shoes. She told her friend Carla.

In a **vague pronoun reference**, the pronoun does not refer clearly to any particular person or thing. To correct a vague pronoun reference, substitute a more specific noun for the pronoun.

VAGUE	After an accident at the intersection, they installed a traffic light.
	[Who installed the traffic light?]
EDITED	After an accident at the intersection, the highway department installed a traffic light.

AVOID REPETITIOUS PRONOUN REFERENCES

In a **repetitious pronoun reference**, the pronoun repeats a reference to a noun rather than replacing the noun. Remove the repetitious pronoun.

The police officer ~~he~~ told me I had not stopped at the sign.

The sign,/~~it~~ was hidden by a tree.

Use the Right Type of Pronoun

As you can see on the chart on page 239, there are several types of pronouns—*subject* pronouns, *object* pronouns, and *possessive* pronouns, each of which has a different function.

Subject Pronouns

For more on subjects, see Chapter 15.

Subject pronouns serve as the subject of a verb.

She took my parking space.

I honked my horn.

Object Pronouns

Object pronouns either receive the action of a verb (the object of the verb) or are part of a prepositional phrase (the object of the preposition).

OBJECT OF THE VERB	Carolyn asked *me* to drive.
	Carolyn gave *me* the keys.
OBJECT OF THE PREPOSITION	Carolyn gave the keys to *me*.

Possessive Pronouns

Possessive pronouns show ownership. Note that you never need an apostrophe with a possessive pronoun.

Giselle is *my* best friend.

That jacket is *hers*.

Certain kinds of sentences can make choosing the right type of pronoun a little more difficult — ones that have compound subjects or objects; ones that make a comparison; and ones where you have to choose between *who* or *whom*.

PRONOUNS USED WITH COMPOUND SUBJECTS AND OBJECTS

A **compound subject** has more than one subject joined by a conjunction such as *and* or *or*. A **compound object** has more than one object joined by a conjunction.

COMPOUND SUBJECT	Tim and *I* work together.
COMPOUND OBJECT	Kayla baked the cookies for Jim and *me*.

To decide what type of pronoun to use in a compound construction, try leaving out the other part of the compound and the conjunction. Then, say the sentence aloud to yourself.

~~Jerome and~~ (me /Ⓘ) like chili dogs.
[Think: *I* like chili dogs.]

The package was for ~~Karen and~~ (she /her).
[Think: The package was for *her*.]

When you are writing about yourself and others, always put the others first, choosing the correct type of pronoun.

INCORRECT	Gene bought the tickets for *me* and my friends.
CORRECT	Gene bought the tickets for my friends and *me*.
	[Sentence puts others first and uses the object pronoun, *me*]

If a pronoun is part of a compound object in a prepositional phrase, use an object pronoun.

> Please keep that information just between you and *me*.
>
> [*Between you and me* is a prepositional phrase, so it uses the object pronoun, *me*.]

Many people make the mistake of writing *between you and I*. The correct pronoun is the object pronoun, *me*.

PRONOUNS USED IN COMPARISONS

Using the wrong type of pronoun in comparisons can give a sentence an unintended meaning. Editing sentences that contain comparisons can be tricky because comparisons often imply words that are not actually included in the sentence.

To find comparisons, look for the words *than* or *as*. To decide whether to use a subject or object pronoun in a comparison, try adding the implied words and saying the sentence aloud.

> Bill likes Chinese food more than *me*.
>
> [This sentence means Bill likes Chinese food more than he likes me. The implied words after *than* are *he likes*.]
>
> Bill likes Chinese food more than *I*.
>
> [This sentence means Bill likes Chinese food more than I like it. The implied word after *I* is *do*.]
>
> The professor knows more than (us / we).
>
> [Think: The professor knows more than *we know*.]
>
> Jen likes other professors more than (he / him).
>
> [Think: Jen likes other professors more than *she likes him*.]

CHOOSING BETWEEN WHO AND WHOM

Who is always a subject; use it if the pronoun performs an action. *Whom* is always an object; use it if the pronoun does not perform any action.

WHO = SUBJECT   Janis is the friend *who* introduced me to Billy.

WHOM = OBJECT   Billy is the man *whom* I met last night.

In most cases, for sentences where the pronoun is followed by a verb, use *who*. When the pronoun is followed by a noun or pronoun, use *whom*.

The person (who / whom) spoke was boring.

[The pronoun is followed by the verb *spoke*. Use *who*.]

The person (who / whom) I met was boring.

[The pronoun is followed by another pronoun: *I*. Use *whom*.]

Whoever is a subject pronoun; *whomever* is an object pronoun.

Make Pronouns Consistent

Pronouns have to be consistent in **person**, which is the point of view a writer uses. Pronouns may be in first person (*I, we*); second person (*you*); or third person (*he, she, it,* or *they*). (See the chart on page 239.)

INCONSISTENT PERSON	After *a caller* presses 1, *you* get a recording.
	[The sentence starts with the third person (*a caller*) but shifts to the second person (*you*).]
CONSISTENT PERSON	After *a caller* presses 1, *he or she* gets a recording.
CONSISTENT PERSON, PLURAL	After *callers* press 1, *they* get a recording.

Adjectives and Adverbs

Adjectives describe nouns (words that name people, places, or things) and pronouns (words that replace nouns). They add information about what kind, which one, or how many.

City traffic was *terrible* last night.

The highway was *congested* for *three* miles.

Two huge old tractor trailers had collided.

Adverbs describe verbs (words that tell what happens in a sentence), adjectives, or other adverbs. They add information about how, how much, when, where, why, or to what degree. Adverbs often end with *-ly*.

MODIFYING VERB	Dave drives *aggressively*.
MODIFYING ADJECTIVE	The *extremely* old woman swims every day.
MODIFYING ANOTHER ADVERB	Dave drives *very* aggressively.

Adjectives usually come *before* the words they modify; adverbs come either before or after. You can also use more than one adjective or adverb to modify a word.

adj   adj   adj noun verb   adv   adv

The happy, funny, old man spoke quickly and humorously.

Choosing between Adjective and Adverb Forms

Many adverbs are formed by adding *-ly* to the end of an adjective. To decide whether to use an adjective form or an adverb form, find the word you want to describe. If that word is a noun or a pronoun, use the adjective form. If it is a verb, an adjective, or another adverb, use the adverb form.

ADJECTIVE	ADVERB
The *new* student introduced himself.	The couple is *newly* married.
That is an *honest* answer.	Please answer *honestly*.

Adjectives and Adverbs in Comparisons

To compare two persons, places, or things, use the **comparative** form of adjectives or adverbs.

Sheehan drives *faster* than I do.

Francis is *more talkative* than Destina is.

To compare three or more persons, places, or things, use the **super-lative** form of adjectives or adverbs.

Sheehan drives the *fastest* of all our friends.

Francis is the *most talkative* of the children.

Comparative and Superlative Forms

ADJECTIVE OR ADVERB	COMPARATIVE	SUPERLATIVE
ADVERBS AND ADJECTIVES OF ONE SYLLABLE		
tall	taller	tallest
fast	faster	fastest
ADJECTIVES ENDING IN Y		
happy	happier	happiest
silly	sillier	silliest
ADVERBS AND ADJECTIVES OF MORE THAN ONE SYLLABLE		
graceful	more graceful	most graceful
gracefully	more gracefully	most gracefully
intelligent	more intelligent	most intelligent
intelligently	more intelligently	most intelligently

NOTE: Use either an ending (*-er* or *-est*) or an extra word (*more* or *most*) to form a comparative or superlative—not both at once.

One of the ~~most~~ easiest ways to beat stress is to exercise regularly.

It is ~~more~~ harder to study late at night than during the day.

Good, Well, Bad, and *Badly*

Four common adjectives and adverbs have irregular forms—*good, well, bad,* and *badly.*

People often are confused about whether to use *good* or *well. Good* is an adjective, so use it to describe a noun or pronoun. *Well* is an adverb, so use it to describe a verb or an adjective.

Forms of *Good, Well, Bad,* and *Badly*

	COMPARATIVE	SUPERLATIVE
ADJECTIVE		
good	better	best
bad	worse	worst
ADVERB		
well	better	best
badly	worse	worst

ADJECTIVE	She is a *good* friend.
ADVERB	He works *well* with his colleagues.

Well can also be an adjective to describe someone's health:

I am not *well* today.

Misplaced and Dangling Modifiers

Modifiers are words or word groups that describe other words in a sentence. If a modifier is not near the words it modifies, the sentence can be misleading or unintentionally funny.

Misplaced Modifiers

A **misplaced modifier,** because it is not correctly placed in the sentence, describes the wrong word or words. To correct a misplaced modifier, move the modifier as close as possible to the word or words it modifies. The safest choice is often to put the modifier directly before the sentence element it modifies.

MISPLACED   Rudy saw my dog *driving on the highway.*

[Was my dog driving a car? No, Rudy was, so the modifier must come right before or right after his name.]

CORRECT   *Driving on the highway,* Rudy saw my dog.

Four sentence constructions in particular often lead to misplaced modifiers:

1. Modifiers such as *only, almost, hardly, nearly,* and *just*

Molly ~~almost~~ slept for ten hours.   *almost*

[Was Molly awake, *almost* sleeping for ten hours? No, she slept for just under ten hours.]

2. Modifiers that start with *-ing* verbs

Using cash,
Timothy bought the car, ~~using cash.~~

[Note that when you move the phrase beginning with an *-ing* verb to the beginning of the sentence, you need to follow it with a comma.]

3. Modifiers that are prepositional phrases

With binoculars, we
~~We~~ saw the rare bird, ~~with binoculars.~~

4. Modifiers that are clauses starting with *who, whose, that,* or *which*

who call people during dinner
Telemarketers are sure to be annoying, ~~who call people during dinner.~~

Dangling Modifiers

A **dangling modifier** "dangles" because the word or words it is supposed to modify are not in the sentence. Dangling modifiers usually appear at the beginning of a sentence and may seem to modify the noun or pronoun that immediately follows—but they do not.

Correct dangling modifiers either by adding the word being modified right after the opening modifier or by adding the word being modified to the opening modifier. Note that to correct a dangling modifier, you might have to reword the sentence.

DANGLING	*Talking on the telephone,* the dinner burned.
	[Was the dinner talking on the telephone? No.]
CORRECT	*While Sharon was talking on the telephone,* the dinner burned.
	The dinner burned *while Sharon was talking on the telephone.*
DANGLING	*While waiting in line,* the alarms went off.
	[Were the alarms waiting in line? No.]
CORRECT	*While waiting in line,* I heard the alarms go off.
	While I was waiting in line, the alarms went off.

Coordination and Subordination

When you join two sentences, you can use either coordination or subordination.

Joining two sentences with related ideas can make your writing less choppy.

Coordination

In **coordination**, two complete sentences (independent clauses) are joined with a comma and a coordinating conjunction, a semicolon alone, or a semicolon and a conjunctive adverb.

| TWO SENTENCES | This internship is prestigious. Many interns have gone on to get good jobs. |

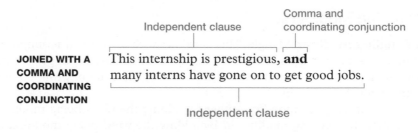

| JOINED WITH A COMMA AND COORDINATING CONJUNCTION | This internship is prestigious, **and** many interns have gone on to get good jobs. |

COORDINATING CONJUNCTIONS

| for | and | nor | but | or | yet | so |

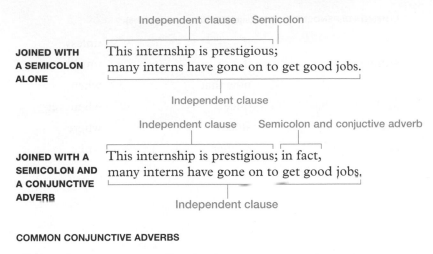

JOINED WITH A SEMICOLON ALONE

Independent clause — Semicolon

This internship is prestigious;
many interns have gone on to get good jobs.

Independent clause

JOINED WITH A SEMICOLON AND A CONJUNCTIVE ADVERB

Independent clause — Semicolon and conjuctive adverb

This internship is prestigious; in fact,
many interns have gone on to get good jobs.

Independent clause

COMMON CONJUNCTIVE ADVERBS

afterward	frequently	instead
also	however	still
as a result	in addition	then
besides	in fact	therefore
consequently		

Subordination

In **subordination**, you put a dependent word **(subordinating conjunction)** in front of one of the two sentences, which then becomes a dependent clause and is no longer a complete sentence.

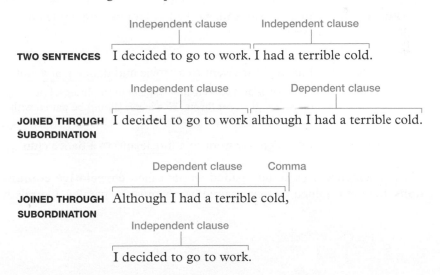

TWO SENTENCES

Independent clause — Independent clause

I decided to go to work. I had a terrible cold.

JOINED THROUGH SUBORDINATION

Independent clause — Dependent clause

I decided to go to work although I had a terrible cold.

JOINED THROUGH SUBORDINATION

Dependent clause — Comma

Although I had a terrible cold,

Independent clause

I decided to go to work.

COMMON DEPENDENT WORDS (subordinating conjunctions)

after	if	unless
although	if only	until
as	now that	when
as if	once	whenever
because	since	where
before	so that	while
even though		

Parallelism

Parallelism in writing means that similar parts in a sentence are balanced by having the same structure. When making comparisons or listing items in a series, put nouns with nouns, verbs with verbs, and phrases with phrases.

NOT PARALLEL   I like <u>math</u> more than <u>studying English</u>.

[*Math* is a noun, but *studying English* is a phrase.]

PARALLEL   I like <u>math</u> more than <u>English</u>.

NOT PARALLEL   In class, we <u>read</u>, <u>worked</u> in groups, and <u>were writing</u> an essay.

[Verbs must be in the same tense to be parallel.]

PARALLEL   In class, we <u>read</u>, <u>worked</u> in groups, and <u>wrote</u> an essay.

NOT PARALLEL   Last night we went <u>to a movie</u> and <u>dancing at a club</u>.

[*To a movie* and *dancing at a club* are both phrases, but they have different forms. *To a movie* should be paired with another prepositional phrase: *to a dance club*.]

PARALLEL   Last night we went <u>to a movie</u> and <u>to a dance club</u>.

When a sentence uses certain paired words called **correlative conjunctions**, the items joined by these paired words must be parallel. Correlative conjunctions, shown below, link two equal elements and show the relationship between them.

both . . . and	neither . . . nor	rather . . . than
either . . . or	not only . . . but also	

NOT PARALLEL Brianna dislikes *both* <u>fruit</u> *and* <u>eating vegetables</u>.

PARALLEL Brianna dislikes *both* <u>fruit</u> *and* <u>vegetables</u>.

NOT PARALLEL She would *rather* <u>eat</u> popcorn every night *than* <u>to cook</u>.

PARALLEL She would *rather* <u>eat</u> popcorn every night *than* <u>cook</u>.

Sentence Variety

Having **sentence variety** in your writing means using assorted sentence patterns, lengths, and rhythms. Here are some strategies for achieving more sentence variety in your writing.

Start Some Sentences with Adverbs

Adverbs are words that describe verbs, adjectives, or other adverbs; they often end with *-ly*. As long as the meaning is clear, you can place an adverb at the beginning of a sentence or near the word it describes. An adverb at the beginning is usually followed by a comma.

ADVERB AT BEGINNING *Frequently,* stories about haunted houses surface at Halloween.

ADVERB NEAR A VERB Stories about haunted houses *frequently* surface at Halloween.

Join Ideas Using an *-ing* Verb Form

One way to combine sentences is to turn one of them into a phrase using an **-ing verb form** (such as *walking* or *racing*). The *-ing* verb form indicates that the two parts of the sentence are happening at the same time. The more important idea (the one you want to emphasize) should be in the main clause, not in the phrase you make by adding the *-ing* verb form. In the examples that follow, the idea the writer wanted to emphasize is underlined.

TWO SENTENCES	<u>Jonah did well in the high jump</u>. He came in second.
JOINED WITH -*ING* VERB FORM	<u>Jonah did well in the high jump</u>, coming in second. Doing well in the high jump, <u>Jonah came in second.</u>

Join Ideas Using an *-ed* Verb Form

Another way to combine sentences is to turn one of them into a phrase using an **-ed verb form** (such as *waited* or *walked*). You can join sentences this way if one of them has a form of *be* as a helping verb along with the *-ed* verb form.

TWO SENTENCES	Leonardo da Vinci was a man of many talents. He was noted most often for his painting.
JOINED WITH -*ED* VERB FORM	Noted most often for his painting, Leonardo da Vinci was a man of many talents.

Join Ideas Using an Appositive

An **appositive** is a phrase that renames a noun. Appositives, which are nouns or noun phrases, can be used to combine two sentences into one.

TWO SENTENCES	Elvis Presley continues to be popular many years after his death. He is "the King."
JOINED WITH AN APPOSITIVE	Elvis Presley, "the King," continues to be popular many years after his death. [The phrase *"the King"* renames the noun *Elvis Presley*.]

Join Ideas Using an Adjective Clause

An **adjective clause** is a group of words with a subject and a verb that describes a noun. Adjective clauses often begin with the word *who, which,* or *that* and can be used to combine two sentences into one.

TWO SENTENCES	Lorene owns an art and framing store. She is a good friend of mine.
JOINED WITH AN ADJECTIVE CLAUSE	Lorene, who is a good friend of mine, owns an art and framing store.

NOTE: If an adjective clause can be taken out of a sentence without completely changing the meaning of the sentence, put commas around the clause.

Lorene, who is a good friend of mine, owns an art and framing store.

[The phrase *who is a good friend of mine* adds information about Lorene, but it is not essential; the sentence *Lorene owns an art and framing store* means almost the same thing as the sentence in the example.]

Word Choice

Four common problems with word choice can make it difficult for readers to understand your point. You can avoid them by using specific words that fit your meaning and make your writing clearer.

Vague and Abstract Words

Your words need to create a clear picture for your readers. **Vague and abstract words** are too general to make an impression. Here are some common vague and abstract words.

Vague and Abstract Words			
a lot	dumb	OK (okay)	stuff
awesome	good	old	thing
awful	great	person	very
bad	happy	pretty	whatever
beautiful	house	sad	young
big	job	school	
car	nice	small	

When you see one of these words or another general word in your writing, try to replace it with a concrete or more specific word. A **concrete word** names something that can be seen, heard, felt, tasted, or smelled. A **specific word** names a particular individual or quality. Compare these two sentences:

VAGUE AND ABSTRACT	It was a beautiful day.
CONCRETE AND SPECIFIC	The sky was a bright, cloudless blue; the sun was shimmering; and the temperature was a perfect 78 degrees.

The first version is too general to be interesting. The second version creates a clear, strong image.

Some words are so vague that it is best to avoid them altogether.

VAGUE AND ABSTRACT   It's like *whatever*.

[This sentence is neither concrete nor specific.]

Slang

Slang, the informal and casual language shared by a particular group, should be used only in informal and casual situations. Avoid it when you write, especially for college classes or at work. Use language that is appropriate for your audience and purpose.

SLANG	EDITED
I'm going to *chill* at home.	I'm going to relax at home.
I *dumped* Destina.	I ended my relationship with Destina.

If you are not sure if a word is slang, check an online source, such as **http://www.slangvocabulary.com/wp/** or **http://www.manythings .org/e/slang.html**.

Wordy Language

Using too many words in a piece of writing can obscure or weaken the point.

Wordy language includes phrases that contain too many words, unnecessarily modify a statement, or use slightly different words without adding any new ideas. It also includes overblown language—unnecessarily complicated words and phrases that are often used to make the writer or writing sound important.

WORDY   We have no openings *at this point in time*.

EDITED   We have no openings now.

[The phrase *at this point in time* uses five words to express what could be said in one word—*now*.]

WORDY   *In the opinion of this writer,* tuition is too high.

EDITED   Tuition is too high.

[The qualifying phrase *in the opinion of this writer* is not necessary and weakens the statement.]

Common Wordy Expressions

WORDY	EDITED
A great number of	Many
A large number of	Many
As a result of	Because
At that time	Then
At the conclusion of	At the end
At this point in time	Now
Due to the fact that	Because
In order to	To
In spite of the fact that	Although
In the event that	If
In this day and age	Now
In this paper I will show that	(Just make the point; don't announce it.)
It is my opinion that	I think (or just make the point)
The fact of the matter is that	(Just state the point.)

Clichés

Clichés are phrases used so often that people no longer pay attention to them. To get your point across and to get your readers' attention, replace clichés with fresh language that precisely expresses your meaning.

CLICHÉS	EDITED
Passing the state police exam is no *walk in the park*.	Passing the state police exam requires careful preparation.
I was *sweating bullets* until the grades were posted.	I was anxious until the grades were posted.

COMMON CLICHÉS

as big as a house	last but not least
as hard as a rock	more trouble than it's worth
as light as a feather	no way on earth
best/worst of times	110 percent
better late than never	playing with fire
break the ice	spoiled brat
climb the corporate ladder	spoiled rotten
crystal clear	starting from scratch
drop in the bucket	sweating blood/bullets
easier said than done	24/7
hell on earth	work like a dog

There are hundreds of clichés. To check if you have used a cliché, go to **clichesite.com**.

Punctuation and Capitalization

Commas

Commas (,) are punctuation marks that help readers understand a sentence by introducing a pause at key points. Be sure you understand how to use commas in the following situations.

COMMAS BETWEEN ITEMS IN A SERIES

Use commas to separate three or more items in a series. This includes the last item in the series, which usually has *and* before it.

> Last semester I took *math,* *reading,* and *composition.*

> Students may take the course as a *regular classroom course,* as an *online course,* or as a *distance learning course.*

COMMAS BETWEEN COORDINATE ADJECTIVES

Coordinate adjectives are two or more adjectives that independently modify the same noun and are separated by commas. Coordinate adjectives can be separated by the word *and.*

> It was a *long,* *hard,* *complicated* test.

Do *not* use a comma between the final adjective and the noun it modifies.

> It was a *long, hard, complicated,* test.

✓ LearningCurve For extra practice in the skills covered in this chapter, visit
bedfordstmartins.com/reinteractive.

259

Cumulative adjectives modify the same noun but form a unit and are not separated by commas. Cumulative adjectives cannot be joined by the word *and*.

Our team wants to win the *big regional sales* trophy.

All of the words in italics are adjectives, but they build on each other. Moving left from *trophy,* each adjective becomes part of a larger unit.

COMMAS IN COMPOUND SENTENCES

A **compound sentence** contains two independent clauses (sentences) joined by one of these words—*and, but, for, nor, or, so, yet.* Use a comma before the joining word to separate the two clauses.

Tom missed class yesterday, *and* he texted me to ask what he missed.

I would have been happy to help him, *but* I was absent too.

I told him I wasn't there, *so* he said he would e-mail the professor.

A comma is not needed if the word *and, but, for, nor, or, so,* or *yet* joins two sentence elements that are not independent clauses.

A comma by itself cannot separate two sentences: Doing so creates a run-on (see pages 223–26).

COMMAS AFTER INTRODUCTORY WORD GROUPS

Use a comma after an introductory word or word group. An introductory word group can be a word, a phrase, or a clause. The comma lets your readers know when the main part of the sentence is starting.

INTRODUCTORY WORD   *Finally,* I finished the job.

INTRODUCTORY PHRASE   *According to the paper,* the crime rate went down.

INTRODUCTORY CLAUSE   *As you know,* the store is going out of business.

COMMAS AROUND APPOSITIVES AND INTERRUPTERS

For more on appositives, see page 255.

An **appositive,** a phrase that renames a noun, comes directly before or after the noun.

Dick, *my neighbor,* has a new job.

Apartment prices are high at Riverview, *the new complex.*

An **interrupter** is an aside or transition that interrupts the flow of a sentence and does not affect its meaning.

Campus parking fees, *you should know,* are going up by 30 percent.

A six-month sticker will now be $75, *if you can believe it.*

COMMAS AROUND ADJECTIVE CLAUSES

An **adjective clause** is a group of words that often begins with *who, which,* or *that;* has a subject and verb; and describes the noun that comes before it in a sentence. An adjective clause may or may not be set off from the rest of the sentence by commas depending on its meaning in the sentence.

If an adjective clause can be taken out of a sentence without completely changing the meaning, put commas around the clause.

SuperShop, *which is the largest supermarket in town,* was recently bought by Big Boy Markets.

I have an appointment with Dr. Kling, *who is the specialist.*

If an adjective clause is essential to the meaning of a sentence, do not put commas around it. You can tell whether a clause is essential by taking it out and seeing if the meaning of the sentence changes significantly, as it would if you took the clauses out of the following examples:

The hair salon *that I liked* recently closed.

Salesclerks *who sell liquor to minors* are breaking the law.

COMMAS WITH QUOTATION MARKS

Quotation marks are used to show that you are using a direct quotation, repeating exactly what someone said or wrote. Generally, use commas to set off the words inside quotation marks from the rest of the sentence.

"Excuse me," said the old woman in back of me. "Did you know," she asked, "that you just cut in front of me?"

I exclaimed, "Oh, no. I'm so sorry!"

Notice that a comma never comes directly *after* a quotation mark.

COMMAS IN ADDRESSES

Use commas to separate the elements of an address included in a sentence. However, do not use a comma before a zip code.

My address is 4498 Main Street, Bolton, Massachusetts 01740.

If a sentence continues after the address, put a comma after the address. Also, use a comma after individual elements used to name a geographical location such as a city and state.

The house was moved from Cripple Creek, Colorado, to the lot on Forest Street.

COMMAS IN DATES

Separate the day from the year with a comma. If you give only the month and year, do not separate them with a comma.

She wrote the letter on April 1, 2009.

The next session is in January 2011.

If a sentence continues after a date that includes the day, put a comma after the date.

He waited until April 15, 2010, to file his 2008 tax return.

COMMAS WITH NAMES

Put commas around the name of someone you are addressing by name.

Don, I want you to come look at this.

Unfortunately, Marie, you need to finish the report by next week.

COMMAS WITH *YES* OR *NO*

Put a comma after the word *yes* or *no* in response to a question.

No, that isn't what I meant.

[To express a strong emotion, an exclamation mark is sometimes used instead of a comma: *No! That is not what I meant.* A word or phrase that expresses emotion and stands alone (like *No!*) is called an interjection.]

Apostrophes

An **apostrophe (')** is a punctuation mark that either shows ownership (*Susan's*) or indicates that a letter has been intentionally left out to form a contraction (*I'm, that's, they're*).

APOSTROPHES TO SHOW OWNERSHIP

- **Add *'s* to a singular noun to show ownership even if the noun already ends in *s*.**

  Darcy's car is being repaired.

  Joan got all the information she needed from the hotel's Web site.

- **If a noun is plural and ends in *s*, just add an apostrophe to show ownership. If it is plural but does not end in *s*, add *'s*.**

  Seven boys' coats were left at the school.

  The children's toys were all broken.

- **The placement of an apostrophe makes a difference in meaning.**

  My neighbor's twelve cats are howling. [One neighbor who has twelve cats]

  My neighbors' twelve cats are howling. [Two or more neighbors who together have twelve cats]

- **Do not use an apostrophe to form the plural of a noun.**

  Use the stair's or the elevator.

- **Do not use an apostrophe with a possessive pronoun. These pronouns already show ownership (possession).**

  That basket is our's.

Possessive Pronouns

my	his	its	their
mine	her	our	theirs
your	hers	ours	whose
yours			

The single most common error with apostrophes and pronouns is confusing *its* (a possessive pronoun) with *it's* (a contraction meaning "it is"). Whenever you write *it's,* test to see if it's correct by reading it aloud as *it is.*

APOSTROPHES IN CONTRACTIONS

A **contraction** is formed by joining two words and leaving out one or more of the letters. When writing a contraction, put an apostrophe where the letter or letters have been left out, not between the two words.

I'll go when you come back. = *I will* go when you come back.

Be sure to put the apostrophe in the right place.

Don does'n't work here anymore.

Do not use contractions in papers or reports for college or work.

Common Contractions

aren't = are not	it's = it is, it has
can't = cannot	let's = let us
couldn't = could not	she'd = she would, she had
didn't = did not	she'll = she will
doesn't = does not	she's = she is, she has
don't = do not	there's = there is, there has
he'd = he would, he had	they're = they are
he'll = he will	they've = they have
he's = he is, he has	who's = who is, who has
I'd = I would, I had	won't = will not
I'll = I will	wouldn't = would not
I'm = I am	you'll = you will
I've = I have	you're = you are
isn't = is not	you've = you have

APOSTROPHES WITH LETTERS, NUMBERS, AND TIME

■ **Use _'s_ to make letters and numbers plural. The apostrophe prevents confusion or misreading.**

Mississippi has four i**'s**.

In women's shoes, size 8**'s** are more common than size 10**'s**.

■ **Use an apostrophe or _'s_ in certain expressions in which time nouns are treated as if they possess something.**

I get two weeks**'** vacation next year.

Last year**'s** prices were very good.

Quotation Marks

Quotation marks (" ") are punctuation marks with two common uses in college writing: They are used with direct quotations, and they are used to set off titles. They always appear in pairs.

QUOTATION MARKS FOR DIRECT QUOTATIONS

When you write a direct quotation, you need to use quotation marks around the quoted words. These marks tell readers that the words used are exactly what was said or written.

Quoted words are usually combined with words that identify who is speaking. The identifying words can come after the quoted words, before them, or in the middle. Here are some guidelines for capitalization and punctuation.

■ Capitalize the first letter in a complete sentence that's being quoted, even if it comes after some identifying words.

Quotation mark   Quotation mark

The teacher said, "This assignment is due next Monday."

Capital letter for complete sentence

▪ Do not capitalize the first letter in a quotation if it is not the first word in the complete sentence.

Quotation marks

"If anyone needs help with it," she said, "see me during office hours."

Not the first word in the complete sentence, no capital letter

▪ If it is a complete sentence and its source is clear, you can let a quotation stand on its own, without any identifying words.

Speaker (teacher) known

"My office hours are on the first page of your syllabus."

▪ Attach identifying words to a quotation with a comma; these identifying words cannot be a sentence on their own.

Identifying words attached with comma

A student asked, "May we e-mail questions?"

▪ Always put quotation marks *after* commas and periods. Put quotation marks after question marks and exclamation points if they are part of the quoted sentence.

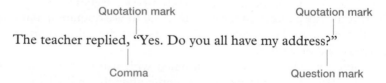

Quotation mark   Quotation mark

The teacher replied, "Yes. Do you all have my address?"

Comma   Question mark

▪ If a question mark or exclamation point is part of your own sentence, put it after the quotation mark.

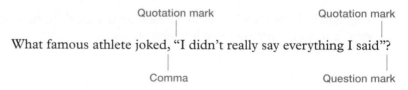

Quotation mark   Quotation mark

What famous athlete joked, "I didn't really say everything I said"?

Comma   Question mark

For information about how to use quotations in research papers, see Chapter 14.

When you quote the exact words of an outside source in a paper, use quotation marks. You also need to cite, or give credit to, the source.

The government needs to ensure that when a company fails, employees' pensions are protected. An article in the *Boston Globe* reported, "When Polaroid collapsed, pension funds and employee stock programs were suddenly worthless. At the same time, however, the chief financial officer walked away with a package worth more than $2 million" (Richardson B3).

For more on citing and documenting sources, see pages 194–200.

SETTING OFF A QUOTATION WITHIN ANOTHER QUOTATION

Sometimes you may directly quote someone who quotes what someone else said or wrote. Put **single quotation marks** (' ') around the quotation within a quotation so that readers understand who said what.

> Terry told his instructor, "I'm sorry I missed the exam, but I would like to take a makeup exam. According to our student handbook, 'Students must be given the opportunity to make up work missed for excused absences,' and I have a good reason."

Terry's entire quotation

Here, Terry is quoting from the student handbook.

NO QUOTATION MARKS FOR INDIRECT QUOTATIONS

When you report what someone said or wrote but do not use the person's exact words, you are writing an indirect quotation. Do not use quotation marks for indirect quotations. Indirect quotations often begin with the word *that*.

INDIRECT QUOTATION   Sophie said that the exam was postponed.

DIRECT QUOTATION   Sophie said, "The exam was postponed."

QUOTATION MARKS FOR CERTAIN TITLES

When referring to a short work such as a magazine or newspaper article, a chapter in a book, a short story, an essay, a song, or a poem, put quotation marks around the title of the work.

NEWSPAPER ARTICLE   "Mayor Warns of Budget Cuts"

SHORT STORY   "Everyday Use"

ESSAY   "Mother Tongue"

Usually, titles of longer works—such as novels, books, magazines, newspapers, movies, television programs, and CDs—are italicized. The titles of sacred books such as the Bible or the Koran are neither italicized nor surrounded by quotation marks.

BOOK   *The Chocolate War*

NEWSPAPER   the *Washington Post*

[Do not italicize or capitalize the word *the* before the name of a newspaper or magazine, even if it is part of the title. But do capitalize *The* when it is the first word in titles of books, movies, and other sources.]

If you are writing a paper with many outside sources, your instructor will probably refer you to a particular system of citing sources. Follow that system's guidelines when you use titles in your paper.

NOTE: Do not put quotation marks around the title of a paper you write.

Semicolon ;

SEMICOLONS TO JOIN INDEPENDENT CLAUSES (SENTENCES)

Use a semicolon to join very closely related sentences and make them into one sentence.

In an interview, hold your head up and don't slouch; it is important to look alert.

Make good eye contact; looking down is not appropriate in an interview.

SEMICOLONS WHEN ITEMS IN A SERIES CONTAIN COMMAS

For more on using semi-colons to join sentences, see page 251.

Use a semicolon to separate list items that themselves contain commas. Otherwise, it is difficult for readers to tell where one item ends and another begins.

I have a cousin who lives in Devon, England; another cousin who lives in Derry, New Hampshire; and a third cousin who lives in Freeport, Maine.

Colon :

COLONS BEFORE LISTS

Use a colon to introduce a list after an independent clause.

In the United States, three ice cream flavors are the most popular: vanilla, chocolate, and strawberry.

COLONS BEFORE EXPLANATIONS OR EXAMPLES

Use a colon after an independent clause to let readers know that you are about to provide an explanation or example of what you just wrote. If the explanation or example is also an independent clause, capitalize the first letter after the colon.

Sometimes, the choice of cereals is overwhelming: My supermarket carries at least five different types of raisin bran.

I use one criterion to choose a cereal: price.

NOTE: A colon in a sentence must follow an independent clause. A common misuse is to place a colon after a phrase instead of an independent clause. Watch out especially for colons following the phrases *such as* or *for example*.

INCORRECT	The resort offers many activities, such as: snorkeling, golf, and windsurfing.
CORRECT	The resort offers many activities: snorkeling, golf, and windsurfing.
CORRECT	The resort offers many activities, such as snorkeling, golf, and windsurfing.

COLONS IN BUSINESS CORRESPONDENCE

Use a colon after a greeting (called a *salutation*) in a business letter and after the standard heading lines at the beginning of a memorandum.

Dear Mr. Latimer:

To: Craig Kleinman

From: Susan Anker

Parentheses ( )

Use two parentheses to set off information that is not essential to the meaning of a sentence. Parentheses are always used in pairs and should be used sparingly.

My grandfather's most successful invention (his first) was the electric blanket.

My worst habit (and also the hardest to break) is interrupting.

Dash —

Use dashes as you use parentheses: to set off additional information, particularly information that you want to emphasize.

> The essay question —— worth 50 percent of the whole exam —— will be open book.

A dash can also indicate a pause, much as a comma does.

> My son wants to buy a car —— if he can find an affordable one.

Make a dash by typing two hyphens together. Do not leave any extra spaces around a dash.

Hyphen -

HYPHENS TO JOIN WORDS THAT FORM A SINGLE DESCRIPTION

Use a hyphen to join words that together form a single description of a person, place, or thing.

> The eighty-year-old smoker was considered a high-risk patient.

If you are unsure about whether or how to hyphenate a word or phrase, consult a dictionary or your instructor.

HYPHENS TO DIVIDE A WORD AT THE END OF A LINE

Use a hyphen to divide a word when part of the word must continue on the next line. Most word-processing programs do this automatically, but if you are writing by hand, you need to insert hyphens yourself.

> If you give me the receipt for your purchase, I will imme-
> diately issue a refund.

> If you are not sure where to break a word, look it up in a dictionary. The word's main entry will show you where you can break the word: *dic • tio • nary.*

Capitalization

There are three basic rules of capitalization: Capitalize the first letter of

- every new sentence.
- names of specific people, places, dates, and things.
- important words in titles.

CAPITALIZATION OF SENTENCES

Capitalize the first letter in each new sentence, including the first word in a direct quotation.

Mary was surprised when she saw all the people.

She asked, "What's going on here?"

CAPITALIZATION OF NAMES OF SPECIFIC PEOPLE, PLACES, DATES, AND THINGS

Capitalize the first letter in names of specific people, places, dates, and things. Do not capitalize general words such as *college* as opposed to the specific name: *Lincoln College*. Look at the examples for each group.

People

Capitalize the first letter in names of specific people and in titles used with names of specific people.

The word *president* is not capitalized unless it comes directly before a name as part of that person's title: President Barack Obama.

SPECIFIC	NOT SPECIFIC
Carol Schopfer	my friend
Dr. D'Ambrosio	the physician
Professor Shute	your professor

The name of a family member is capitalized when the family member is being addressed directly or when the family title is standing in for a first name.

Good to see you, Dad.   I see that Mom is taking classes.

In other instances, do not capitalize.

It is my father's birthday.   My mom is taking classes.

Places

Capitalize the first letter in names of specific buildings, streets, cities, states, regions, and countries.

SPECIFIC	NOT SPECIFIC
Bolton Police Department	the police department
Washington Street	our street
Boston, Massachusetts	my hometown
Texas	this state
the West	the western part of the country
Italy	that country

Do not capitalize directions in a sentence: *Drive south for five blocks.*

Dates

Capitalize the first letter in the names of days, months, and holidays. Do not capitalize the names of the seasons (winter, spring, summer, fall).

SPECIFIC	NOT SPECIFIC
Monday	today
January 4	winter
Presidents' Day	my birthday

Organizations, Companies, and Groups

SPECIFIC	NOT SPECIFIC
Santa Monica College	my college
Toys"R"Us	the toy store
Merrimack Players	the theater group

Languages, Nationalities, and Religions

SPECIFIC	NOT SPECIFIC
English, Greek, Spanish	my first language
Christianity, Buddhism	your religion

Courses

SPECIFIC	NOT SPECIFIC
Nutrition 100	the basic nutrition course

Commercial Products

SPECIFIC	NOT SPECIFIC
Diet Coke	a diet cola

The names of languages should be capitalized even if you are not referring to a specific course: *I am taking nutrition and Spanish.*

Capitalization of Titles

Capitalize the first word and all other important words in titles of books, movies, television programs, magazines, newspapers, articles, stories, songs, papers, poems, legislation, and so on. Words that do not need to be capitalized (unless they are the first word) include articles (*the, a, an*); coordinating conjunctions (*and, but, for, nor, or, so, yet*); and prepositions.

For more on punctuating titles, see pages 267–68. For a list of common prepositions, see page 212.

American Idol is a popular television program.

Newsweek and *Time* often have similar cover stories.

"Once More to the Lake" is one of Chuck's favorite essays.

Acknowledgments

Alex Espinoza. "Still Water Saints." Excerpt from *Still Water Saints*. Copyright © 2007 by Alex Espinoza. Used by permission of Random House, Inc. Any third party use of this material, outside of this publication, is prohibited. Interested parties must apply directly to Random House, Inc. for permission.

Daniel Flanagan. "The Choice to Do It Over Again." Copyright © 2008 by Daniel Flanagan. From *This I Believe: On Fatherhood*, edited by Dan Gediman. Copyright © 2011 by This I Believe, Inc. Reprinted with permission of John Wiley & Sons, Inc.

Michael Gates Gill. "On the Front Lines — Ready or Not." From *How Starbucks Saved My Life* by Michael Gates Gill, pp. 102-6. Copyright © 2007 by Michael Gates Gill. Used by permission of Gotham Books, an imprint of Penguin Group (USA) Inc.

Don H. and Sandra E. Hockenbury. "When the Regulation of Eating Behavior Fails: Anorexia and Bulemia." Excerpt from *Discovering Psychology* by Don H. Hockenbury and Sandra Hockenbury, 3rd ed. Copyright © 2004 Worth Publishers.

Baxter Holmes. "My Date with 15 Women." From *The Boston Globe*, Jan. 11, 2009. Reprinted by permission of the author.

Stephanie Lindsley. "Autism and Education: Who should we focus on — my disabled son or my gifted girl?" From *Newsweek*, February 28, 2009. Copyright © Harman Newsweek LLC, Inc. All rights reserved. Used by permission and protected by the copyright laws of the United States. The printing, copying, redistribution, or retransmission of this content without express written permission is prohibited. http://www.newsweek.com.

Monique Rizer. "When Students Are Parents." From *The Chronicle of Higher Education*, December 16, 2005. Reprinted by permission of the author.

Christopher Shea. "In Praise of Peer Pressure." Originally published in the *Boston Globe*, April 29, 2007. Reprinted by permission of Christopher Shea.

Rob Walker. "Stuck on You." From *The New York Times*, June 6, 2010. Copyright © 2010 *The New York Times*. All rights reserved. Used by permission and protected by the copyright laws of the United States. The printing, copying, redistribution, or retransmission of this content without express written permission is prohibited. http://www.nytimes.com.

Howard White. "The Power of Hello." From the book *This I Believe: Life Lessons*, edited by Dan Gediman. Copyright © 2008 by Howard White. Copyright © 2011 by This I Believe, Inc. Reprinted with permission of John Wiley & Sons, Inc.

Index